WESTERN WRITING IMPLEMENTS

For my friend Philip Poole
who has preserved the ephemera
of the pen for more than half a century,
with respect

Western Writing Implements
in the Age of the Quill Pen

Michael Finlay

PLAINS BOOKS

First published 1990

© Michael Finlay
   Plains Books
   Wetheral, Carlisle, Cumbria

British Library Cataloguing in Publication Data
Finlay, Michael, *1935–*
    Western writing implements in the age of
    the quill pen
    1. Writing equipment, history
    I. Title
    681.6
ISBN 1-872477-00-3

All photographs, other than those otherwise
credited, are by the author of items in, or
formerly in, his collection

Book and jacket design, line drawings and
calligraphy by the author

Text computer-typeset by the author on
software compatible for filmsetting

Filmset in Palatino, printed by Titus Wilson &
Son, Ltd, Kendal and bound by Hunter and
Foulis, Edinburgh

Contents

Acknowledgements

During the past ten years during which I have been intermittently gathering material for this book I have been assisted by a great many people; to all of those below, I wish to record my sincere appreciation. Inevitably, there will be some who have been unwittingly omitted, and to those I offer my apologies and I hope they too will accept my thanks.

J. H. Andrews, Esq, of the Museum of Science and Industry, Birmingham; Christopher Bangs, Esq; G. W. W. Barker, Esq, Director of the British School at Rome; Bernard Barkoff, Esq; Professor Younes A. El-Batrik, Cultural Counsellor, Embassy of the Arab Republic of Egypt, London; Roger Bishop, Esq, and the late William Bishop, Esq, whose weekly telephone conversations over some two years are sadly missed; A. D. H. Bivar, Esq, of the School of Oriental and African Studies, University of London; Staff of the British Museum: Dr Ian D. Jenkins of the Department of Greek and Roman Antiquities, Miss A. Dawson, Miss Angela Evans and Timothy Wilson, Esq, of the Department of Medieval and Later Antiquities, Miss Francis Dunkels and Duncan Smith, Esq, of the Department of Prints and Drawings, and G. Cooper Esq, of the Photographic Services Department; Justin Brooke, Esq; Mrs Peg Brown; W. H. Brown, Esq, for many kindnesses; David Bryant, Esq and the Staff of the Westminster City Archives Department; Peter Cameron, Esq; Christies, London: Anton Gabszewicz, Esq, European Ceramics Department, Charles Truman, Esq, Silver Department, and his secretary, Miss Deborah Reynolds; Christopher Clarkson, Esq, of the Bodleian Library; C. Cook, Esq, of Lloyds of London; Signora Corti of Archivi Alinari, Florence; Staff of the Courtauld Institute, University of London: Ms Tania Jones of the Netherlands School Department and Miss Jane Cunningham, Mrs J. Hervey and Christopher Gatiss, Esq of the Photographic Survey; Staff of Cumbria Record Office, Carlisle: Miss Sheila MacPherson, Bruce C. Jones, Esq, David M. Bowcock, Esq and Jeremy Godwin, Esq; Kenneth Davis, Esq; Mrs J. K. Davies; Beverley P. Dennison, Esq; Alistair Dickenson, Esq, of Asprey, London; Edward Eldred, Esq; Harry Fancy, Esq, Curator, Whitehaven Museum; Mrs Joan Ferguson; Professor T. Gandjei of the School of Oriental and African Studies, University of London; Norman Gandy, Esq, Curator, Fitz Park Museum, Keswick; Mrs V. A. G. Glynn of H. R. Jessup, Ltd; Peter Goodwin, Esq; Laurie Gould, Esq; Mrs V. A. Goulds, National Gallery, London, Reproductions Section; Miss Maureen Greenland; Miss M. E. Grimshaw; Colin Gross, Esq; Staff of the Guildhall Library: Mrs Irene F. Pollock, Richard M. Hervey, Esq and Godfrey Thompson, Esq; Michael Gullick, Esq; Donald F. Hale, Esq; John W. B. Hall, Esq; Dr John Hardman; Miss Alison Hems, Keeper of Leathercraft, The Museum of Leathercraft, Northampton; Thomas Heneage, Esq; A. Eric Hennell, Esq; Christopher Hollett, Esq, and R. F. G. Hollett, Esq; Martin Hopkinson, Esq, Curator, the Hunterian Museum and Art Gallery, University of Glasgow; the late Dr Leslie B. Hunt of Johnson Matthey for a tragically short but illuminating acquaintance and a memorable lunch at the Athenaeum Club; Donald Jackson, Esq; Bob and Sue Beresford-Jones, for much encouragement over the years; George W. Keates, Esq and Roddy McRoberts, Esq, of Maurice Dodd Books, Carlisle; Paul B. Kebabian, Esq, of the Early American Industries Association; W. H. Lapthorne, Esq; D. S. Lavender, Esq; Miss G. E. Lee of Ronald A. Lee, (Fine Arts) Ltd; Mrs Cynthia Lennon for her generous gift of a box of quill pens; Oldrich Lenz, Esq, Cultural Attaché, Embassy of the Czechoslovak Socialist Republic, London; M. J. Leppard, Esq, Honorary Curator, East Grinstead Town Museum; William H. Longenecker, Esq of the National Agricultural Library, Beltsville, Maryland; Frans Maathuis, Esq; David Mander, Esq, of the Rose Lipman Library, Hackney Archives Department; Dr Rosalind K. Marshall and Mrs S. Kerr of the National Portrait Gallery of Scotland; Michael Moon, Esq; Susan, Viscountess Mountgarret; Bruce A. Nichols, Esq; Mike Notman, Esq and Miss Julie Winspear; J. Martin Olive, Esq, Sheffield City Libraries; the late Dr A. S. Osley; Staff of the Museum of Fine Arts, Boston, Mass: Karen L. Otis and Sandra M. Mongeon; Ralph Parr, Esq; Miss Molly Pearce, Principal Keeper, Applied Art and David Sier, Esq, Sheffield City Museum; Phillips, London: John Sandon, Esq, European Ceramics, and Eric J. Smith, Esq, Silver Department; 'His Nibs' Philip Poole, Esq who has been a constant source of encouragement and information; Miss Judith Prendergast of the Picture Library, National Portrait Gallery, London; Staff at the Public Record Office: Dr Meryl R. Foster, J. Crawford, Esq, R. C. Kershaw, Esq and N. Pointer, Esq; Oliver Ray, Esq; L. Renner of the Bayerische Staatsbibliothek, Munich; John Reynolds, Esq of A. C. Cooper, Ltd; Colin Richardson, Esq, Carlisle City Museum and Art Gallery; J. Allan Robinson, Esq; Dr Geoffrey E. Roe; Mrs M. M. Russell, Cumbria Family History Society; Gerald Sattin, Esq; Dr Erich Schleier of the Staatliche Museen Preussischer Kulturbesitz Gemäldegalerie, West Berlin; Staff at the Museum of London: Mrs I. E. Shaw and Gavin Morgan, Esq of the Picture Library and Peter Stott, Esq of the Medieval Department; Dr D. J. Smith, Keeper of the Museum of Antiquities, University of Newcastle-upon-Tyne; Sothebys, London: Miss Iona Cairns and Miss Elizabeth Wilson, European Works of Art, and Richard Came, Silver Department; Jack Sowerby, Esq; John Storrs, Esq of Berol, Ltd; James C. Sullivan, Esq; Peter Thornton, Esq; Mrs Fiona Thwaytes; Oliver Turnbull Esq, Raymond Fielding, Esq; and the staff of Messrs Titus Wilson and Son Ltd; Raphael Valls, Esq; The Staff of the Kunsthistoriches Museum, Vienna; Dr Jan Várra and staff of the Metropolitan Chapter Library, Prague; Staff of the Victoria and Albert Museum: Miss Bathsheba Abse, Miss Clare Graham and A. North, Esq; Edric van Vredenburgh, Esq; D. F. Wallis, Esq; Mrs Maryanne Wilkins of Wilkins and Wilkins, London; Miss M. Y. Williams, Lambeth Archives Department; the late Bruce Woodcock, Esq; Mrs Judy Wormall.

My thanks are also due, for many helpful suggestions, to my daughter Fiona Dix who valiantly read the entire manuscript during a week's 'holiday'. Finally, to my long-suffering wife Ann, for her never-failing patience and support, my especial gratitude.

Preface

In spite of having been the instrument with which the entire history of western civilisation and culture was both developed and recorded over some thirteen hundred years, the quill pen has until now been largely ignored by the social historian in modern times. The notion of this book was born out of the frustration of the author, as a collector of the writing implements surrounding the quill, at the dearth of information available on the subject. There are excellent instructional accounts of quill-cutting as practised by the modern calligrapher, but until now little has been written on the detailed history of the quill pen or the artefacts which accompanied its use. It is hoped that this work will go some way towards filling that gap.

The days of the quill pen as the main instrument of the scribe were numbered from the beginning of the mass-production of the steel pen in the 1820s but it was not to be a sudden death. Within living memory the quill was still the only acceptable writing instrument in many lawyers' offices. Nevertheless, although they were well-established in what was technically still the 'age of the quill pen' I have excluded from this work both the mass-produced steel pen and the modern fountain-pen which are both perhaps better seen as successors to the quill rather than contemporary imitations of it.

1

The History of the Quill Pen

From the Dark Ages until the nineteenth century, the quill pen was the means by which every aspect of the growth of civilisation in Europe was recorded. Almost every written work of religion, philosophy, literature, history, science, medicine, commerce and administration relied upon the humble goose feather for its existence. Yet little is, or can ever be, known of its beginnings; the date of the earliest use of the quill pen will always be a matter of conjecture.

An excellent account of the development of writing instruments from the earliest times, which also describes the use of styli, reed and metal pens, is the chapter on 'Writing Pens' in Beckmann's *History of Inventions,* published in 1797.[1] In this scholarly account, which quotes and examines critically many earlier sources, the author concludes that the earliest certain reference to the quill pen is that by Isidore, Bishop of Seville, (560-636 AD),[2] who, in his *Etymologia*, distinguishes between the reed and the quill pen:

> *Instrumenta scribae calamus et penna. Ex his enim verba paginis infiguntur, sed calamus arboris est, penna avis, cuius acumen dividitur in duo, in toto corpore unitate servata*

which may be freely translated as

> The tools of the scribe are the reed and the quill. By them, words are written on the pages of books, but the reed is a plant, the quill from a bird; the point is divided in two, coming together in the body.

The general consensus of later writers, including the author of perhaps the most comprehensive nineteenth century account of the history of writing materials, that of *The Saturday Magazine,* (1832-1838),[3] (which, for its information regarding the quill pen, owes much to Beckmann's article), is that the quill pen was probably introduced in the seventh century, prior to 636. Earlier references to pens are generally thought to concern reed or metal pens.

As far as illustrations of the quill pen are concerned, it is sometimes difficult to discern from early illuminated manuscripts with their beautifully stylised depictions of scribes, whether the pen in use is made from a quill or from a reed. Among the earliest which may represent a quill, is that depicting St Matthew, of the *Lindisfarne Gospels,* dating from about 700.[4] Another illumination of St Matthew, using what is undoubtedly a quill pen, is that of the *Ms Barberini, Lat 570*, dating from the late eighth or early ninth century.[5]

A considerably earlier depiction of a quill pen, and what may be the earliest evidence of its use so far discovered, is to be found in a mosaic which forms part of the mural decoration of the Byzantine Church of San Vitale in Ravenna. This church was built between 526 and 547 AD by Bishops Ecclesio and Massiniano, and was dedicated on May 17th, 547 or 548.[6] Forming part of the decoration of the sides of the upper triforium in the right wall of the presbytery, a panel depicts St Matthew at work on his Gospel, seated behind a small table on which there are both quill and reed pens and an ink-pot,(1) this mosaic is thought to have been among the last executed prior to the completion of the church in 547.[7] The particular significance of this datable evidence for the use of the quill pen does not appear to have been previously noted.[8]

The reed pen was first used mainly on papyrus, but survived long after the advent of parchment as a writing surface, which was certainly known to the Romans before the first century AD,[9] and perhaps earlier. It is not unreasonable to suppose that a culture familiar with the cylindrical form of a hollow reed, would quickly see the potential of the barrel of a bird's feather for a similar purpose, and it may be that the quill pen was already in use in Imperial Rome. Circumstantial evidence for this possibility is provided by the existence of a number of bronze pens with slit nibs, found in London in the nineteenth century and then ascribed to the Roman period, which conform exactly to the form of a trimmed quill pen.(270) If indeed these are Roman, it is difficult to sustain the possibility that such a pen was designed and made by someone familiar only with the straight cylindrical reed pen and those metal pens of similar form used at Pompeii in the mid-first century BC, now in the Naples Museum. However, a similar bronze pen in the Museum of London has more recently been excavated from a late medieval context in London, throwing considerable doubt on the earlier attribution. It has also to be said that in spite of the survival of many artefacts of a perishable nature, including wooden writing tablets and leather shoes, at Vindolanda on Hadrian's Wall, for instance, no example of a quill pen seems to have survived from Roman times.

We can be certain, however, that the quill, once discovered, because of its improved elasticity over the reed, its greater durability, and the ease with which it could be cut for finer writing, would quickly become the main source material for the making of pens; the quill pen was in fact to become the scribe's chief writing instrument from this time until the nineteenth century, and survived, as an alternative to the mass-produced metal pens which eventually brought about its demise, well into the twentieth. It is, of course, still the fundamental tool of modern calligraphers and illuminators.

In the early Middle Ages, when writing was mainly the prerogative of the Church, (hence the term *cleric*), there would have been little demand for pens outside the monasteries; individual scriptoria and those itinerant Clerks in Holy Orders who served the laity, no doubt made their own local arrangements for the procuring of quills for this purpose. In the later medieval period, with the establishment of more stable town life and a consequent expansion of business and commerce, the professions of the law, medicine and scholarship developed, and with them a wider literacy among the laity, the increasing demand for writing

being met both by the professional lay scribes or scriveners, and by a growing number of individuals who were learning to write, for the better conduct of their own business and domestic affairs. All of this, of course, required an increased supply of quills to provide pens.

An interesting example of the difficulties which could arise in obtaining a ready supply of quills, and the value accorded such a humble requirement, is given in a letter, written in Venice in 1433 by Ambrosius Traversarius, a monk of Camaldule, to his brother, to accompany the gift of a bundle of quills:

> They are not the best but such as I received as a present. Show the whole bunch to Nicholas that he may select a quill, for these articles are indeed scarcer than at Florence.[10]

The reason for this paucity of quills in Venice is not apparent, and was probably due to a purely local problem; at any rate, the stationer's shop was well-established in Italy by the fifteenth century.(2)

The trade of the stationer in medieval times was associated, as it often is today, with that of the bookseller. The word derives from the medieval Latin *stationarius*, a tradesman having a regular 'station' or shop, as opposed to an itinerant hawker.[11] The production of the medieval book involved many different craftsmen, whose work might be co-ordinated by a 'stationer' who stayed in one place and performed the function of agent between the various workshops and the customer, possibly commissioning books on his own account for sale in his shop, during slack periods.[12] As the demand for parchment, quills, ink and other writing equipment increased with the spread of literacy, it was natural that the stationer-bookseller should supply this need.

The invention of printing in the mid-fifteenth century accelerated this spread of literacy as many professional scribes, whose work as copyists could now be done much more quickly and cheaply by the new technology, turned to the teaching of writing for their livelihoods, and printed manuals on writing started to appear. The first printed writing book was Sigisimondo Fanti's *Theorica et Pratica*, published in Venice in 1514; it comprised four sections, the first on handwriting, the remainder on lettering,[13] and Johann Neudörfer's *Fundament*, a collection of models of *Fractur* letters, appeared in 1519.[14] The book which was, perhaps, to have the greatest influence on future handwriting styles, the first Italian manual devoted entirely to handwriting, was Ludovico Vincento degli Arrighi's *La Operina*, which bears the date 1522 but probably came out a year or so later.[15] It taught the *littera Cancellarescha*, the cursive hand used by the Chancery of the Roman Church, which spread rapidly across Europe through the vehicle of Papal documents, and by the adoption of its style by the Italian printers for their typefaces. The Chancery hand is now widely imitated, largely through the influence of Arrighi's style on Alfred Fairbank, (1895-1982), the driving force behind the modern revival of the italic hand.

Writing manuals of other masters quickly followed, notably those of Giovannantonio Tagliente (1524), Giovambattista Palatino (1540) and Giovan Francesco Cresci (1560) in Italy, Gerard Mercator (1540) in Flanders, Caspar Neff (1549) in Germany, and Juan de Yciar (1548) in Spain. In England, John de Beau Chesne's and John Baildon's *A Booke containing divers sortes of hands . . . .*, the first treatise on handwriting in English, appeared in 1570,[16] the first of what was to prove a long tradition of writing masters' copy books in England, stretching into the nineteenth century.[17] Most of these copy books included instruction in the preparation of quills and other writing materials.

The spread of education in schools also produced an increased demand for quills for pens. In Chaucer's time there were already some three to four hundred grammar schools, teaching reading, writing and Latin, mainly for the education of clerks. Unlike the grammar schools of modern times, many of which sprang from them, these fourteenth-century schools were mainly very small, under the control of the monasteries, cathedrals, hospitals, trade guilds or chantries, and the masters who taught in them were secular clergy. In the fifteenth century there were even more schools, still mainly catering for the sons of the more well-to-do, but in the sixteenth and seventeenth centuries, the grammar schools did take pupils from all social classes, including particularly bright children from very poor backgrounds. It was not, however, until the eighteenth century, with the advent on a wide scale of charity schools for the poor, and the spread of village schools, that there was any real effort to educate the general mass of the population.[18]

The degree to which literacy had become widespread by the early nineteenth century, is reflected in the numbers of quills for pens which were imported into the country. In 1832, in spite of the ready availability of mass-produced steel pens, the number of goose quills 'entered for home consumption' was thirty-six million, six hundred and sixty-eight thousand, which were mainly imported.[19] Imports of quills into London alone during the preceding years were:

In 1828 – – – 22,418,600
1829 – – – 23,119,800
1830 – – – 19,787,400
1831 – – – 23,670,300
1832 – – – 17,860,900
1833 – – – 23,976,600
1834 – – – 18,732,000,

this in spite of the fact that the Birmingham manufacturers were by then producing vast quantities of steel pens. From the beginnings of industrial mass-production in the early 1820s, the annual output of these steel pens, or pen nibs as we now prefer to call them, had grown by 1838 to a staggering two hundred and twenty millions, not all, of course, for the domestic market.[20]

The main types of quills used for pens were those of the goose, turkey, swan, crow and duck. Raven quills, although very much more difficult to obtain, were occasionally used, and there are instances recorded of the use of those of other birds, including the pelican and the peacock. The vast majority of quills, however, came from the humble goose, quills which have all the qualities most suitable for a good pen: elasticity, hardness and durability.

The goose, as an excellent source of fresh meat, was widely raised in medieval and later England, each village maintaining its communal pond and each cottager his flock of geese; no doubt for many centuries this provided an adequate supply of quills for such pens as were needed. As demand increased, however, to a point where it could no longer be met by such husbandry, huge flocks of geese were farmed mainly for their quills, both in this country, where, in 1812, about nine million geese were plucked to supply the domestic market with pens, and abroad, notably in Germany and Russia. Ireland also produced large quantities of quills. The usable feathers which could be plucked annually, without discomfort to the birds, at the time of their natural moulting, were of sufficient value to encourage the inhumane practice of removing these large flight feathers from the living birds, two or three times a year, a practice frowned upon even then by the more sensitive.[21]

In England, the main supply of quills was from the fens of Lincolnshire and from Norfolk, whose geese were white; those of the other main producing county, Somersetshire, were of a very dark hue. Each wing of a bird provides five good quills and a single goose might therefore produce up to twenty or more quills annually. To satisfy the ever-increasing demand, a great many quills had to be imported to supplement the domestic production. In 1812, these imports were largely from Russia, Sweden and North Germany; B. Pride, a professional quill-cutter, writing at that time, suggested that the best quills came from the coldest countries. Quills from the Continent were generally known as Hamburg quills because of that port's importance to the European export trade in general, to distinguish them from English or Irish quills.[22] Quills from Holland were also prized; an advertisement in the *Edinburgh Evening Courant*, in 1787, offered 'Genuine Dutch Quills' for sale, suggesting that it was not unknown for quills from other sources to be misrepresented as Dutch.(3)

The quills of the North American wild goose, also imported in large numbers, were particularly highly regarded, and perhaps because of the trading monopoly of the Hudson's Bay Company, and the distances involved, generally more expensive than their European counterparts. Marketed as Hudson's Bay Quills, they had black barbs, long barrels of particular elasticity, and were very durable.[23](4) By the 1830s, an immense number of goose quills was also being imported from Holland, Germany, Russia and Poland.[24]

Swan quills were the largest generally used for pens, those from Russia being of particularly large dimensions, some having a barrel of up to nine inches in length. They were therefore much more durable than those of the goose, a single swan pen outlasting as many as fifty made from goose quills.[25] Turkey quills were very hard but short-barrelled and consequently not so durable as those of the swan, but were widely used. Crow quill pens, by virtue of their small size, were recommended for use by ladies, and generally for fine writing. They were, of course, black, and very short in the barrel, which distinguished them from the longer-barrelled duck quills which were also useful for fine work.

The quills used for pens were, and still are, the bird's five largest feathers from each wing. The first quill in the wing, called a Pinion, has the shortest and hardest barrel and is distinguished by the extreme narrowness of the barbs on that side of the feather which in flight is the leading edge and is exposed to the wind. The next quill in the wing is called a Second; its barrel is longer than that of the Pinion and is not so hard. Its shape is also distinctive, each side of the feather having broad barbs except on the leading edge from the point at which the Pinion ceases to overlap it, to the tip. This part of the Second is also exposed in flight and the barbs quickly taper away. Oddly, the third and very similar feather is also called a Second. These two quills are regarded as the best in the wing. The fourth and fifth feathers, somewhat confusingly called Thirds, have no narrowing of the barbs of their leading edges; their barrels are nearly as long as those of the Seconds but are smaller in diameter, and they also make very good pens.(5 and 6) The remaining feathers on the wing were sometimes used for cheaper pens of poorer quality. The sixth and seventh, because of their broader barbs are called Flags, have smaller and thinner barrels, and while they make good pens for fine writing, they do not last long. The remainder, called simply Feathers, become progressively smaller away from the extremity of the wing, and are of little use for pens.

The greatly differing qualities of the various grades of quills, according to their positions in the wing, gave rise to a dishonest practice known as 'plating', among itinerant hawkers of pens. Pens were sold in tied bundles, and it was therefore a simple matter to conceal low-grade pens within an outer layer of better quality. Goose pens, in 1812, for example, varied in price from one to eighteen shillings a hundred, and remained much the same for most of the century; it is clear, therefore, that large profits could be made by the perpetrators of such a fraud.[26] Very few pens were ever repaired, and no doubt the pens sold in stationers' shops would generally be of high quality, with a view to repeated orders.

The grading of raw quills from Europe was carried out by the exporters themselves and was called 'lothing', from the German *Loth*, a unit of weight approximating to just over $5\frac{1}{2}$

English ounces. The quills were exported in bundles of a 'long thousand' (twelve hundred), and a quill in a bundle weighing say twenty-four loths would be called a twenty-four loth pen. Nine loth quills upwards were considered suitable for pens, goose quills ranging up to eighteen loths and those of swans from twelve to twenty-six. Queen Victoria is said to have preferred a swan quill of twenty-five loths.[27]

Quills supplied by the farmer, and the majority of those imported from the Continent, were in the raw state, as plucked from the bird. Before they could be retailed for use as pens, they had to be prepared by the quill-dresser, who cleaned, trimmed and hardened them, after which they might be sold either as prepared quills to those who preferred to cut their own pens, or having passed through the pen-cutter's hands, as finished pens. Prepared quills or pens were sold in bundles, by size and quality, usually in twenty-fives, fifties or hundreds, although in the late eighteenth century, as we have seen, an enterprising stationer in Edinburgh offered a discount on the price of a parcel of a thousand or more.(3) James Woodforde, in his diary, for the 8th October, 1759, records the purchase, along with other writing materials, of 'Half a Hundred of Pens', from his Oxford bookseller, unfortunately omitting to note the cost.[28]

Quills and pens were widely available from booksellers, stationers, and in some provincial towns from the local newspaper printers' offices, which often sold related goods as a sideline. They were graded according to quality, excluding the cheaper pinions, in as many as nineteen grades, the bundles being bound in different coloured strings, to signify the grade and price. The examples which follow, in each case for bundles of one hundred pens, and taken mainly from the price-lists or catalogues of a number of wholesale stationers, illustrate the range of goose quills and pens available during the century from 1812. All used different colour-coding with the exception of the final two, whose colours corresponded exactly, differing only in that Causton's prices were cheaper, suggesting a common supplier:

1812 –	B. Pride, Pen-cutter, 31 Chancery Lane, London.	– Several grades 1/- to 20/-
1837 –	John Shaw and Sons, 137-138 Fetter Lane, London.	– 17 grades 1/6 to 19/-
1860 –	Waterlow and Sons,	– 5 grades
	24 & 25 Birchin Lane, London	4/- to 12/-
1880 –	Aberdeen Quill Company, 47 Queen St, Aberdeen.	– 12 grades 1/- to 12/-
1880 –	W. F. Matthews, 12 Swift's Row, Dublin.	– 16 grades 1/- to 12/-
1882 –	Waterlow and Sons, 49-50 Parliament St, London.	– 6 grades 4/- to 15/-
1890 –	Sir Joseph Causton, 89, 91, 93 and 114 Southwark St, London.	– 6 grades 4/- to 15/-
1893 –	W. Hawtin and Son, 24-25 Paternoster Row, London.	– 19 grades 1/- to 16/-
1911 –	Sir Joseph Causton, 9 Eastcheap, London.	– 12 grades 2/6 to 15/-
1912 –	Shaw and Sons, Fetter Lane, London.	– 12 grades 3/- to 18/-

This comparison is a somewhat arbitrary one, dictated by the catalogues available. During those days of little or no inflation, however, prices do not seem to have altered greatly over the period covered. The figures shown relate only to common goose quills and pens, there being apparently no difference in price between prepared quills and finished pens. Turkey quills were sold at prices comparable with the lower range of goose quills, while Hudson's Bay quills were more expensive than the best common goose quills, and swan quills were dearest of all.(7) Quill pens were also sold in decorative cardboard boxes, a practice which seems to have become more popular in the latter part of the nineteenth century.(8 to 14) Although some have makers' names, most are anonymous, presumably supplied wholesale to retailer stationers around the country who would naturally not wish to advertise their suppliers and risk losing their customers to them. Quill pens from London were generally considered the best available, many boxes carrying this description, and it would seem that pens 'Warranted Cut With a Knife' were preferred to those cut by machine.

In 1822, there were twenty-seven Quill and Pen Manufacturers and Dealers listed in *Pigot's London Directory*; in the same year *Pigot's Directory for Northumberland* lists three Quill and Pen Dealers working in the city of Newcastle-upon-Tyne. Liverpool, at this time, boasted a 'Royal Pen-Cutting Chambers' in the firm of A. Hayes and Company, who advertised their Royal Appointment in *Pigot's London Directory* for 1832.[29] No doubt there were quill and pen dealers in most of the larger cities, the smaller towns and the rural areas relying on general stationers, supplied from London. One pen-cutting establishment, in Shoe Lane, London, in the mid-1830s, whose name is unfortunately not recorded, was producing about six million pens a year.[30] As a skilled pen-cutter's output was about six to eight hundred pens a day, the firm must have employed a work-force of about twenty-five or thirty, making pens from pre-pared quills. (In about 1823, the firm of Walk-den, Darby and Terry were pen-cutters at 5 Shoe Lane, Fleet Street, London,[31] and remain-ed the only quill pen manufacturers in Shoe Lane until at least 1838; they were succeeded at the same address by Cooper and Company, which firm, under various styles, continued to make quill pens into the twentieth century).

A particularly successful firm of provincial pen-cutters was that of Palmer's, Stationers, of East Grinstead, Sussex, who were established in the reign of George III and quickly became 'Pen-Cutters to the Royal Family'. The firm was founded by Thomas Palmer, (1752-1821), a miniature portrait of whom is still in the possession of his descendants.(Colour plate V(ii)) He was the father of Thomas Palmer, (1775-1841), who was Warden of Sackville College, East Grinstead, and William Palmer, (1784-1861), who succeeded him in the pen-cutting business. There were also six other children, one of whom, Frederick, fell at Waterloo.[32] A turned cedar screw-lidded box in the author's collection, which from its neo-classical printed label may be dated circa 1805, in which year the Princess of Wales granted to Palmer per-mission to use her name in his advertising, still contains a few quill nibs, which were sold as Palmer's 'Royal Portable Pens'. (Chapter IV).(15) Another wooden box of the same period, which formerly contained fifty 'Gentle-mens Pens', is now unfortunately empty. It is rather short to have contained full-length pens but just the right length to have held two rows of quill barrel pens for use over an inserted handle.(16) Its printed label is very similar to Palmer's trade-card, which may also be dated to this period.(18) 'Ladies Pens', also in fifties and in similar boxes, were sold by William Palmer.(17) Advertising broadsheets in the Banks Collection, show that Palmer had a countrywide network of agents selling his products.(19,20) The firm was still flourishing in the 1860s under the ownership of Thomas J. Palmer, whose price list shows the wide range of pens he produced.(21)

The decline of the quill pen in the wake of the commercial production of the steel pen, from the 1820s, was not perhaps as swift nor as total as might be imagined. From a study of London directories it can be seen that there was a substantial market for the quill for many years; the numbers of firms in business under the head 'Quill Pen Merchants and Manufacturers' were:

1822	*Pigot's*	27	1899	*Post Office*	6
1832	-do-	34	1910	-do-	4
1840	*Post Office*	21	1915	-do-	3
1848	*Kelly's*	16	1925	-do-	2
1856	*Post Office*	15	1950	-do-	2
1874	-do-	11	1951	-do-	1
1890	-do-	8	1954	-do-	1
			1955	-do-	Nil

It is clear that many writers preferred the quill pen, which could be cut to suit their particular hands, to the steel pen. In an adver-tising booklet, for Windle's Steel Pen Depot, on London Bridge, which is dated in ink on the cover, 'December, 1857', the writer deplored the former prejudice against the steel pen, allowed that there were some very bad pens on the market, but suggested that this reluctance to change old habits had by then been largely overcome by the public's acceptance of the im-provements which had been made in the manu-facture of steel pens.[33] Not all the public shared his view, however; some half a century after the commercial production of the steel pen, in 1875, a writer to *Notes and Queries* sheds further light on the survival of the quill pen:

> From the introduction of steel pens to the present time, I have sought with more or less success for a good one; but neither in gold nor iron have I found anything so pleasant to write with as a good or even middling goose quill.[34]

It is equally clear that, amongst professional scribes, too, the quill pen was still preferred by some. In 1889, a law writer was still able to write:

> Up to within the last ten years, Law Writers executed engrossing hand and text with turkey quills, but there have been steel pens introduced with broad points, with which both engrossing hand and Ger-man text are executed. But many prefer the old-fashioned quill, as it enables an expert Scribe to both text and engross in a better style, and to cut the letters more clearly.[35]

As late as 1968, quill pens were still being advertised for sale in the catalogue of Cooper, Dennison and Walkden of London, a firm of wholesale stationers, the successors of Cooper and Co above, established in 1735. Their last quill-cutter had died some fifty years previously, and they had subsequently obtained stocks of quill pens from Henry Hill and Sons of Peckham, one of the last firms to make quill pens on a commercial scale.[36] In 1894, three quarters of a century after the advent of the commercial steel pen, Hill's quill business was still flourishing to such a degree that Henry Hill was later able to refer to that time as 'the palmy days of the quill trade'. In that year the firm had supplied HM Stationery Office with 400,000 new pens and about 60,000 recut, and the India Office with over 2,000,000 quill pens.[37] A box of Hill's 'Metallised' quill pens, datable to 1908 from the printed testimonials enclosed in the box, contains a number of swan pens with gold- and silver-plated tips.(22) A patent for 'Gilding and Preparing Quills and Pens by Manual Labour and Chemical Operations, so as to render them more durable and useful', was granted to Charles Watt, a Surgeon, in 1818, which may also have been the process adopted by Messrs Hill.[38] The firm continued to appear in the *Post Office London Directory* up to and including 1950, as a maker of quill pens.

One of those who cut quills for Hill and Company and for several other firms, was William Southgate, who was born in 1853, the son of a Norwich shoemaker who came to Haggerston in London in the 1860s to find work; William was trained as a quill dresser and towards the end of his life, in 1919, he was one of very few still carrying on the trade. In the late 1870s, he signed a contract with the Aberdeen Quill Company and spent about three years in that city. He later worked for Francis Mordan and Company of the Albion Works, City Road, London for some two years, leaving their employ in May, 1889. He was approached in 1893, with an offer of employment as a parcel wax hand, by Henry Morrell of Hatton Garden, for whom he also cut quill pens. William Southgate lived with his wife Elizabeth, and their seven children, only four of whom were to survive infancy, in two adjoining cottages at 47 and 49 North Street, Bethnal Green, where he also carried out his cottage industry, using the copper boiler common to all such cottages to har-

den his quills in hot silver sand. His son Walter, in his autobiography, recalls that after school, he would sometimes earn 'tuppence' by delivering parcels of prepared quills to a firm of wholesale stationers in Paternoster Row in the City.[39] This firm was probably Watkins and McCombie, whose 'Royal Quills' were supplied to Queen Victoria and other members of the Royal Family, the Czarina of Russia, Gladstone, Disraeli, Balfour and many other notable persons. These pens were, according to a pencilled annotation by his son on the back of an advertising leaflet from a box of 'Royal Quills', usually cut by William Southgate.(23) In the early twentieth century, the revival of interest in calligraphy which followed the establishment of the Central School of Arts and Crafts, and the setting up by W. R. Lethaby, the first Principal, of classes under Edward Johnston, provided Southgate with another market for his quill pens, and these were supplied with carefully hand-written instructions.(24) He also supplied Lloyds of London with the quill pens with which entries in their Shipping Loss Book have always been recorded. In 1971, after some 230 years, this tradition was endangered when Lloyds were no longer able to find a professional source of quill pens after the retirement of their supplier up to that time. Walter Southgate, by then 82 years of age, who although he had not been allowed to follow his father into what the latter considered a dying trade, had learnt the art of quill-cutting by observing his father at work, was able to step into the breach and supply Lloyds with pens for a time, using his father's tools to prepare them.(118) Happily, this tradition is still carried on at Lloyds, the pens now prepared and cut from swan quills, by Mr Charles Stooks.[40]

The only quill pen firm listed after 1950 was Barton, Gray and Co, Ltd, of Mamora Street, East Dulwich, who were the last firm of quill pen manufacturers to appear in the *London Directory*, whose pen-cutting business survived until 1954, and it is interesting to note from the same directory, that the computer age was by then already in evidence, in the form of 'Punched Card Systems'.

11

Preparing & Cutting the Quill

The prepared quill has all the qualities necessary for a good pen: elasticity, durability, hardness and a form and weight which can be comfortably held, without fatigue, during long periods of writing. We have seen that the quill as imported, or as supplied by the farmer, was usually in its raw state, just as it left the bird. In this condition, the quill is resilient but soft and the barrel is covered by a membranous skin which prevents it being accurately split. It is also opaque and has a vascular membrane on the interior of the barrel which is not easily removed while the quill is in this raw state. It was the business of the quill-dresser to take the raw quills and to prepare them to be cut as pens; they had to be hardened, and by removing the membranous coverings, clarified.

Quills could be bought 'in the rough', prepared, or as finished pens. Richard Green, a 'Pen-Cutter and Dealer in Quills', whose early to mid-eighteenth century trade card,(25) and a later receipt for pens to Mr Gibbon, (presumably Edward Gibbon, the author of *The Decline and Fall of the Roman Empire*), are both in the Banks Collection, offered for sale a wide variety of quills and pens. In the same collection is a fine rococo trade card, dating from circa 1760, which advertises a similar range of quills and pens.(26) It was patently common practice, as one might expect, for the dressing of the raw quills and the making of the finished pens to be carried out in the same establishment. E. Crabbe, on his early-nineteenth century trade card, described himself a 'Pen and Quill Dresser'.(27)

Some quills imported from Holland were, unlike those of Eastern Europe or North America, shipped in an already hardened and clarified condition. The process used to prepare these Dutch quills was adopted by some quill-dressers in England, probably during the second half of the eighteenth century, and became known as 'dutchifying' or 'dutching'. The quills to be dutched were first gradually dampened by being placed in a moist cellar with their points directly touching the earth, or were wrapped for a number of hours in a damp cloth. (When thoroughly dampened, a quill is so elastic that it may be bent double without damage, and it is important that a degree of this elasticity is retained in the finished pen). A hole, about six inches square and the same deep, was then made in a glowing coal fire, and the dampened quill inserted in the centre, care being taken that it did not touch the coals. After a second or two, the entire quill barrel having been uniformly heated, it was then removed, placed on a warm steel plate, and drawn beneath a metal dutching-hook, a heavy tool with a fine edge, which flattened the quill and removed its outer covering, shrivelling and crumbling the inner membrane, and extracting any oily substances or moisture still present. The flattened barrel was then re-inserted into the cavity of the fire, which restored its roundness. The process could be repeated if necessary until the barrel of the quill was clear and hard, care being taken not to overdo the heating to the point of causing brittleness. Any remaining traces of grease or membrane were removed by rubbing the quill with a piece of the skin of the dog-fish.[1]

Contemporary accounts of this dutching process do not mention cutting off the end of the quill barrel to allow the escape of air during heating, but an examination of prepared but uncut quills reveals a small ragged hole in each tip, caused by the explosive release of the air compressed towards the end as the quill passed beneath the dutching-hook, which was ac-

8

companied by a sharp report, known in the trade as 'snapping'. A group of such quills, one still bearing lateral indentations from the tool, and all containing loose fragments of the shrivelled inner membrane, is bound with coloured string, as sold in the early nineteenth century.(28) The dutching-hook has been described as resembling the instrument used by cutlers to burnish their hardware.[2]

A somewhat simpler method of clarifying, degreasing and hardening the quill involved the use of hot sand or ashes, and is the basis of the method still used by calligraphers today. The quills, their tips removed, were first soaked in water, either by having only their ends covered and allowing capillary action to fill the barrels, or by immersing the latter totally. After a period of hours, when they were thoroughly damp and pliable, taking a few at a time, the water was shaken from them and they were plunged briefly into a pan of hot sand or ashes, which shrivelled and removed the membranes and any oily substances, and left the barrels clear and hard. A final rub with a piece of fish-skin finished them off. (Some modern scribes recommend a piece of sack-cloth impregnated with pumice powder for this purpose). The term 'dutching' had, by the 1830s, become synonymous with the hardening and clarification of quills, whether by the hot sand method or with the use of the dutching-iron,[3] and is still used today.[4] Another recommended method of clarifying quills was to scrape off the outer skin of the quills and cut off their ends; the barrels were then placed in boiling water in which small quantities of salt and alum had been dissolved, for a quarter of an hour, after which they were dried in a pan of hot sand or in an oven.[5]

The colour of a well-cured quill is similar to that of blond cow-horn, and the cut edge of such a quill often has a slight amber cast to it; some quills, particularly in the early nineteenth century, were artificially coloured, for purely cosmetic purposes, in a solution of turmeric which produced a yellowish tint, or were soaked in mild nitric acid, which had the same effect but tended to make them more brittle.

The clarification and hardening of quills using heat does not appear to have met with general approval much before the mid-eighteenth century, but was nevertheless sufficiently widespread in the sixteenth to cause Palatino to express his disapproval of the practice. Writing in 1540, he advocated the choice of a quill which was already hard and clear, from which the fatty membrane should be scraped away, using the back of the pen-knife blade. He goes on to warn the reader not to rub quills with a cloth, nor to 'put them under hot ashes as many do, to make them round.'[6] His contemporary, Juan Vives, in his *Lingue Latinae Exercitatio* of 1538, in a dialogue between writing master and student, implies his approval of the suggestion that the latter should make his quills smooth by spitting on them and rubbing them on the inside of his coat or on the thigh of his hose.[7] Fanti, in 1514, and Tagliente, ten years later, merely advise the scraping away of the fatty membrane with the back of the knife.[8]

Other writing manuals which advocate the choice of a quill which is round and clear, are those of Arrighi, circa 1523, and Amphiareo, of 1548.[9] Augustino da Siena, in 1568, suggests one which is round and strong,[10] while Hamon, in a dialogue on handwriting in Plantin's *Première et la seconde partie des dialogues françois pour les jeunes enfants*, of 1567, advises a barrel which is long, clean, dry and not too greasy.[11] Scalzini, in 1581, warns against quills that are too fresh and consequently too fatty.[12] In England, Peter Bales, in *The Writing Schoolemaster*, of 1590, advises the reader to 'clens your quill well'.[13]

It would seem that, among writing masters at least, the natural tempering of the quills through the passage of time, followed by scraping to remove the unwanted membranes, was considered preferable to any form of artificial curing. Martin Billingsley, in his *Pens Excellencie* of 1618, gives the same instruction, and the method was still being advocated in much the same terms in 1714, when, in his *Second Part of Natural Writing*, George Shelley writes:

> choose a round hard and clear Quill, and with the back Edge of your Knife, scrape off the Scurf or Film from the Pipe,

words repeated verbatim a century later by C. Bradbury, who, in his *The Penman's Companion*, of circa 1815, also writes that 'age best mellows and meliorates a quill'.

Pride suggests that the clarification of quills in England, using hot sand or dutching-iron, dates in both cases, from about 1775; in 1812, he writes:

I do not know how long we have been in the habit of preparing Quills by either of these methods but it has not been much used till within these last fifty years.

He adds, throwing further light on previous methods,

In an old school book I remember meeting with instructions to prepare Quills, which was simply by holding them over a charcoal fire, and then scraping them with a knife, and to this direction was added This is the best mode, probatum est.[14]

Dutching was, however, practised in England somewhat earlier, at the latest by 1760, when R. Hopwood, a Soho 'Bookseller and Pen-Cutter' advertised for sale a 'newly-invented Dutching Instrument' by which 'You may make Feathers or bad Quills as hard as you please, and the most specky Quills as transparent as Glass by this Method'. He sold the instrument with a book of instructions for six shillings. The cutting of this advertisement, in the possession of Phillip Poole, although dated, gives no clue as to the newspaper in which it appeared.

The quill pen quickly lost its sharpness in use and required frequent re-cutting. In skilful hands this operation could be repeated many times to extend the useful life of a pen, and there are recorded instances of prodigious feats of writing using the same quill. Philemon Holland, (1552-1637), a Coventry schoolmaster and self-styled physician, is said to have written the whole of his translation of Camden's *Britannia* with the same pen, commemorating the fact in verse:

With one sole pen I wrote this book
Made of a grey goose quill;
A pen it was when I it tooke,
And a pen I leave it still.[15]

The story may be apochryphal; another version records his translation of the whole of Pliny's *Natural History* with one pen, the event commemorated by the same rhyme.[16]

In 1834, it was estimated that not more than one pen in ten sold was ever mended, and although a skilled professional pen-cutter could cut up to 'two-thirds of a long thousand' (twelve hundred) pens in a day, it is clear that most people found difficulty in learning how to make or repair a pen.[17] Writing in 1812, a London pen-cutter, B. Pride, confirms this:

The simple Art of making a Pen is not generally known; I have often been astonished at hearing

persons who are in the constant habit of using Pens, lament their inability to make or mend one, and I have frequently observed good writers very inexpert in performing this little office for themselves.[18]

Even amongst professional clerks who would no doubt be trained to repair their worn pens, a single pen might only be expected to last perhaps a day. In the Exchequer accounts showing the quarterly allowances of stationery to the various departmental clerks, each clerk received at least 100 pens per quarter and some double or treble that number; most clerks were also allowed a new pen-knife each quarter.[19]

A prepared quill is very tough, and the knife used to shape it had to be very sharp, the blade ground to a curve at the back to facilitate curved or scooping cuts, but left flat at the front to make straight cuts, both necessary to form a pen. The barbs of the feather were removed by holding a portion near the tip between thumb and knife blade and peeling it away, using the knife to cut it off at the lower end, to avoid tearing into the usable barrel; the newly-bared shaft was usually cut off at a length convenient to the user. In the case of commercially-cut pens, the narrow barb of the leading edge of the feather was often left intact in the case of pinions, for instance, or lightly trimmed in the case of seconds or thirds, towards the barrel, and in most cases the length of the quills was also shortened. Although those full-feather pens flourished by actors on the stage engender a certain theatrical quality, in practice they would present some difficulty to the user, if not a degree of danger to his eyes as he bent over his desk, especially in the case of the larger swans' feathers; notwithstanding, there is a tradition that swans' quill pens are often left full-feather. Most portraits of scribes of all periods do, however, show quills which have been at least partially trimmed and shortened.

The quill was then held firmly in the left hand, and with the ball of the right thumb pressed hard against the opposing second finger to ensure support, the shaping of the pen was carried out in a series of careful cuts, towards the body. As Juan de Yciar observed, in his manual of 1550, it is relatively easy to demonstrate practically the art of cutting a pen, but almost impossible to describe it adequately in words;[20] no doubt for this reason, a number of later books on the subject included step-by-step illustrations of the method. One such manual, Paillason's *L'Arte d'Écrire*, published

10

in several editions in the late eighteenth century, shows clearly the sequence of cuts.(29) The end of the barrel was first cut off at an angle, the quill turned over and a similar cut made, forming 'horns'. By introducing the knife blade between these points, edge uppermost, and exerting gentle leverage upwards, a short slit would be made in what would become the top of the pen in use. Turning the quill once more, the scoop of the pen was next formed by a single curved cut through the end of the barrel, at a depth of about half its diameter. Two further carefully curved cuts formed the shoulders of the pen, converging towards their points. The final trimming of these points, or 'nibbing', was then carried out, using another quill inserted into the barrel on which to cut. Some masters preferred a piece of ebony or ivory for this purpose, or even the scribes's own thumbnail, with or without a black thimble, an operation calling for a steady hand and strong nerves! The colour of the ebony or thimble, against the lightness of the quill, was an aid to accurate cutting.

Accounts in other writing manuals varied in accordance with the preferences of their authors, Paillason's stage C often being dispensed with altogether. Some scribes made only a tiny incision with the knife blade at stage D, extending the slit to the required length by a quick upward flick of the peg, or pointed end of the knife handle, while a strong pressure was maintained on the top of the barrel with the thumb of the left hand, at the intended limit of the slit. Finally, the nibbing of the pen was performed by making first an oblique cut and then a final vertical cut, near and in the direction of the points. *(Figure 1)*. (In practice, the pressure of this vertical cut, even with an extremely sharp knife used with a slight rocking movement, can cause a slight distortion of the horn-like material; many modern scribes, therefore, make a second infinitesimal vertical cut to remove any slight 'burr').

The vertical cut was made either at right angles to the slit of the pen, producing a square-cut pen, or for a left- or right-oblique pen, at the appropriate angle. The angle of the nibbing was varied according to the nature of the hand to be written, as was the length of the slit, which radically affected the flexibility of the pen. Other factors which affected the character of the writing, and had therefore to be modified for each of the different hands in vogue at any

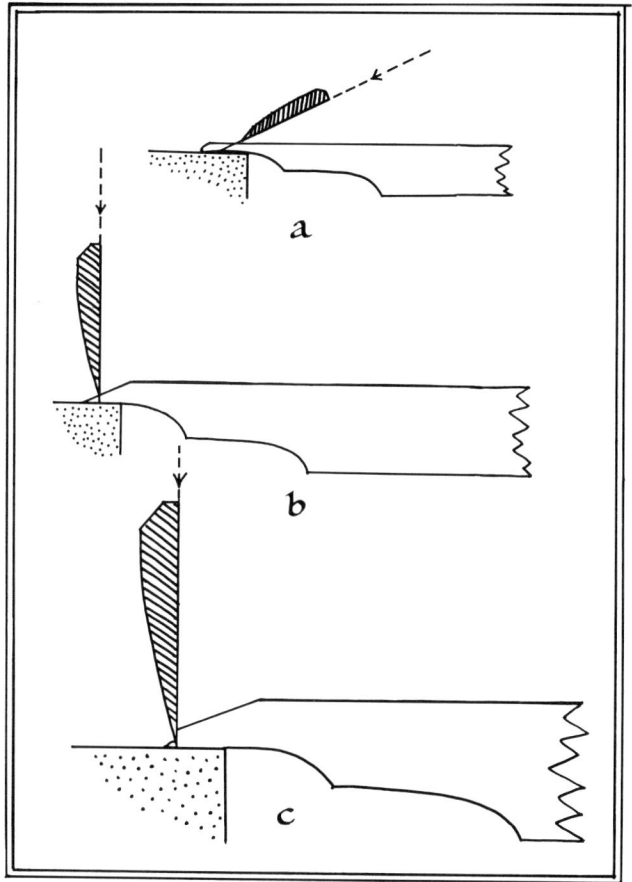

Figure 1

particular period, were the breadth of the nib and the angle at which it was held in relation to the writing line. George Shelley, who was Writing Master to Christ's Hospital in the reign of Queen Anne, produced a number of writing manuals, in one of which, *The Second Part of Natural Writing*, published in 1714, he showed graphically the variations of nib-angle needed to perform the hands commonly written at that time.(30) He also specified the degree of broadness of the nibs for each hand, and the length of slit. Among these hands, taught for general or commercial purposes, and still fashionable a century later, were the Round Hand and the similar but less formal and more flourished Running Hand, either of which would now be recognised as Copperplate.(31 and 32) These hands relied for their distinctive thick downward strokes and their thin hair-line upward strokes, on the degree of hand pressure applied by the writer, and the consequent degree of spreading of the flexible nib, which therefore required a long slit. Shelley recommended a square-ended pen [(30) pen 4] with a narrow

11

nib, for the Round Hand, and the slightly left-oblique pen [pen 5] for the Running Hand. For the Square or German Text Hands, the thick strokes were achieved without pressure, using a right-oblique nib, [pens 2 or 3], cut slightly broader than the intended stroke, and because less flexibility was required, the slit was shorter.(33) For the legal hands, left-oblique pens were used. The Engrossing Hand used Shelley's pen 6, cut with a nib slightly broader than the minim strokes. This hand was used until the early 1890s for the engrossing of copies of wills and other legal documents, along with the German Text for the introductory phrases, exactly as it had been in Shelley's time.(34) In his memoirs of some forty-two years on the copying staff of the Probate and Divorce Registries at Doctors Common, and later at Somerset House, J. W. Knight reminisces:

> We were supplied with bundles of turkey quills, which we ourselves had to cut and shape to enable us to write the Engrossing Hand.[21]

The archaic legal Court Hand, virtually unchanged from medieval times, and significantly almost indecipherable to the legally untrained eye, was still being used for some legal documents in the nineteenth century.(35) It required a markedly left-oblique pen, [pen 7], and a stiff nib with a short slit.

These considerations of the various elements of the cutting of the pen, its nib angle, breadth and slit length, were crucial to the satisfactory writing of any particular hand, and in the eighteenth and nineteenth centuries, it was the practice among pen-cutters to keep specimens of those pens which had found favour with their customers, as patterns to be copied in the event of repeated orders. John Wilkes, a London pen-maker, complaining, in 1799, of his difficulty in obtaining good quills, writes:

> I spare neither expence or trouble in procuring them, and pay every possible attention to the making of them into pens, so as to please and suit the writer, if I know the hand they are wanted for; and whenever I succeed in this point, I always keep a few for patterns, that I may not mistake afterwards when more are wanted.[22]

The chance and possibly unique survival of a group of such pattern pens, dating from the early nineteenth century, and each marked with the name of the individual or trade customer, is worthy of note.(36) Still in the possession of a descendant of William Frederick Hennell of Haggerston Old Town, Shoreditch, whose occupation, on the birth certicate of his son, in 1874, is given as 'Quill Pen Cutter', these goose quills are inscribed in ink: 'Spencer Brunton', 'Secretary Devonˢ Club', 'Adams Bros', 'C.R. Left Hand Brown', 'Brook's Club April 1805' and 'Waterlow', the latter a firm of wholesale stationers, established in 1810.[23]

III

The Scribe's Knife

The term 'penknife' is widely used today to describe any small general purpose folding pocket-knife, and many people have probably never considered that it owes its origin to the late Georgian folding pen-knives of similar design, themselves the final development in a long tradition of pen-knives going back even beyond the use of the quill pen, when scribes first cut the barrel of a reed to fashion a pen. Folding knives for the pocket or writing-case, however, were purely a convenience for the personal use of the private writer; the professional scribe, to whom the knife was an essential tool of his trade, has always preferred a more substantial rigid-handled knife.

We are fortunate that there are many contemporary representations of scribes at work in early manuscripts, often depicting the Gospel writers. The importance to the scribe of his penknife is evident in the frequency with which the writer is shown with the pen in his right hand and his knife, the point holding down any slight undulation in the parchment, but immediately available to repair the pen, in his left.(37) Parchment, the prepared skin of animals, has a number of layers, and the erasure of errors by scraping was the other main function of the scribe's knife.

In the sixteenth century, some writing masters, among them Palatino, and Juan de Yciar, who quoted and endorsed the former's view, advocated that the knife should be kept exclusively for the cutting and repair of the pen.[1] B. Pride, writing in 1812, demonstrates his perception of human nature when he warns that

> . . . Pen-knives are very unfit for cutting pens if used for other purposes, such as erasing writing from parchment or paper, peeling apples, picking nails, cutting corns, or any other purpose except the one intended, but very often a Pen-knife is made to serve in lieu of a dozen other instruments, and the

cutler is blamed for bad knives, and the quill dealer for bad quills.[2]

It is probable that some medieval scribes also subscribed to this view and kept a separate knife for erasing, but a secondary knife designed specifically for this purpose seems to have been an innovation of the early seventeenth century. Pairs of scribal knives, of South German or Italian origin, often with extremely long but well-balanced ivory handles, date from this time, one knife having a single cutting edge, the other a double-edged leaf-shaped blade, designed for scraping.(38 and Colour plate II(i)l and m) These knives are usually etched with classical figures, animals and birds in vigorous scrollwork, and many retain at least some of their original gilding; they were clearly not merely the working tools of an ordinary scribe and seem to be more suitable to the preparation of parchment. A third variety of knives with straight-sided blades and chisel edges may have served a similar purpose and would also be very suitable for the opening of wax-sealed letters.(39) An example of the single-edged type, formerly in the Hever Castle Collection, and inscribed with the name of its original aristocratic owner, Signore Barone Bartolemeo Braschini, has an ornamental serration on the back edge of the blade, a feature which is common to all the single-edged knives of this type and probably more than mere decoration; placing the index finger on this point would greatly improve the scribe's grip while using the knife to cut his parchment to size.(40) Another example, this time with an eraser blade, in the Charles Thomas Collection, is etched with the armorial of a cardinal and is dated 1615. A number of similar knives may be seen in the Sheffield City Museum Collection.(41 to 43) Knives of a similar type were used in the Low Countries.(317) An eighteenth century erasing knife, the leaf-shaped blade by then of squatter proportions, and the handle much shorter, appears in an engraving with other scribe's knives in *L'Arte d'Écrire*, part of Paillason's *Dictionaire des Arts*, of circa 1780.(44) By the nineteenth century such erasers were commonplace and some Victorian desk-knives had both cutting and erasing edges on a composite blade.(117)

Many writing masters from the sixteenth century onwards have described the essential features of a good pen-knife, and in general the majority are in agreement, although in practice surviving knives show considerable variations. The shortish blade should be narrow, pointed and of finely-tempered steel, capable of taking a very fine edge. Tempering to an overall blueish colour was considered by one professional pen-cutter of the early nineteenth century to be the optimum,[3] while a few years later, in 1827, a London cutler, Mr Smith of Cheapside, formerly of Sheffield, tempered his knives only to a straw colour.[4] The blade should be ground to a curve on one side and remain flat on the other, to facilitate the shaping of the pen, which requires several curved or scooping cuts and a number of straight ones. The back edge of the knife should not be rounded; its square edge was needed to scrape the outer covering of the quill, as we have seen in the previous chapter. *(Figure 2)*.

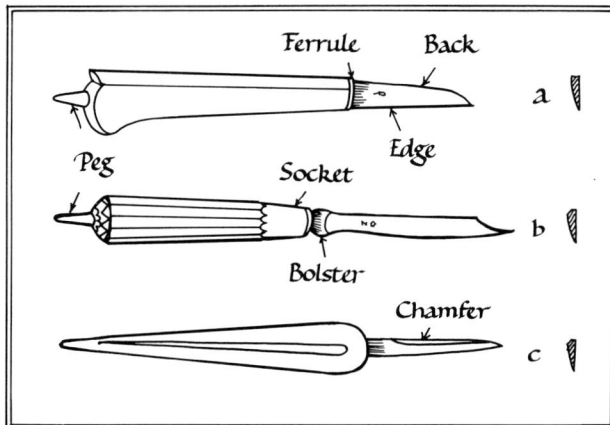

Figure 2

The handle of the knife, ideally as long as the breadth of the user's palm, should be of such a section, usually rectangular, octagonal or oval, as to ensure a firm grip. Such a knife was also unlikely to roll off the desk, causing damage to itself or injury to the scribe. Some knife handles tapered away from the blade,

terminating in a point, which could be used to extend the slit of the pen during its making or repair. *(Figure 2c)*. This shape, however, did not meet with general approval before the mid-nineteenth century, when the majority of quill-knives are of this form. From the late sixteenth to the early nineteenth century, most pen-knife handles either had no taper, or tapered towards the blade, and many had a small point or peg inset into the end, for the extension of the pen's slit. *(Figure 2a and b)*. The earliest reference to such a peg seems to be that of Martin Billingsley, an English writing master, in 1618, when in his description of pen-making, he writes:

> . . . When you have done so, take the end of your knife if it have a pegg, or else another quill, and make a slit up suddenly, even in the cut you gave before.[5]

Evidence for its even earlier use is provided by a Friesian silver pen-knife handle formerly in the author's collection, unfortunately lacking its blade; the sides are engraved with armorials and the owner's name, along with the date 1576.(45)

The earliest recorded knife which can be positively identified as a quill-knife has scales of ornamented brass which may originally have been gilded, with a ring terminal for suspension from a cord.(**Colour plate III(i)a**) The blade is flat at the front and has been ground to a curve at the back, the classic form for cutting a quill. Dating from the twelfth to fourteenth century, the knife was excavated in the early 1980s from the mud of the Thames at low water. No other knives of earlier date than the sixteenth century appear to have been positively identified as pen-knives, and when we consider the scribal knives of the Dark Ages and the later medieval period, we must rely upon the evidence of manuscript illuminations for their forms. *(Figure 3)*. It is difficult to see any obvious pattern in the development of these medieval knives, but one or two features are worthy of note. A number of twelfth-century knives have either a raised button or ball, or a serration, on the back edge of the blade near the point, which would act as a stop on which the scribe could rest his index finger when using the knife to hold down the surface of his parchment, or to enhance his grip while cutting the skin to size. Another feature of a number of knives of the same century is a distinctive ball terminal to the handle, which may have

A Chronology of the Pen-knife

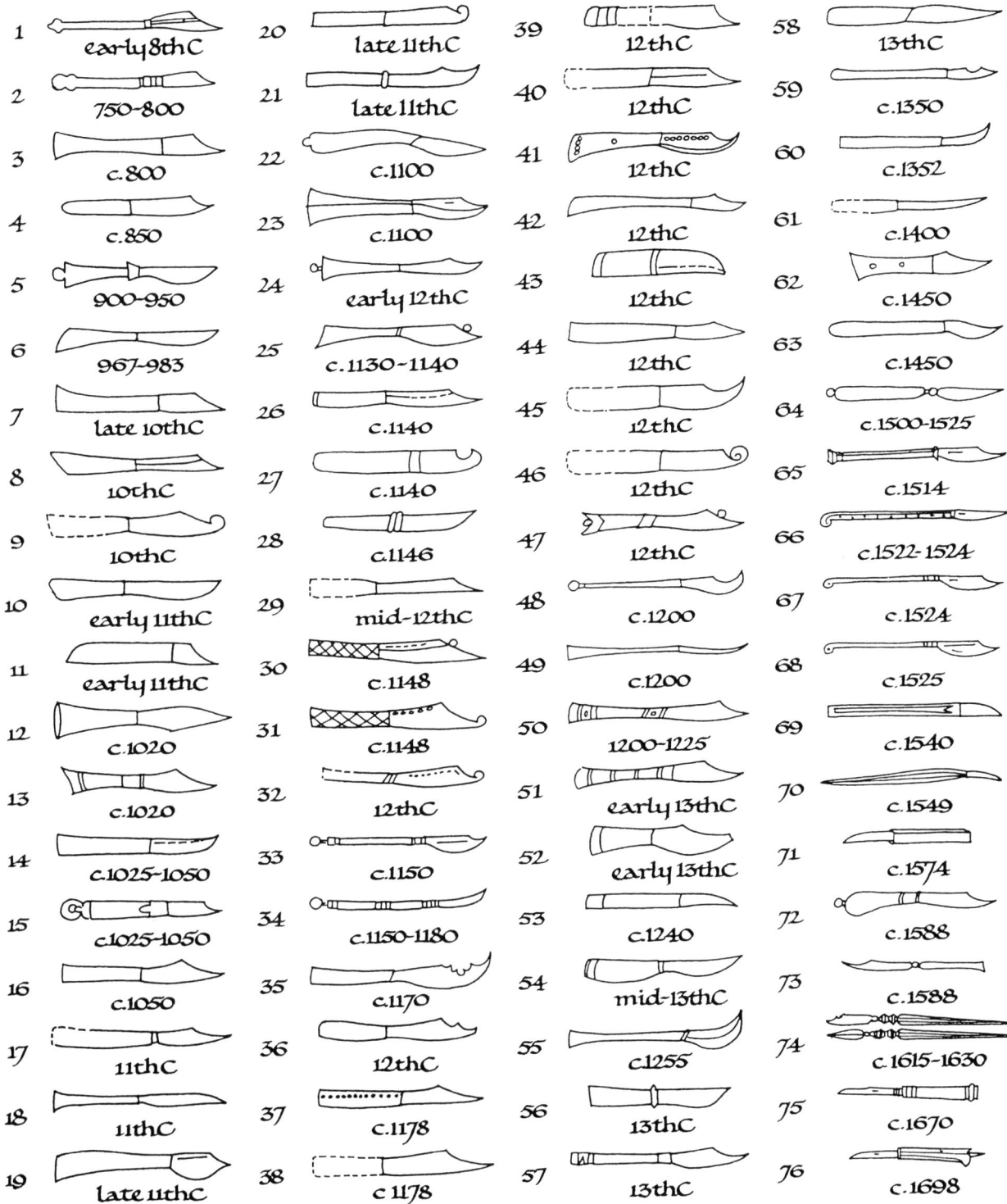

1 — early 8th C	20 — late 11th C	39 — 12th C	58 — 13th C
2 — 750–800	21 — late 11th C	40 — 12th C	59 — c.1350
3 — c.800	22 — c.1100	41 — 12th C	60 — c.1352
4 — c.850	23 — c.1100	42 — 12th C	61 — c.1400
5 — 900–950	24 — early 12th C	43 — 12th C	62 — c.1450
6 — 967–983	25 — c.1130–1140	44 — 12th C	63 — c.1450
7 — late 10th C	26 — c.1140	45 — 12th C	64 — c.1500–1525
8 — 10th C	27 — c.1140	46 — 12th C	65 — c.1514
9 — 10th C	28 — c.1146	47 — 12th C	66 — c.1522–1524
10 — early 11th C	29 — mid–12th C	48 — c.1200	67 — c.1524
11 — early 11th C	30 — c.1148	49 — c.1200	68 — c.1525
12 — c.1020	31 — c.1148	50 — 1200–1225	69 — c.1540
13 — c.1020	32 — 12th C	51 — early 13th C	70 — c.1549
14 — c.1025–1050	33 — c.1150	52 — early 13th C	71 — c.1574
15 — c.1025–1050	34 — c.1150–1180	53 — c.1240	72 — c.1588
16 — c.1050	35 — c.1170	54 — mid–13th C	73 — c.1588
17 — 11th C	36 — 12th C	55 — c.1255	74 — c.1615–1630
18 — 11th C	37 — c.1178	56 — 13th C	75 — c.1670
19 — late 11th C	38 — c.1178	57 — 13th C	76 — c.1698

With acknowledgement to Michael Gullick for several examples from unpublished medieval manuscripts, and to d'Haenens, Albert – "Écrire, un couteau dans la main gauche" from Mélanges d'histoire de l'art et d'archéologie offerts à Jaques Stiennon, Liège 1982, also drawn to my attention by Michael Gullick · MF

Figure 3

been used as a burnisher after the erasure of mistakes; on the other hand, it may have been no more than a decorative finial, such as is often found on later knives.

In considering the more general forms of medieval pen-knives, the first thing which is self-evident is that narrow blades were not usual, most knives conforming to the types used for eating and other purposes, which calls into question the assertion of most sixteenth century and later writers that a narrow blade is an essential feature of a good pen-knife. Perhaps more important than the breadth of the blade is the way it is ground. It is obvious that a broad straight-sided blade could not smoothly cut a curved scoop, but a knife ground to a curve on one side is equally capable of negotiating such a scoop, irrespective of its breadth. *(Figure 4)*. An interesting letter on this

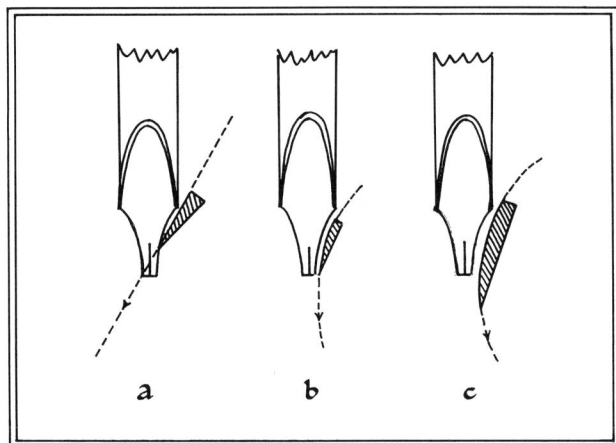

Figure 4

question from an anonymous reader appeared in *Nicholson's Journal*, in March, 1804:

Sir,

Useful discoveries are sometimes derived from the common occurences of life and that which I am now going to mention is a mere accident of this kind. About three years ago I took up a large pocket knife which had been newly ground and used it for making a pen, and was not a little surprized to find that it answered the purpose much better than my penknife ever had. I mentioned this circumstance soon after to the cutler who made the knife. He said he had no doubt of the truth of my observation, as he could harden and temper a large blade better than a small one; because there is more difficulty in ascertaining the proper degree of heat in the latter than in the former.

And it may be perhaps a mechanical truth, that a strong knife will overcome the resistance of a hard

quill with less exertion of the hand than a weak one. The blade of the knife that I use, and which gave rise to these observations, is four inches in length and half an inch in breadth.

It may perhaps be supposed that a knife of these dimensions is improperly constructed for cutting the sides of a pen into a curve, but it will be found on trial, that the breadth of the blade is no impediment, for it is the form of the edge which it receives by whetting, that renders a broad blade quite as manageable as a narrow one.

I am, Sir,
A constant Reader of your
Truly Valuable Journal,
W[6]

The knives of the early to mid-sixteenth century tend to have handles proportionately longer and more slender than those which preceded or followed them, not, one might think, conducive to a firm grip. *(Figure 3, 65-68)*. An all-steel pen-knife of similar form, and of this period, was excavated in the early 1980s from the mud of the Thames.**(Colour plate III(i)b)** To assist its successful shaping of the scooping cuts, it has a chamfered back edge, a feature incorporated in the design of many later pen-knives. A similar knife can be seen, along with other contemporary writing implements, in a portrait of Margaret Tudor, (1489-1541), in the Scottish National Portrait Gallery.**(46 and detail)**

Another interesting pen-knife found in the bed of the Thames has an ivory or bone handle, stained by its burial to a rich brown, and having an unusually bold peg, suitable for burnishing the parchment after an erasure. The simple straight-edged blade has the appearance of having been cut down, perhaps from a domestic eating knife. From the style of the cutler's mark, a Roman Y, it can be dated not later than the early seventeenth century.**(47)** A knife of similar slab-sided form with a straight-edged blade is illustrated by Hercolani in his *Lo Scrittor' Utile et brieve Segretario*, of 1574.[7]

For a writer whose work required his movement from place to place, a knife which could be safely carried on his person was an essential. Many pen-knives had fitted paper or *cuir bouilli* cases, but another solution to the problem, in the mid-seventeenth century, was to have a reversible blade which could be unscrewed and fitted into the handle when not in use. Two very similar examples of such knives, with different London cutlers' marks, one in horn, the other in engine-turned bone, both date from this period; each has a peg attached to the blade, which also acts as a handle when unscrewing the blade for use, and in each case the narrow blade is chamfered on both sides of the back edge, which would allow its use by either a right-handed or a left-handed person.(48, 49)

A documentary pen-knife with an ivory handle of lozenge section, prick-engraved with ownership initials and the date 1698, has a simple straight-edged blade with a collared handle-joint but no bolster.(50) An almost identical knife is depicted in a number of *trompe l'oeil* paintings of about this date, by Edwaert Collyer, a Dutch painter working in London under the anglicised name Edward Collier, one of which is in the Smiley Collection at the Hunterian Art Gallery of the University of Glasgow.(51) Collier seems to have specialised in such still-life paintings, which usually include other writing equipment and materials, such as sealing wax, quill pens, seals and portable pen-cases or penners. Another pen-knife, which also appears in several of his works, has a curved claw-like peg, a type which does not appear to be recorded on a surviving pen-knife; its form would suggest the likelihood of its breakage in use, which may be the reason.(52)

Pen-knives having straight blades without a bolster at the handle-joint remained in fashion for some years. George Shelley, in the engraved frontispiece portrait of his *Second Part of Natural Writing*, published in 1714, is depicted with such a knife, the handle apparently of hardstone, with a peg.(53) Of course, there is no way of knowing how long Shelley had owned it and he would certainly have been unlikely to replace a trusted and serviceable knife.

In common with eating knives, however, the bolstered handle-joint became popular on pen-knives from about 1700, and is found on the majority of knives for the rest of the century. Blades from the early eighteenth century usually have a curved edge, sometimes of distinctly scimitar-like form. In trying to discern a pattern of development in the styles of pen-knife blades and handles used during the eighteenth century, a useful source is the cutler's trade card. The majority of cutlers seem to have included pen-knives in their stock-in-trade, which may be seen in the engraved illustrations of their wares which most trade cards display.(54 to 61)

Many of the handles follow the designs of contemporary eating cutlery, with or without the addition of a peg. Such handles, usually silver-mounted, are found in various hardstones, particularly agate and jasper,(62 to 65) ivory,(66, 67) foiled tortoiseshell and ivory,(69) or die-stamped silver,(68 and 70) all of which types may be found in the handles of eating knives and forks of the period.[8] Another type of handle popular in the first half of the eighteenth century was of tortoiseshell, inlaid with scrolling foliage in silver piqué,(71,72) while a humbler brass-handled pen-knife of the same period has wriggle-engraved decoration reminiscent of the decoration commonly found on late seventeenth century pewterwares.(73)

A type of die-stamped silver-handled pen-knife has previously been attributed to the last quarter of the eighteenth century.[9] Such knives would, however, appear to be of somewhat earlier date. A very large example, complete with its *cuir bouilli* covered case, has a blade impressed with the cutler's mark SPOON.(68) This mark was entered in the Register of the Sheffield Cutlers' Company by John Spooner, in 1723; the same mark, with the addition of an anchor above, was entered, also by a John Spooner, possibly his son, in 1736. Neither mark was still in use by 1773, when the first Sheffield directory was published,[10] and it seems likely that this knife dates from the second quarter of the century, a dating which is supported by the style of the blade. The maker's mark on the handle, I.S. in an oval, presumably for John Spooner, is found on another smaller knife with a similar blade, also marked SPOON.(70b) A different maker's mark, I.S. above a six-pointed star in a heart, is on the handle of another similar knife,(70d) and is also the maker's mark of the silver handle of a pen-knife in the Victoria and Albert Museum, the blade of which is marked SPOON,[11] and is therefore also attributable to John Spooner. Another die-stamped silver-handled knife of Sheffield origin,(70c) has a cutler's mark Z under a heart, a mark entered by George Harrison in 1670, again by Cotton Watkin in 1705, and by another Cotton Watkin in 1731. It would seem likely that this knife was made by one or other of the Watkins. A further, and particularly small example of this type of knife, perhaps made for a lady or child, and unmarked on either blade or handle, is unusual in having a steel peg.(70a) In the second half of the eighteenth century quill knives were also made with handles of Sheffield Plate.(74)

Blades, when badly worn through repeated sharpening over a long period, would be replaced, and it is not unusual to find examples of pen-knives with a handle type earlier than one would expect from the style of the blade. The cutler's mark RAVEN, for example, which appears on the replacement blade of a fluted ivory-handled knife of the early eighteenth century,(67) was entered at Sheffield by Joshua Morton in 1760, while the mark EVANS under a crown, on the blade of a knife whose handle may also be dated to the early years of the eighteenth century,(65) is possibly that of the London cutler of that name who worked towards the end of the century.

By the end of the eighteenth century, blades had become quite short, and in the case of those made in France, distinctly curved, a form also adopted by a minority of English cutlers. Knives from this time were sometimes provided with a number of blades which could be brought into use as each dulled through use, thus avoiding the need for the constant re-sharpening of a single blade. A French pen-knife of sectional construction in black horn, with ivory collars, unscrews to reveal three spare blades at one end and a needle-sharp spike at the other, suggesting that this was a scrivener's knife, the pricker intended for the marking out of the parchment prior to the ruling of the guidelines, or as a bodkin or *broche* for the piercing of several sheets of parchment to enable their tying together as a *brochure*, which is, incidentally, the origin of that term.(75 and detail)

A sectional English pen-knife, in ivory, also has three of its original four interchangeable blades, which screw into the threaded socket of the handle, as required. In addition to its perpetual calendar, this knife conceals a rounded peg-burnisher, a cavity containing wafer seals and a chequered seal-matrix with which to impress them.(76 and detail) It was made by John Wilkes, an inventive business-man who ran a Quill and Pen Warehouse at 57 Cornhill, London, in the late eighteenth century, until the business was taken over, in 1803, by Thomas Lund. Wilkes wrote a treatise on pen-cutting which he published in 1799, and in which he is described as John Wilkes, MAP, presumably 'Master of the Art of Pen-cutting'.[12] In it, as well as instructions for the preparation and cutting of pens, he gives details of his 'Penman's Boxes', 'Pen-knives' and his 'recently invented Pen-nibber'. An example of this nibber, interchangeable with the pen-blade, is attached to a knife in the Charles Thomas Collection,(77) and the same instrument is found in different and independent forms.(Chapter IV). Another knife by Wilkes in the Thomas Collection has an eraser blade.(78)

The idea of a knife with multiple blades was one which would have found favour with those who wrote a great deal, clerks, scriveners or law-writers in particular, and there were several ingenious solutions to the problem. Towards the end of the eighteenth century, there were some sixty-six pen-knife cutlers in Sheffield, many of whom were making folding pen-knives using a variety of materials for the handle scales, including ivory, bone, stag-horn, cow-horn and tortoiseshell. A five-bladed folding knife, the blades interchangeable, with stag-horn scales, has the cutler's mark REES.(79) Its steel peg moves through ninety degrees to allow the release and replacement of the blade. Knives of this type are illustrated in Smith's *Key to Sheffield Manufactures* of 1816,(80) from which it will be seen that more conventional multi-bladed pen-knives were also available.[13] Knives with several detachable blades were sold in leather-covered wooden pocket-cases with slots for the spare blades; a typical example, with four interchangeable blades, is marked on each blade with the name of the previously-mentioned Thomas Lund, of 57 Cornhill.(81)

An unusual four-bladed folding pen-knife, by Joseph Rodgers of Sheffield, its handle a complete roe-buck antler, is impressed with the Royal Cypher of George IV on each blade and can therefore be dated to the 1820s.(82) Also of this period is a London-made knife with four folding blades and finely engraved mother-of-pearl scales, reminiscent of, and possibly inspired by, the Chinese gaming counters made for the European market during the Regency.(83) A feature of these multi-bladed knives is that one of the blades usually differs slightly from the remainder in having a distinctly curved edge, presumably for the purpose of erasing.

Another type of multi-bladed pen-knife had sliding blades, housed within the handle when not in use, which were particularly popular in France.[14] Some had as many as four blades; a late example dating from the mid-nineteenth century, with typically French curved blades, was recently purchased in a street market in Paris, but has also very strong affinities with some contemporary Sheffield-made desk-knives and quill-cutting machines, such as those made by Rodgers, and it may be that these were imported into France.(84)

A late eighteenth-century folding single-bladed pen-knife, with ivory scales and a steel peg, has a curved blade with a cutler's mark in the form of a pen-knife, and is of French origin.(85) A somewhat later example with tortoiseshell scales and a peg of the same material, by Rodgers of Sheffield, has a second spring-loaded general-purpose blade which also acts as a nibber.(86) Similar folding knives are illustrated in *Smith's Key*, as is a wide range of small folding pocket pen-knives.(87, 88) A 'hollow-pointed' example with tortoiseshell scales,(89) is very similar to several illustrated in the *Key*. Ivory and mother-of-pearl scales are also commonly found on this type of knife.(90) Novelty pen-knives, in combination with pens or pencils, were popular at this period; an example with mother-of-pearl scales, combined with a silver porte-crayon, has a blade marked CARRS, with the Royal Cypher of George IV.(91) Another novel and amusing late Georgian folding pen-knife has an ivory handle carved as a human leg, a goose, presumably attempting revenge on behalf of its species for the liberties taken with its quills, pecking at the toe.(92) Novelty pen-knives in the form of percussion muskets, which are found with design registration marks dating from the early 1840s, are typical of the many 'form' pen-knives which became increasingly popular during the Victorian period.(93) Joseph Rodgers of Sheffield, in the firm's catalogue of the 1860s, were still offering such knives, at two pounds six shillings a dozen in ivory and two pounds two shillings in cocoa-wood. These and the multi-purpose small pocket-knives, which provided work for the pen-knife cutlers as the demand for quill pen-knives declined, were, of course, aimed at a market other than the scribe.

True pen-knives were, of course, still made, with handles in a variety of materials, including ivory, pressed horn and stag-horn, sometimes with perpetual calendars and wafer-seal terminals, each incised, grooved or fluted for a better grip.(94 to 98) B. Pride, in 1812, was not in favour of handles which tapered to a point, preferring a taper towards the blade, with a peg. The material of the handle was not important;

> those of black ebony with an ivory peg look neat and are not expensive.[15]

He would, no doubt, have approved of a black pressed horn pen-knife of about this time.(99)

For the well-to-do, knives were made with gold-mounted handles of semi-precious gem-stones, such as malachite, heliotrope and different forms of quartz. A high quality example, of the George IV period, with a finely-faceted handle of citrine, has a gold-sheathed blade by John Thomas, an Oxford Street working cutler whose name appears in *Pigot's Commercial Directory* for 1822/3.(Colour plate III(ii)) Animals' teeth have always been used by scribes as burnishers, and the handle of a pen-knife by Moseley and Simpson, of Covent Garden, dating from about 1875, and made from a tiger's entire tooth, would serve this secondary purpose admirably.(100) A pen-knife made from the silver-mounted bone of a favourite racehorse is inscribed 'Rosebery 1872-1894'.(104) Another somewhat exotic knife, following the style of French examples found as part of elaborate desk sets, but with a distinctly English blade, has a well-carved mother-of-pearl handle.(102) A pen-knife with a highly decorative handle of polished steel etched in the rococo style with songbirds in floral scrollwork, dates from the 1830s and was made by Evans of Old (Ex)Change, London.(101) The majority of pen-knives of this period were, however, of a simpler nature.(103,105)

From the mid-nineteenth century, the quill pen-knife, or desk-knife as it came to be known, was designed mainly for the office and was usually of a very functional form, although a range of handle materials and designs was available, as may be seen in a page from Joseph Rodgers' catalogue of the 1860s, re-issued in 1870 with price revisions.(106) A group of such desk-knives and erasers, which were sold in paper or skiver-covered cases, illustrates typical Rodgers' productions, which must have been made in very large quantities, to judge by the numbers which survive.(107 to 111) Similar pen-knives were made by many other firms, in Sheffield and elsewhere; those made for Civil Service use are impressed with either the Royal Cypher VR, or SO for the Stationery Office, in both cases under a crown.(112 to 116) These types of knives ceased to be issued in Government Departments in 1869.[16] They were still available in the catalogues of wholesale stationers, well into the twentieth century, often combined with erasers.(117)

The knife used by a working quill-dresser and pen-cutter would of necessity be more stoutly made to cope with the task of cutting many hundreds of pens each day, than those made for general use, and we are fortunate that such a knife, with the cutler's mark of John Sellers and Sons of Sheffield, dating from the mid-nineteenth century, has survived. It belonged to William Southgate, a London pen-cutter who died in 1919, and was preserved and occasionally used by his son Walter, until his death at the advanced age of 98 years in 1986, along with a number of other tools of his trade.(118) (Chapter I). This knife, whose simple wooden handle is fitted with a robust steel peg, has a brass ferrule and a blade ground to a form precisely similar to that favoured by another professional pen-cutter, Mr Cotmore, of Stangate, Lambeth, some years previously, in 1827.[17]

The cost of a pen-knife in 1614 was sixpence; a domestic account book of that date records such a purchase:

to Sagar for his penknyffe   vjd[18]

Parson Woodforde, in 1786, records a similar transaction:

For a pair of Scissars and a Penknife today p[d] 0.5.0. Nancy also bought a neat P[r] of Scissars for 0.4.6.[19]

from which it would seem, if the two pairs of scissors were comparable, that the pen-knife cost about sixpence. In 1812, specially made pen-knives could be had from a professional pen-cutter for two shillings or three shillings and sixpence,[20] while in the Rodgers Catalogue of 1877 already referred to, prices ranged from eightpence to three shillings and tenpence halfpenny each (sold wholesale by the dozen), according to quality. Messrs Myers were still, in their catalogue of 1902, charging eightpence each, little more than the price obtaining three centuries earlier.[21]

IV

Mechanical Quill-cutting & the Quill Nib

We have seen in Chapter II that many people found great difficulty in learning to repair a worn quill pen satisfactorily and that very few bought pens were ever repaired. It is not therefore surprising that the manufacture of a mechanical device which would obviate the need for skill, by cutting a pen automatically, should concern such an inventive brain as that of Joseph Bramah (1749-1815), whose catalogue of major inventions in the field of engineering is well-documented.[1] Bramah's patent of 1809, for *Pens for Writing*, which includes a mechanical quill-cutter, is the first to give a detailed specification for the design of the cutting blades of such an instrument.[2] These consisted of a pair of bevelled and diverging blades forming a curved triangular or pen-shaped mouth, working against a concave bed or anvil to cut the profile of the pen, a vertical lancet blade mounted centrally between the bevelled cutters making the slit necessary for the satisfactory flow of ink. The scoop of the pen was first cut with a knife in the normal way, and the resulting U-shaped section placed on the concave anvil; the cutters would then be brought down on the quill, forming the profile of the pen and slitting it, in one operation of the machine.**(Colour plate IV(i))**

Although Bramah's patent is the first to give detailed specifications, an earlier patent for what can only have been a mechanical quill-cutter does exist. In 1729, Isaac de la Chaumette, in an extensive patent covering his inventions ranging from small-arms to a machine 'to cure chimneys that smoak in windy weather', includes 'A pen knife yᵗ make ye pen at one cut', which in the 1857 printed version of the patent has been transcribed as 'a pen knife that makes a pen at once'. Unfortunately no details are specified.[3]

The actual invention of the device, however, pre-dates both patents. A very rare example which may be dated to the first half of the seventeenth century, uses exactly the same principle as that described in Bramah's patent a century and a half later.**(119)** Of extremely fine workmanship and engraved with exotic birds in scrolling foliage, this quill-cutter has its cutting blades and opposing anvil mounted in the plier-like jaws, one of the arms incorporating a folding knife blade for the cutting of the scoop of the pen. The same arm is also extended as a peg similar to those found on the end of some pen-knife handles, and used for extending the slit in the pen at the time of its repair. Another example of this type of cutter is illustrated in the *Catalogue of the Spitzer Collection*.[4] Much simpler quill-cutting 'pliers' were made in England, circa 1800, some of which have a folding pen blade in one of the jaws, while in others it is incorporated into one of the handles.**(120)** Examples have been noted with the maker's mark OSBORNE. A fine French example, in its gold-tooled green leather carrying case, dates from the early eighteenth century.**(Colour plate IV(iv))**

In the British Museum is a very rare type of standing quill-cutter, dating from the end of the seventeenth century.**(121)** In this type, the cutting device, of exactly similar design to the previous examples, is operated by a screw, rather than by leverage as in the case of the 'pliers'. The quill, having had its scoop cut with the folding knife blade incorporated in the engraved handle or key, is inserted through a U-shaped opening on to the anvil of the cutter inside the body of the device. A few turns of the key bring the cutters down on to the quill, cutting the profile of the pen and also slitting it. This machine, made largely of brass, has no marks but is almost certainly of Continental origin, probably German, as is a similar, perhaps slightly later brass example in the Victoria and Albert Museum, which does have a maker's mark impressed twice, so far unidentified.(122) A brass-mounted turned-ivory example, in the author's collection, and dating from the early to mid-eighteenth century,(123) is still in excellent working order, as is the fine silver example by George Adams, No 60 Fleet Street, London, which like the ivory example, uses the same system of cutters as those previously discussed, in this case operated by a steel screw.(Colour plate IV(ii)) The Adamses, father and son, were scientific instrument makers to King George III and the Prince Regent. George Adams, the elder, died in 1773, and as this quill-cutter can be dated by its silver-mounted shagreen case to about this time, it may have been made either by him, or by his son, George Adams the younger, who died in 1795.

A contemporary if somewhat brief mention of a quill-cutting machine appears in a book by a professional pen-cutter, John Wilkes, published in 1799; he was obviously not very impressed with its performance:

> ... their pens were cut with an engine, an attempt that was once made, but by which many thousand quills were spoiled, without any benefit to the sagacious inventor or improvement to the Public.[5]

John Wilkes ran a Pen and Quill Warehouse; his successor, in the same business at the same address, from 1803, was Thomas Lund, who had no such misgivings about the efficacy of mechanical cutters, and whose name appears as maker on a pocket quill-cutting machine in the author's collection, about which more later.

The quill-cutter of Bramah's patent of 1809 must be seen, at best, as a refinement of an earlier invention; perhaps the patent's importance lies more particularly in his ideas for cutting pens with greater efficiency and economy.

The specification describes the cutting of a nib at each end of a severed quill barrel, into which could then be inserted a tapered handle, which he called his 'first class of compound pen'. He developed this into his 'double compound pen' merely by having a similar barrel on each tapered end of a single handle, giving four usable nibs. An example of such a penholder, turned in horn, was found in a pocket pen-case of about 1820.(124a) A simple tapered pen-stick, for insertion into a severed quill

barrel, was sometimes used. A typical example, the work of French prisoners during the Napoleonic Wars, dates from the early nineteenth century.(124b) Bramah goes on to describe his 'tribble-compound pens', which were made by dividing the barrel in two lengthwise and thereby producing two double-ended pens for use in special holders. Finally, in this section, he goes on to describe probably the most significant commercial aspect of his patent, the making of quill nibs, by first dividing the quill barrel longitudinally twice or more, depending on the circumference of the quill, and then into short sections, on each of which a nib was cut. He called these his 'fragment forms', to be mounted for use 'on handles, either with brass or otherwise'. A box of these quill nibs, sold as Bramah's Patent Pens, at three shillings, contains its original complete contents of twenty-five nibs.(125a) The holders for these nibs were made not only in very simple materials such as brass with plain wooden handles,[6] but also in more exotic materials. A beautifully turned ivory-handled example has a silver holder impressed 'J. BRAMAH PATENT'.(125b) Holders using the principle of Bramah's patent are found in many materials, well into the Victorian period.(126) To produce his quill nibs commercially, Bramah's quill-cutter was to have been mounted in 'a small fly-press, such as are used for cutting and stamping in the common way of other manufactures', which unfortunately does not seem to have survived, so far as is known.

Although Bramah's patent 'fragment forms' were possibly the first quill nibs to be produced by machine, the idea of the quill nib was certainly not new. Thomas Palmer of East Grinstead was already producing such nibs, which he called his Royal Portable Pens, before July, 1806, the date of a testimonial to their efficacy from one Cosmo Gordon, which appeared in a printed advertising broadsheet published by Palmer, and some three years before the date of Bramah's patent.(19) In another similar advertisement, of 1810, Palmer states his firm's claim to be 'The Sole Inventors of the Royal Portable Pens', presumably a response to Bramah's patent. An inspection of the few remaining quill nibs in a box of Palmer's Royal Portable Pens, suggests that they were cut with a knife.(15) It would appear that later in the nineteenth century the warranty that quill nibs were 'cut by hand' or 'made with knife' was considered a valuable selling point.(127) A box of quill nibs, by Cooper and Co, of 5 Shoe Lane, London, dates from about 1840, prior to the firm's expansion to occupy the adjoining properties at numbers 6 and 7.(128)

A holder for quill nibs, beautifully fashioned from tortoiseshell with a gold-mounted partridge-wood handle, may have been the sort of holder used with the earliest quill nibs, prior to Bramah's patent.(129a) Another interesting holder impressed with the name of the maker 'WEST LATE PALMER', has a spring-loaded lower 'jaw' which opens to accept the nib, and like Bramah's, is kept closed by a sliding ring.(129b) The Palmer in question was George Palmer, Cutler and Dressing Case Maker to the Royal Family, of 1 St James's Street, whose trade-card shows him to have also been an agent for 'PALMER'S PORTABLE PENS FROM EAST GRINSTEAD'.(130) He was the son of Thomas Palmer, Quill Pen Manufacturer, and Elizabeth, his wife, and was baptised at East Grinstead in 1781.[7] It was only natural that when he became a successful London cutler he should have promoted his father's products. He was succeeded at the same address by Fitzmaurice West in the late 1830s.

At a lecture delivered by Mr Faraday at the Royal Institution, reported in the *Literary Gazette* of April 4th, 1835,[8] a machine which must have been somewhat similar to that used by Bramah, transported specially from Morden's (sic) factory, where it was used to manufacture their 'Portable Pens' by a process involving fourteen stages, was exhibited and demonstrated by his workmen. A box of Mordan and Co's 'Patent Portable Pens', dating from circa 1830-40, which originally contained fifty quill nibs, was priced at one shilling and sixpence.(131c) Mordans, as well as making holders for their 'Portable Pens' which followed the Bramah design, registered the designs of several holders in more exotic forms, including a serpent's head, and a hand which appears to grip the nib.(131a and b)

The intensity of competition for business in the supply of pens during the 1820s is well-illustrated by the records of the Bank of England,[9] which at that time employed a staff of about a thousand and had been spending sums in excess of £2000 per annum providing pens for their use. In 1820, for example, more than a million and a quarter quill pens were purchased for a staff of one thousand and two, at a cost of £2021. For the previous half-century or so, the firm of Walsh, (father and son), had supplied the Bank with quills at prices which had obtained since 1734; there were four grades of pen, priced from 2s 8d to 10s 0d per hundred.

In 1822, Bramah's patent pens were being sold by Joseph Bramah's son at 3s 0d per hundred, and during trials at the Bank, each pen was found to outlast five of the third quality of Walsh's pens costing 3s 6d per hundred. In spite of price reductions by Mr Walsh, the Committee of the Bank, confident of making a saving of fully fifty per cent in their costs, adopted Bramah's patent pens for the majority of their needs, and by 1830 the consumption of full quill pens had dropped to under sixty thousand, while that of the patent pens had increased to over four hundred thousand, in spite of the fact that many of the clerks thought little of the patent pens and continued to use the full quill pens supplied free for their private use.

When the protection afforded by Bramah's patent expired after its fifteen-year currency, competitors were able to undercut his prices, offering quill nibs at 2s 0d and 1s 6d per hundred, against Bramah's 3s 6d and 2s 9d for comparable grades. As Bramah continued to enjoy the patronage of the Bank, he was no doubt able to satisfy the Committee on the relative merits of his pens in relation to price. In 1828, George Palmer, of 1 St James's Street, who, as we have seen, was an agent for Palmer of East Grinstead, offered to supply the Bank with patent pens at Bramah's prices less '15% Discount for Cash'. Once more Bramah must have successfully met the challenge, as his pens continued to be purchased until 1845, by which time the steel pen had largely supplanted the quill at the Bank for most purposes, although some full quill pens continued to be provided until as late as 1907.

No mechanical quill-cutting device bearing Joseph Bramah's name appears to be recorded, but from the 1820s, presumably after the expiry of his patent in 1824, many makers made pocket quill-cutters on the same principle. One such machine, apparently made during the currency of Bramah's patent, and the earliest of this type so far recorded, is that previously mentioned, made by Thomas Lund, which bears the address 57 Cornhill.(132) By 1817, Lund had already taken over the adjoining premises, and from this time his address appears as 56 & 57 Cornhill, which premises are depicted in his trade-card.(133) He remained in business there until about 1845,[10] when the premises were taken over by his son William Lund, cutler, ivory-turner and pencil-maker, who was already in business at 23-24 Fleet Street, and whose patent propelling pencils are discussed in Chapter X.

Two other early pocket quill-cutting machines, from the 1820s, are worthy of note.(134, 135) One, of particularly fine quality, in ivory, with engraved gilt-brass mounts, bears the name Thornhill, Cutler, 144 New Bond Street; the other is by Savigny and Co, a noted firm of cutlers and surgical instrument makers, of 67 St James's Street, whose Huguenot founder Paul Savigny was 'successor to the late Widow How of St Martin's Churchyard'.(58) A feature of many of the pocket quill-machines of this period is that the lever which operates the cutters is of squared-off tapering form.

Most pocket machines also incorporate a nibber, a tiny guillotine operated by the depression of a button and used to cut off the extreme points of the nibs to create a slightly square-ended pen. All the cutters so far described produce a sharply-pointed pen which would tend to snag the fibres of the paper or parchment, and would also quickly distort with wear and pressure. The initial cut with the nibber produces a barely discernible squareness, for fine writing, which can be increased as required by repeating the operation until the correct degree of broadness for any particular hand is achieved. It can, of course, also be used to cut an oblique pen.

These nibbers, working on the principle of a spring-loaded guillotine, are based on an invention of John Wilkes, of 57 Cornhill, in the late eighteenth century, examples of which are found in brass and ivory and also in steel.(136, 137) Each has a ring or recess for the thumb and is operated with the index finger by depressing a spring-loaded button attached to the guillotine blade which 'nibs' the inserted points of the pen. Although the ivory and brass examples, which each incorporate a wafer seal, are stamped 'PATENT', together with Wilkes's name and address, no such patent appears to have been granted. The steel example, which was advertised at 4s 6d,(138) is still attached to its contemporary steel watch-chain and was clearly intended for the pocket. The invention is referred to by Wilkes in his book of 1799, as my newly-invented Pen-Nibber (which instrument has met the decided approbation of many of the first penmen in this Kingdom.[11]

It was advertised along with his 'complete Box of PEN CUTLERY'.(139)

The invention of this nibber was a particular boon to those with the use of only one hand. Between 1818 and 1820, various mechanical devices, including several clamps for holding quills firmly while cutting a pen, for the use of those unfortunate enough to have lost an arm or hand, were placed before the Society for the Encouragement of Arts, Manufactures and Commerce. An ex-officer so disabled in the Peninsular War, Captain George FitzGerald Stack, late of the 54th Regiment, was awarded the Society's Vulcan Gold Medal for his inventions, and Mr T. Lane received the Society's Silver Medal for his efforts.[12] Wilkes's pen nibber could be readily used in combination with any such quill-holding device.

A very fine and unusual combined pocket-knife and quill-cutting machine, silver-mounted with mother-of-pearl scales and retaining its original gold-tooled red morocco case,(140) has one folding general-purpose blade and two folding pen-blades, all of which are impressed 'DOUGHTY, 19 West Strand'. The quill, its scoop already cut, is inserted into the end of the handle with the lever raised, and the cutter operated as the lever is depressed. An otherwise identical example, the blades marked 'Hurst' with a crowned Royal Cypher WR, for William IV, dates this type to circa 1830-35. Also dating from about this time is a smaller than average quill-cutting machine which has a dustproof cover over the quill hole.(141)

Perhaps the most prolific maker of pocket quill-cutting machines, if one is to judge by the frequency with which examples are encountered, was the firm of Joseph Rodgers of Sheffield, examples of whose machines are found with the crowned WR cypher of William IV, circa 1835. Victorian examples are also found in small sizes, perhaps for ladies.(142) A catalogue of their wares, mainly domestic cutlery, issued in the 1860s and re-issued with pencilled price revisions in 1877, illustrates a variety of quill-cutting machines, and may be compared with an almost similar group of Rodgers' quill-cutters,(Colour plate IV(iii)) examples of which may be found with ivory, ebony, cocoa-wood, horn, tortoiseshell, mother-of-pearl or nickel scales, some having sliding pen-blades, some folding. A de-luxe model was produced in mother-of-pearl with nickel mounts.(143) These machines were originally sold in morocco leather or pressed paper cases, according to quality, and as can be seen from the firm's catalogue, prices ranged from 6s 0d to 13s 6d each. They enjoyed a long vogue; the simplest ebony and brass version was still being offered commercially well into the twentieth century, and Rodgers' final stock clearance of the last remaining carton of these machines, to one of our leading calligraphers who had the initiative to enquire, did not take place until the late 1970s. The firm, whose origin can be traced back to at least 1672, when their now famous mark, the star and Maltese cross, was first registered, was taken over and lost its identity at about the same time.[13]

In the Charles Thomas Collection of writing equipment, in the Museum of Science and Industry, Birmingham, is a most unusual quill-cutting machine of French manufacture, which is impressed 'Lassèrre Brevette', dating from about 1822.(144) The cover at one end unscrews to reveal a sliding blade to cut the scoop, which is then inserted through a U-shaped opening at the other end, which also has a screw-on cover; the cutters, of conventional design, operate when the spring-loaded end is sharply depressed. The patent specifications with coloured drawings are still extant.[14]

V

Ink, Parchment & Paper

The ink of the ancient civilisations of China, Egypt, Greece and Rome was simply a mixture of fine soot such as lamp-black or ivory-black, mixed with gum, roughly in the proportions of three to one, formed into cakes with a little water and dried in the sun, to be rubbed down with water when required for use. Chinese stick-ink, which is also widely used by modern western calligraphers, is still made in this way. An anonymous Victorian writer, in *Pens, Inks and Inkstands*, published as a thinly-disguised advertising medium for Francis Mordan's Gold Pens, quotes Demosthenes, referring to the lowly origins of Aeschines:

> When a youth he was in a state of great want, assisted his father in the school, rubbed the ink, washed down the forms and swept the schoolroom.[1]

This cake ink was no doubt similar to the Roman *atramentum*, which in its undried state was used as a rather viscous liquid. Inkwells containing this type of ink have been found at Herculaneum and Pompeii, sometimes of double form to accommodate also the red ink made from vermilion or cinnabar. Ink made from carbon in this way is densely black, and if used on unbleached materials has little tendency to fade; examples of Egyptian writings from about 3000 BC retain their directness and freshness to this day. It has, however, the serious disadvantage, especially in the case of legal documents, that water, by dissolving the gum with which it is bound, will tend to remove it.

The Romans also used the word *encaustum*, from which our term ink is derived, suggesting a more biting fluid, and it has been said that this more penetrating quality may have been imparted to the ink by the substitution of a mild acid such as vinegar, in place of water, during its making.[2] The carbon-based inks of the ancients were probably more akin to paint than the fluid we think of as ink; they were used on papyrus with the soft reed brush in Egypt and later with the split reed pen, as they were in Greece and Rome.

Of more concern to us, in relation to the quill pen, is the iron-gall ink which came into use in the early medieval period. By mixing the tannin extract of natural galls with iron salts, a strong free-flowing black ink is formed, whose density is increased by oxidisation in contact with the air, and which has a high degree of indelibility. Tannins can be extracted from a wide variety of vegetable matter, including gall nuts, elm, logwood, hawthorn and other woods and barks, sloes and the berries of buckthorn, but the best source is the common gall formed on the leaves of oak and other trees, as well as the oriental gall which forms on the leaf-stalks of various kinds of *Rhus*. The familiar oak-apple, for instance, is a typical gall, formed when the young oak bud is used by the gall-wasp (*Cynips*) to deposit an egg. Instead of developing normally as a leaf, the bud becomes an excrescence in the form of a spherical gall, in which the embryo wasp develops through its larval stage, pupates, and finally emerges as a wasp.

The best galls for the making of ink are those from which the wasp has not yet escaped, which can contain up to seventy-seven per cent of tannin. In former times, those from the Levant, known as Aleppo galls, were the most highly regarded; Istrian galls, and those from Morea, Smyrna and Mamora were next in quality, while those from France, Italy, Hungary, Senegal and the Barbary Coast, although widely used, were of poorer quality. Chinese galls, formed by the action of aphides on the leaf-stalks of *Rhus*, also have a high tannin content.[3]

The other main constituent of iron-gall ink is one of the salts of iron, usually Copperas or Green Vitriol (*Ferrous Sulphate*). The crushed galls are infused in boiling water, filtered and exposed to the air; over a period of weeks the gallotannins are converted into gallic acid, which, when mixed with ferrous sulphate produces a dense blue-black ink, which in use becomes blacker as it oxidises. A small proportion of gum arabic is often added to inhibit the separating out of the fine particles of solid matter as a sediment. This type of free-flowing iron-gall ink was entirely suitable for use with the quill pen, on both parchment and paper, and remained the basis of European writing inks until the advent of the commercially produced steel pen in the second quarter of the nineteenth century. Such inks, because of their acid nature, quickly corroded the steel nib, and inks were developed using dyes, to overcome this problem.

A fifteenth century recipe, written in an English *Bastarda* hand, for iron-gall ink, is in the Public Record Office.[4](145) It reads, ignoring expunged and deleted words:

To make hynke take galles
and coporas or vitrial (*quod idem est*)
and gumme, of everyche a quartryn
other helf quatryn and a halfe
quatryn of galles more and
breke the galles a ij other a iij
and put hani togedere everyche on in a pot and stere hyt
often and wythinne
ij wykys after ze mow
wryte therwyth
Yf ze have a quatryn of
everyche take a quarte of
watyr yf halfe a quartryn of
everyche than take half
a quarte of watyr

Similar recipes are to be found in many writing masters' manuals. Francis Clement, for instance, in his *The Petie Schole*, of 1587, gives one:

To make inke
Put into a quarte of water two ounces of right gumme Arabick, five ounces of galles, and three of copras. Let it stand covered in the warme sunne, and so it will the sooner prove good inke.

He goes on to say that it can be made more quickly by boiling but that 'the unboyled yeldeth a fayrer glosse'.[5] Edward Cocker, in his *The Pen's Triumph*, of 1658, gives a similar recipe, adding

to make your Ink shine and lustrous, add certain pieces of the Barque of Pomgranat, or a small quantity of double-refin'd Sugar, boyling it a little over a gentle fire.[6]

The addition of gum arabic to these recipes was to prevent the particles of tannate and gallate of iron in the oxidised ink from settling to the bottom of the container.[7] Such a sediment, however, even though dried, could be reconstituted as ink simply by the addition of water. One of the earliest patents for writing materials was that of Charles Holman, for Ink Powder, granted on 7th February, 1688:

A new art or invencion of making a certaine powder, which being put into faire water, beer, ale, or wine, doth immediately turne the same into very good black writing ink. . .[8]

The composition of this ink-powder is not known, but it was almost certainly an iron-gall preparation, which would probably behave in this way. Holman's trade label for 'The London Ink Powder',(146) of about 1690, to judge by the style of the engraving, describes him as a 'habidasher' in Southwark.[9] An advertisement in the *London Gazette* in 1695 shows that this ink-powder was sold in

Papers fit to make a gallon of the best durable writing ink, by stirring in so much (Plain or River) water. . .

and his sixpenny papers of near two ounces made a pint, or a pint and a half 'for Shopkeepers' Common Writing'.[10] That his ink-powder met with considerable success is demonstrated by an advertisement in a Whitehaven newspaper in 1776:

The Printers of this Paper Sell
WHOLESALE AND RETALE
MOLYNEUX'S SMELLING
MEDICINE
And HOLMAN'S BRITISH INK-
POWDER
**Orders from Shop-keepers and Dealers
in the County
will be duly attended to.[11]

The device of a broad arrow-head or *pheon* in the arms of Holman's label was also used by George Westerman, whose Ink Warehouse was at the King's Arms, No 2 Black Swan Alley, London Wall.[12](147) It is clear that Westerman was in business before 1760 from another of his advertisements which incorporates the Royal Cypher of George II in its engraved Royal

Arms.[13] He sold both ink and ink-powder, black and red, and was successful enough for unscrupulous hawkers to offer, as Westerman's, 'a vile Liquor for INK (which is nothing but Hatter's Dye)', against whose conviction he offered a reward of two guineas. His cart, its sides painted in gold letters with warnings to the public against such imitations, visited a different part of London each day, selling and delivering ink ordered 'by the penny post'.

The somewhat more arduous task of an earlier hawker of ink and quills is the subject of an engraving in a series of *Cries of London*, circa 1700, which shows him bent over under the weight of his ink-barrel, while from his belt is slung his pewter pint measure and funnel.(148) George Westerman was obviously in a much larger way of business and was succeeded at the same address by Joshua May and Samuel Amess.[14](149) Another London ink-maker was Sarah Smith, who made and sold her 'CAKE-INK . . . . greatly superior to any INK-POWDER', at 13 Sweetings Alley in the later eighteenth century. She claimed the grant of His Majesty's Letters Patent as Sole Patentee.[15] No such patent is recorded in her name, and it is possible that she purchased it from one John Dring, whose patent for cake-ink, the only such patent of this period, was granted in 1768. The recipe for this ink is given in the specification:

> Take sweet oyl, vinegar, gauls, coperas, gum arabac, and allam, mix them well together, and pour it into tin moulds to harden for use.[16]

Other makers of inks were Harwoods, of Fenchurch Street, whose name is found impressed on salt-glazed stoneware inkwells of about 1820, and Walkden, whose late eighteenth century trade label for British Ink Powder, at sixpence for a paper of two ounces, is in the Heal Collection.[17] This made a pint of ink and it is worth noting that in 1614, a pint of ink cost precisely the same. In a book of domestic accounts for that year, there appears the entry:

> for on pynt pot of Incke . . . . 0. 0. vjd[18]

Incidentally, in 1858, Walkden's Black Inkpowders at half-a-crown a dozen and Red, at three shillings, were being supplied to the Hudson's Bay Company.[19] In 1830, Charles Terry, a Quill and Pen Manufacturer and Merchant, of 5 Shoe Lane, is listed as the manufacturer of Walkden's British Ink-Powder.[20] He was succeeded at the same address by Cooper and Philips, also in the quill and pen business, whose successors were still trading, as Cooper, Dennison and Walkden, in 1975. The inks supplied to the Hudson's Bay Company would have been chemically formulated to overcome the problems of the corrosion caused to steel pens by the acidity of iron-gall inks. James Perry was producing non-corrosive ink, containing his 'Limpidum', a substance for 'neutralising the ill-effects of common ink when used with metallic pens', by 1833.[21] In 1837, Henry Stephens and Ebenezer Nash were granted a patent for

> improvements in manufacturing colouring matter and rendering certain colour or colours more applicable to dyeing, staining and writing,

the basis of Stephens's subsequent huge success in the field of ink manufacture.[22] Such developments and the discovery of aniline dyes in 1856, which revolutionised ink-manufacture, are however, more relevant to a study of the steel pen, than to the quill.

Papyrus, made from the stems of the papyrus plant (*Papyrus antiquorum* or *Cyperus papyrus*), was the main writing material not only of ancient Egypt from the third millenium BC, but also of the Greeks and the Roman Empire. There is a tradition, stemming from an account by Pliny the Elder in the second century BC, that the invention of parchment was the direct result of an embargo on the export of papyrus from Egypt to Pergamum in Asia Minor, where King Eumenes, a great book-collector, was forming a library which threatened to surpass in importance the library at Alexandria, thus incurring the jealousy of the Egyptian King, Ptolemy V. The need for an alternative writing material is said to have resulted in the invention of parchment, which took its name, *Pergamena*, from the city and kingdom of Pergamum, (now Bergama in Western Turkey), around the beginning of the second century BC. (The name is still retained in the German *Pergament* and the Italian *Pergamena*). Although this account is not considered historical, it seems likely that parchment was known at that time and that its appearance was more probably the result of a slow development from the more primitive single-sided hides and skins, in various dried and tanned forms more appropriately called leather, which had been in use for writing in Egypt since at least the twenty-fourth century BC.[23]

Parchment can be made from the skins of many animals, but in practice usually from those of the sheep, goat and calf, which as well as being particularly suitable, are readily available; it differs from leather in that, whereas the latter is simply tanned, parchment involves a more complex process which results in a fine white double-sided writing material of great beauty, which is probably the most sympathetic surface on which to write, especially with the quill pen, which has ever been used.

The method of manufacture of parchment has probably not changed significantly since its first use, and apart from the use of a degree of mechanisation is still used today. The following description is based on an account of the process in 1838.[24] The newly-flayed skins were taken by a workman called a skinner and first divested of the bulk of their usable wool or hair, washed and liberally coated on their fleshy sides with quick-lime, folded lengthwise and placed in heaps to ferment for about two weeks. After a further washing they were half-dried and stretched on a frame called a herse, carefully scraped with a half-moon-shaped blunt-edged tool to remove any remaining hair or flesh, and then rubbed with chalk and a pumice stone, a process known as grinding, to remove any traces of oil; after a final scraping with the knife, known as draining, the skin was once more treated with powder and pumice. Both sides of the skin having been similarly treated, a final powdering of chalk was rubbed in using a piece of lambswool, the skin was thoroughly dried while still under tension, and was then cut from the frame.(150) The finishing of the parchment was carried out by the parchment-maker, a highly skilled workman who placed it on a summer (a calf-skin stretched on a frame) and, using a much sharper half-moon-shaped knife than that used by the skinner, scraped and shaved the parchment to its final even smoothness.

Parchment is any animal skin treated in this way, the term vellum, from the Latin *vitulinium*, being correctly reserved for the parchment made from the skin of a calf, which is of high quality; there is, however, some confusion in the modern usage of these terms, the term parchment usually referring to split sheepskin and vellum to all other quality parchments.

Parchment has a number of advantages over papyrus: its toughness and therefore durability, its capability of accepting writing on both sides, and the fact that being a layered material, errors can be erased by scraping. (It was common practice to re-use valuable parchment by first erasing a manuscript, when it was no longer of use, the rewritten parchment being known as a palimpsest).(2) In spite of its advantages, the adoption of parchment in favour of papyrus was a slow transition over several centuries. During the height of the Roman period, it was regarded more as an alternative to the wax-tablet, for informal writing, rather than to papyrus, which was clearly seen as the superior material, and used for formal purposes. By about AD 350, however, parchment had superseded papyrus as the writing material for the best books, largely as result of the growth of Christianity under the Emperor Constantine the Great, and the corresponding increase in book production.[25]

Early parchment books were of roll form, following the tradition of their papyrus and leather counterparts, and were therefore cumbersome to use, it often being necessary to unroll large quantities of unwanted material to find the required place. By the middle of the fourth century, books were more conveniently of codex form, which allowed immediate access to any page. The great Greek Uncial bibles, the *Codex Sinaiticus*, for example, which is now in the British Museum, and the *Codex Vaticanus*, both written on fine vellum, are of fourth century date. From this time, the manuscript books of the dark and middle ages, in the Insular, Carolingian and Gothic styles, up to the development of printing in the late fifteenth century were to be written on parchment, and from at least the sixth century, by the use of the quill pen.

The art of making paper originated in China sometime before the end of the first century AD. It was to take a further millennium for these skills to reach Europe, by way of Persia, where there was a mill at Baghdad by 793, Damascus, Egypt, (where in the ninth century, paper gradually supplanted papyrus after some three thousand years of its usage as the main writing material), and Morocco; the Moors had set up a paper mill at Xativa in Spain by 1150, and the spread continued gradually northwards and eastwards through Europe.[26] The earliest surviving European manuscript on paper, no doubt imported, is a Sicilian deed dated 1109.[27]

The first paper mill in France is thought to

29

have been that established at Herault by about 1189; there were mills in Italy at Fabriano by 1260, in Germany by 1389 and in Holland by 1428.[28] In England, although imported paper had been known for about two hundred years, the first recorded paper maker was John Tate, a London merchant, whose name appears in a household book of Henry VII in 1498 and whose mill was established at Stevenage in Hertford-shire before this date. Tate produced good paper which was used for his printing by Wyn-ken de Worde, who mentions the mill in the colophon of his *De Proprietatibus Rerum*,[29] in spite of which, the business does not seem to have been successful. By 1588, Sir John Spiel-man had a paper mill at Dartford, together with a monopoly on the collection of rags, the basic raw material of hand-made paper, by virtue of Royal Letters Patent from Queen Elizabeth I.[30]

Paper is made from the bonding of indivi-dual cellulose fibres into a thin sheet, under pressure, and as cellulose is the basic structural material of all plants, paper can be made from many different kinds of vegetable matter. The traditional European material for hand-made papers has always been linen or cotton rags, and as the demand for paper grew, particularly after the development of printing, the supply of sufficient quantities of rags became a perpetual problem to the paper makers. In 1774, adverti-sing for sale their paper mill in Cockermouth, Cumberland, the proprietors took pains to em-phasise that 'foreign rags may be imported on very easy terms'.[31] In the 1830s, according to the *Saturday Magazine*, most of the rags used in Britain were imported from Italy, Germany, Hungary and Sicily, supplying an industry em-ploying an estimated 27,000 workers in some 700 mills in England and 80 in Scotland. It is probable that these figures are on the high side; at the end of the eighteenth century there had been 416 paper mills in England, 49 in Scotland and 60 in Ireland,[32] not substantially different from the numbers listed in the mid-nineteenth century, 430 in England, 51 in Scotland and 52 in Ireland.[33]

The making of paper is essentially the break-ing down of vegetable cellulose into individual fibres by maceration, the washing out of non-cellulose materials and the reconstitution of the fibres into thin flat sheets. Prior to the use of bleaches, discovered towards the end of the eighteenth century, white paper could only be made from very clean white rags, and the first stage in the making of paper was the sorting of the rags into different qualities, after which they were carefully denuded of any buttons or other extraneous matter, cut up into small pieces, and placed in a 'duster', a revolving mesh drum which removed any loose dirt or dust from the fragments. The rags were then boiled in a solution of carbonate of soda for several hours to soften them before being washed again and reduced by means of a 'hol-lander'; this was a rag-engine, a Dutch inven-tion of the mid-eighteenth century which replaced the earlier stamping mill and whose blades crushed and beat the fibres into a fine pulp. As the fibres were broken down, they became more and more capable of absorbing water and in this state, known as 'wet pulp' they passed through a 'stuff chest', a last clean-ing process known as a 'knotter', and finally into a 'vat' to be used to make paper, by a process not dissimilar to that used to make hand-made paper today.

A thin layer of pulp which will form a sheet of paper is taken by the 'vatman' directly from the vat, using a mould, a frame with either a base of fine parallel wires, or a finely woven wire mesh, the former producing 'laid' paper, the latter 'wove'. With great skill he judges the correct amount of pulp to take to ensure the consistent thickness of the sheets, and by care-fully shaking the mould horizontally, arranges the water-laden fibres in an even layer across the frame. The wet paper sheet is allowed by the vatman to drain a little; he then removes the detachable edge of the mould, known as a 'deckle', and passes the mould to the 'coucher', who, after further draining, rolls the waterleaf, as the wet unsized paper sheet is known, care-fully on to a piece of felt on a board. Further sheets, on their felts, are stacked, forming a 'post' of up to about 200 sheets, which is then pressed hydraulically to remove the remaining water. Another workman, the 'layer', then re-moves the sheets carefully from their felts and stacks them in 'packs' which are pressed again, before being separated into individual sheets to be dried over ropes made from cow-hair. The surfaces of the dried sheets of paper are sized using gelatine made from the hooves and skins of animals, which imparts extra strength to the surface, an advantage not obtained by internal sizing (adding the size to the pulp) which is the method normally used today. Some papers, known as 'hot-pressed' are given a final pressing between metal plates which produces a polished surface.

Watermarks on paper are achieved in a similar way to the lines of laid paper, caused by the contact with the wires of the mould while the fibres are wet, which reduces the thickness of the paper at the point of contact. Any particular device, of fine wires soldered together to form the design, could be attached to the wires or mesh of the mould. Watermarks, the use of which may have originated as indications of size or quality, have been used since the thirteenth century, mainly as distinguishing trade marks. Some watermarks incorporate dates but caution must be exercised in trying to date papers from such marks, which may be no more than indications of the dates of establishment of their makers.

Paper-making by machine was the invention of Louis Nicholas Robert, at the Didot Frères paper mill at Essones, in France, a model of which machine is in the Science Museum in London. The London stationers Henry and Sealy Fourdrinier engaged the services of the engineer Bryan Donkin, to improve upon Robert's invention and the resulting machine was set up at Frogmore in Hertfordshire in 1803. It made paper on a continuous wire mesh which was transferred to felt and reeled up in the wet state, the unreeled paper later being cut into sheets and loft-dried. Although the Fourdriniers encountered such difficulties and expense that their firm failed in 1808, many of the principles embodied in their machine are still the basis of modern paper-making machinery. A machine using a wire mesh-covered brass cylinder, revolving above and just in contact with a sluice-controlled tank of prepared pulp, was patented by John Dickinson,[34] in 1809; by 1830 half of the paper made in England was made by machine.

Because of the lack of whiteness of the rags from which they were made, prior to the invention of bleaches, most writing papers made before the early nineteenth century tend to have a cream or slightly yellowish tint. From about this time, to produce a pale blue writing paper, considered by some to be more pleasing, a small amount of smalt (powdered cobalt silicate) could be added to the pulp.

Papers were made in a vast range of qualities, with varying surfaces according to the purpose for which they would be used. Writing papers, naturally, need to be smooth and free of loose fibres which may be picked up by the pen and because they often carry printed letterheads, they must also be suitable for printing. From the 1830s and throughout the mid-Victorian period it was fashionable to use writing paper headed with a steel engraved landscape view, which might also depict a particular house or other building, printed usually in black or occasionally in puce.(151,152) Embossed borders were also popular with the Victorians, but the technique had been used from at least the beginning of the century. A rare example of cream wove writing paper, by Butterworth and watermarked 1801, is embossed with a neo-classical frieze of Cupids and a female figure representing Hope, within a border of scrolling acanthus leaves and a yellow-printed edge.(153)

VI

The Pounce-pot or Sander

From medieval times until the early nineteenth century, the application of pounce to the writing surface both of parchment and of paper would have been a familiar procedure to anyone engaged in writing. The word 'pounce' would not, however, have meant the same thing to all scribes throughout that period, since both the nature of the substance and the reasons for its use have been quite different at different times.

In the medieval period, pounce was used in the final preparation of the parchment prior to writing, any major roughness having been first scraped away with the knife. Parchment, as we have seen in the previous chapter, is the general term for writing material made from animal skins, usually those of sheep, goats or calves, which have been treated with lime to de-hair, cure and whiten them, then stretched, degreased with the further use of alkalis, and scraped to a fine even surface.

Being of animal skin, and in spite of the removal of most of the fatty substances during its preparation by the parchmenter, newly-made parchment still retains an element of greasiness, which during prolonged storage will eventually rise to the surface, and without further treatment would cause problems for the scribe, whose water-based inks would be repelled, making writing virtually impossible.

The pounce used by medieval and later scribes to overcome this problem was either finely ground pumice stone or powdered cuttle-fish bone, both of which by their chalky nature absorbed and removed any grease from the surface of the parchment. The pounce, being also slightly abrasive, tended to raise an even velvety nap on the surface of the skin, which allowed the hard quill to 'bite' and helped to produce fine, sharp writing, as well as making the surface fibres of the parchment more receptive to the ink, for a greater permanence. It is thought that the medieval scribe may have also added to his pounce a small proportion of powdered gum-sandarach, a resin exuded by the North-West African arar tree (*Tetraclinis Articulata*), which has the property of inhibiting the spreading of the ink, and used sparingly, can help to produce sharp, crisp writing. The surplus pounce was, of course, removed before the parchment was ruled up for writing.

Contemporary illustrations of medieval scribes at work, in the illuminations of their manuscript books, give us no clue to the nature of their pounce boxes or their method of applying the pounce. They may have sprinkled it on to the parchment, rubbing it into the surface with the palm of the hand, a method still used. They may, perhaps, have employed some sort of pounce-rubber, a device used by their nineteenth-century counterparts, the scriveners or law-writers, who, having first rubbed down their parchment with a pumice-stone, applied a pounce made from whiting mixed with resin, using a rubber made from a tightly rolled strip of cloth.[1] Such pounce rubbers, made of rolled felt glued to a domed wooden handle, were still being offered for sale at 4d each, with tins of prepared pounce at 6d, by Messrs Shaw and Sons, Manufacturing Stationers of Fetter Lane, London, in their catalogue of circa 1912.

As we have seen in the previous chapter, by the sixteenth century paper was in general use for writing. Early papers, made from the fibres of cotton and linen, were naturally absorbent, and to give them strength and a surface capable of accepting ink satisfactorily, they were treated to some extent with a size made from gelatinous materials such as animal skins and horns; (the use of vellum and parchment offcuts to make size for some later Whatman papers, effectively produced a surface of reconstituted membrane).[2]

Printing papers had very little size, because the inks used by printers, not being water-based, have no tendency to run in the way that writing inks do, on absorbent surfaces. One result of this was that the practice of scholars of annotating their books in the margins, required the paper to be pounced with gum-sandarach, which, for localised applications of this nature, was tied up in a piece of fine cloth and dabbed on. Sir Hugh Platt (1552-1611?), a writer on agriculture, in his *The Jewell House of Art and Nature*, published in 1594, gives detailed instructions:

> Rub your paper wel over with the fine powder or dust of Rosen and Sandarach in equall parts before you write therwith. Note that you must tie the powder hard in a rag of Laune or Cambrick, and therwith rub the paper throughly well. This is a necessarie secret for students, whereby they may note in the margentes of their bookes if the paper should happen to sinke, which is an especiall fault in many of our late yeere bookes of the Law.[3]

The use of sandarach in the pouncing of paper does not seem to have been favoured by the majority of sixteenth-century writing masters, most of whom, in their manuals, mention the practice; some, among them Fanti (1514), were positively against it. Palatino (1540), advised its use, 'to write well and distinctly', but sparingly, because of its tendency to impede the flow of the ink. He also suggested the use of finely-crushed eggshells mixed with powdered incense, as a better pounce than that which could be bought. The pounce should be applied lightly and evenly with a hare's foot kept exclusively for the purpose, and removed after use by rubbing with bread. Tagliente (1524), in a list of tools and materials for the student, included pounce, but implied his disapproval of the practice by adding the words '. . . if you want to write with it'. One writing master who defended the use of pounce to improve the sharpness of the writing was Cresci, who, in his *Avertimenti*, his answer to Scalzini's criticisms of his writing manuals, suggested that letters written without the use of pounce might look 'as if they had been written with a stick'. He did not insist upon its use, but recommended it, especially for beginners. Scalzini, on the other hand, in his *Il Secre-*

tario (1581), was firmly against pouncing, because it reduced the speed of writing, a view shared by Pedro Madariaga, who, in his *Libro Subtilissimo* (1565), warned against the practice, which slowed up the writing 'as snow does on a path when you walk'.[4]

In England, Peter Bales, in his *Writing Schoolemaster*, (1590), advocated the softening of the paper by 'rubbing the same with stanch graine', but was clearly not in favour of pouncing greasy parchment:

> As for your parchment, chuse it not chaulkie.
> Nor let it be greasie, for that is more faultie.
> If chaulkie, then write not till it be gone
> First with a knife and last with pumice stone:
> If greazie it be, then let it alone:
> For other remedie sure know I none.

The 'stanch graine', to staunch the spreading of the ink, was also mentioned in John de Beauchesne's *A Booke containing divers sortes of hands*, published twenty years previously in 1570, where, in the 'Rules made by E.B. for his Children to learne to write bye', is given the recipe:

> Make stanche graine of allome beaten full smalle,
> And twise as much rosen beaten with all.
> With that in a fair cloute knit verye thinne,
> Rubb paper or parchment, or ye begyn.[5]

We have seen that pounce in the form of rosin or sandarach might be applied to the paper using a hare's foot or tied in fine cloth. It would appear that the powder was kept in bottle-shaped containers or casters. Tagliente, in his *Lo presente libro* (1524), and Palatino, in his *Libro nuovo d'imparare a scrivere* (1540), each gave a woodcut illustration of the instruments of writing which included such a container.(154, 155) It has been suggested that the casting bottles with perforated covers, of the type commonly used for spices or for sprinkling perfumed water, in Elizabethan England, may also have been used for pounce.[6] Certainly, there are marked similarities between these bottles and the pounce-pots of Tagliente and Palatino.

The form of pounce-pot with which we are most familiar, sometimes called a sand-dredger or sander because of its association with sandarach, was also in use by the early sixteenth century.(156) Many have dished tops so that any surplus pounce, after being lightly sprinkled on to the writing surface and rubbed in, could easily be returned to the sander through the same holes in the saucer-shaped depression.

Coming from North Africa, sandarach would be neither cheap nor easy to obtain, and would be far too valuable to waste.

Examples of sanders may be found in a variety of materials, ranging from the humble to the exotic, to suit every pocket. Naturally the most commonly found are of turned wood, often pear or other fruitwoods, but oak examples are occasionally found.(157, 158) *Lignum vitae*, that favourite of the wood-turner, was often used for high quality sanders. Eighteenth century cedar sanders, made from the left-over cedar 'offal', as it was known, of the pencil-makers, are not uncommon.(159) Less common are those turned in ivory or bone.(160) Brass, gilded or plain,(161) pewter and other base metals were all used to make sanders; they were made in lava-stone in Italy, for the Grand Tourist.

Some of the most elegant sanders are found in the painted enamels of Battersea and South Staffordshire,(162) and in the pottery and porcelain of many factories in Europe, as well as in the export porcelains of China, ordered and delivered through the Honourable East India Company.(163 to 168) Glass examples made in the United States of America are well-documented.[7] Many sanders, particularly those of the eighteenth century and later, would originally form part of a standish with a matching inkwell, and perhaps a shot-holder which cleaned and held the quill when not in use, a taperstick or bell. Silver examples are rarely found separated from their standishes. Small Sheffield Plate sanders sometimes formed part of a Regency gentleman's fitted travelling case.

We have considered the use of powdered pumice or cuttle-fish bone as pounce for parchment, and the use of rosin or gum sandarach on paper. In the late eighteenth century, the pounce-pot was given a new lease of life and a third entirely different function. With the advent of glazed papers, which were much less absorbent than the partially-sized papers which had hitherto been made, there was no longer any need for sandarach as the ink did not spread into the fibres of the paper more than was desirable. At the same time, this particular virtue had the drawback that the ink remained wet for a considerable time, and it was to overcome this difficulty that the pounce-pot found its new use. Chalk, which as all schoolboys know, is an excellent blotting agent, was powdered and sprinkled from the sander, which continued to be known by that name, on to the writing. An alternative to chalk, which has much the same drying property, was powdered biotite, a magnesium mica, which also imparted a metallic sparkle to the writing, and was used for this effect. In America, at the time of the gold rush of 1849, a preparation sold as 'California Gold Writing Sand', which probably gave a similar effect to the writing as it served its primary function of drying it, was an alternative to the 'Black Writing Sand', also available, in eight-ounce packets.[8]

The development of modern blotting paper has been described as the chance result of the accidental omission of size from a batch of paper during its making, at John Slade's paper mill at Hagbourne in Berkshire, about 1840, although blotting paper of a sort, used by Matthew Boulton, the great engineer, still remains in his cash-book for 1788.[9] Blotting paper was, however, known much earlier. Its use as an alternative to sandarach, which suggests the use of the latter as a blotting agent after writing, as well as to pounce the paper beforehand, can be dated as early as 1567. In Plantin's dialogue between Grevin and Hamon, the former asks, 'But do you use blotting paper?', and is answered, 'Yes, we use it instead of sand'.[10]

It was, nevertheless, the production of high quality blotting paper on a commercial scale towards the mid-nineteenth century which resulted in the disappearance of the pounce-pot or sander from the equipment of the scribe.

VII

Inkhorns, Inkwells & Standishes

The earliest surviving containers for ink are the wooden palettes and faience godets of ancient Egypt which were designed for the thick carbon-based inks of that time.[1] Roman inkwells for the more liquid *'encaustum'*, dating from the destruction of Pompeii and Herculaneum by the eruption of Mount Vesuvius in 79 AD, are preserved in Naples Museum, together with the reed pens found with them.[2]

During the earliest period of the quill pen, it is probable that the most commonly used receptacle for ink was the end of the horn of a cow, readily available, naturally waterproof and suitably tapered to be held in the hand or in a hole in the scribe's desk. Some of the earliest depictions of scribes which illustrate inkwells show the widespread use of a horn for the purpose. The scribe Hugo, a Norman monk, in a late eleventh century Saint Jerome from Exeter, has his inkhorn lodged in a socket designed for the purpose in the stile of his chair.[3] The twelfth-century lay artist-scribe Hildebert, in his delightful self-portrait, has two such inkhorns resting in holes in his desk, along with his quills in smaller holes,(169) while another scribe, in Gregory the Great's commentary on Ezekiel, is seen holding a similar inkhorn in his hand.(170) Sections of the natural horn with inset bases were also used for inkwells of standing form, their sides incised with simple compass-scribed decoration, during the late medieval period.(171)

Although other forms of inkwells, such as simple cylindrical pots or small bowls, were used,(1) the general use of the horn is further evidenced in the continued use of the term 'inkhorn' for any portable inkwell, irrespective of the material from which it might be made, down to the nineteenth century. In the Rev James Woodforde's diary for 21st November, 1783, is the entry:

Gave Nancy one of the Ladies' Pocket Books for 1784. Gave her also a pretty pocket Leather Inkhorn.

Another favourite material for inkwells, again because of its ready availability, was *cuir bouilli* or boiled leather, often with a waterproof liner of pottery, metal or glass. A fine inkwell of this material, its surface tooled with figures of saints, dating from the late Tudor period, is in the Museum of London.(172)

As we have seen in Chapter I, many scribes were itinerant, and even those who worked in one place would no doubt also find it convenient to have a portable form of inkwell or inkhorn, often attached by draw-strings to a penner or case for the quill pens. The Arms of the Company of Law-Writers or Scriveners are blazoned as:

Azure, an eagle volant or, holding in his mouth a penner and inkhorn sable stringed gules, standing on a book gules, garnished or.

This is an allusion to the eagle of Saint John, which was sometimes depicted in representations of the Evangelist writing his Gospel, holding in its beak his inkhorn and penner.[4] A late fifteenth-century representation of Saint John, from the *Hours of Margaret de Foix* is in the Victoria and Albert Museum.[5]

The inkhorn, when not in use, was no doubt worn for convenience and possibly as an advertisement of his trade, slung from the scribe's girdle or around his neck. In Shakespeare's *Henry VI, Part II* the fate of the unfortunate Clerk of Chatham, during Jack Cade's Rebellion of 1450, graphically demonstrates the odium in which the trade of scrivener was generally held:

Cade: . . . Dost thou use to write thy name? or has thou a mark to thyself, like an honest plain-dealing man?
Clerk: Sir, I thank God, I have been so well brought

up that I can write my name.
All: He hath confessed: away with him! he's a villain and a traitor.
Cade: Away with him, I say! hang him with his pen and inkhorn about his neck.[6]

A *cuir bouilli* penner of this period, said to have belonged to Henry VI himself, gold-tooled with the Tudor rose and other royal heraldic devices, was traditionally held to have been left at Waddington Hall by the king during his period as a fugitive after his defeat at the battle of Towton Moor in 1461.(173) It has also been suggested, however, that it is more probably associated with Henry, Prince of Wales, son of James I, whose book-bindings are stamped with a similar design of a rose under a princely coronet. It must also be noted that gold-tooling on leatherwork was introduced into England only in about 1530-40.[7] Although the penner, formerly in the Victoria and Albert Museum, is now unfortunately no longer in existence, as a result of war damage, we are fortunate in having both an account of its provenance and a wood-cut illustration of its interior showing three compartments, two presumably for quills and the third possibly for a pen-knife.[8] Similar penners, attached by their cords to covered inkpots, continued to be fashionable during the following century; in Holbein's portrait of *An Unknown Man at his Desk*, painted in 1541, we have one of the best depictions of such a penner.(174)

In a discussion between two youths, Mauricus and Mendoza, and their writing master, written by Juan Vives as part of his series of conversations *Linguae Latinae Exercitatio* (1538), the relative merits of the portable inkhorn and a 'fixed' inkwell are considered. The master points out that with a portable inkhorn, a stopper of cotton, silk or linen is necessary, and this causes problems with loose fibres attaching to the pen. He concludes that it is far better to pour the ink from a bottle into a fixed inkwell, perhaps of lead.[9] Lead was often used for inkwells as it was little affected by the iron-gall ink; a favourite shape, for stability, with a narrow opening to reduce the chance of dust finding its way into the ink and to reduce the rate of evaporation by presenting a smaller surface area to the atmosphere, was the simple 'beehive', sometimes attached to a holder for quills.(175,176) Later lead wells had holes in the shoulders to accommodate the quills when not in use.(177)

There seems little doubt, however, from the evidence of contemporary illustrations of scribes at work, that the portable inkhorn, with or without a penner attached, was the preference of most writers until perhaps the sixteenth century.(178,179) For those professional scribes, law-writers, manorial stewards, merchants' clerks and the like, who travelled in the course of their work, an inkhorn was the only satisfactory answer to their need of a portable supply of ink and pens, and although pens which carried their own supply of ink are recorded much earlier, this was to remain the case until the development of a reasonably cheap and efficient fountain-pen in the second half of the nineteenth century. The common practice of stoppering the inkhorn with natural fibres is illustrated in the words of a character in Ben Jonson's play *Everyman in His Humour*, Act I, Scene I, who is made to say: 'say that thou com'st but to fetch wool for thine inkhorn'. Ink absorbed into wool inside the well would also be less apt to leak.

By the seventeenth century the pen-case had ceased to be attached by draw-strings to the inkhorn and had become an integral part of it. A portrait of Charles I dictating despatches to his Secretary of War, Sir Edward Walker, his table a drum, provides an early illustration of this type of inkhorn, in silver.(180 and detail) The ends of many of these metal inkhorns incorporate armorial seals, and from the middle of the seventeenth century a compartment for pounce was often included. Examples of inkhorns, penners or portable inkstands are found in a wide variety of materials: precious metals, brass, pewter, wood, ivory, bone, enamels, shagreen, boiled leather and even paper, according to the purse or the preference of the owner.(181 to 215)

In the Victoria and Albert Museum is a particularly fine silver penner of trefoil section, its end engraved with the arms of Luttrell impaling Baker, for Narcissus Luttrell (1657-1732), annalist and bibliographer, who married Sarah Baker in 1681, providing us with an approximate date for this type of penner.(187) A similar example, in the Sattin Collection, has a screw thread under the base to which the pen-case may be attached to form a handle for the inkwell.(188)

Another group of dated penners, in brass with punch-engraved decoration of animal heads in floral scrollwork, was made in Sheffield in the 1650s, by a somewhat whimsical craftsman calling himself Virgo, who is thought to be one of the Madin family who were Sheffield metalworkers at that time. An early penner, with its pen-case and inkwell side by side, is inscribed 'Virgo me fecit in Sheffeild (sic) 1652';(181) another similar penner may be seen in the London Museum.(182) In later examples the inkwell was simply a lead box incorporated in one end of the pen-case. Several examples of this latter type are known, dated either 1655 or 1656, each inscribed 'I was in Sheffeild made & many can Wittnes I was not made by any man', a play on the maker's name of Virgo or Madin.(183) A unique variation of this type, made for Ann Day in 1657, is inscribed with the words of encouragement 'Scribendo dicsis Scribere' on one side and the somewhat pessimistic sentiment 'Quod nulla est in terra Charitas. Et Odium parit ipsa Varitas', with the date, on the other. The seal terminal on one of the hinged ends is engraved with the arms of the Day family.(184)

Such penners, although perfectly functional, must be regarded as works of art; the amount of painstaking work lavished on them would no doubt have made them expensive. Similar scrolling flowers were also used on a particularly fine ivory penner, which may also be dated to the mid-seventeenth century, whose decoration is incised and reserved on a stained brown ground. Needless to say such items are exceedingly rare.(185) This example retains its original boiled leather and paper case as does a simpler penner with ornamental lathe-turned decoration.(186)

Penners in horn, similar to that of Edward Collier's still life,(Colour plate II(ii)) were made from about 1700 and throughout the eighteenth century.(189, 190) Two examples in the Charles Thomas Collection retain their leather straps with buttonholes for attachment to the person. Horn was sometimes used to line the inkwells and pen compartments of turned wooden penners,(193) although glass or pottery ink-bottles were more usual. A common type of bottle, of reddish earthenware with black lead-glazed shoulders, of oval section with semi-circular grooves in the sides to accommodate the quill barrels, is found in both leather and paper penners where the bottle is flanked by two quill holes.(204, 206) Similar bottles were also used by the Sheffield makers in their brass penners of this form.(207a) The Sheffield Directory of 1787 lists five makers of 'INKPOTS,

Leather and Brass', including Mycock of Burgess Street and Jessop of Carver Street, examples of whose work are known.[10](207) Similar penners, then called 'BRASS INKSTANDS', are illustrated in Smith's 'Key', an early nineteenth-century catalogue of goods manufactured in Sheffield.(208)

Later penners naturally tend to be more sophisticated, particularly during the early years of the Industrial Revolution, when in common with most areas of activity, writing equipment attracted the attention of men of great inventiveness. A late Georgian 'inkhorn' was often a complete writing compendium, fitted with a gold-nibbed pen for convenience and a quill knife to provide pens for more serious writing, a pencil or porte-crayon, an inkwell, a pounce pot, a wafer box and seal, and some even include a ruler, dividers and scissors.(211, 212, 214) Others were less elaborate.(213, 215)

A much simpler answer to the problem of a portable ink-supply was the excise bottle, so called because it was used by the Excisemen who travelled the country collecting the duty imposed on just about everything that the Treasury's drafting lawyers could think up, to finance the war with France. In 1799, for instance, there were taxes on male servants, carriages, horses, houses, windows, dogs, salt, hair powder and a host of other convenient sources of state income. The excise bottle was made spill-proof without the need for a stopper by a simple interior funnel of glass which allowed the bottle to be inverted or even shaken quite vigorously without the risk of spillage. They were made both with a flattened collar for use in a buttonhole, or with a groove to which a cord could be attached for suspension from the belt.(216) Human caution being what it is, some excise bottles are found with a double arrangement of interior funnels, and some with stoppers, but these additional precautions are quite unnecessary. Excise bottles were still being advertised for sale into the present century.(217)

Screw-topped inkwells of glass with metal lids were in use in the latter part of the seventeenth century,(218) and the type was to remain popular while the need for portable inkwells existed, into the present century. Throughout the nineteenth century, well-to-do travellers and military and naval officers on campaign service were often equipped with portable lap-desks or dressing-cases which were usually fitted with glass inkwells; these often had rubber-lined screw-on covers or hinged lids secured by winged screws to render them spill-proof.(217, 219)

No doubt inkwells which were intended to stay in one place, in the scriptorium, office or home, have existed alongside portable ink-horns throughout history, but it is not until the sixteenth century which saw a marked increase in the literacy of the land-owning classes that the inkwell or inkstand became part of the general furnishings of the domestic house and therefore a vehicle for greater decorative embellishment. Jan Gossaert's *Portrait of a Merchant* is interesting in showing the use both of a penner and inkhorn, a separate pounce pot and one of the earliest depictions of a desk inkstand, which has vertical tubes to hold the quill pens (with their nibs upwards to avoid damaging them), and another tube housing a roll of parchment ready for use.(220) A similar inkstand, with the addition of a pounce-pot, may be seen in Holbein's portrait of the Hanseatic merchant George Gisze of Danzig, painted in 1532, and now in the Staatliche Museen, Berlin.(Colour plate I) Inkstands of similar design were still being used a century later. An English silver example, of 1630, probably the earliest such still extant, is now in the Museum of Fine Arts, Boston.(221)

In post-Renaissance Italy, inkwells of fine art quality were produced in the studios of some of the leading sculptors of the time, cast in bronze in many forms, in the late fifteenth, sixteenth and early seventeenth centuries.(222 to 226) Highly decorative maiolica inkwells were also made in Italy at this time.(227)

Elaborate inkstands, or as they were then called, standishes, which incorporate a tray for pens, an inkwell, usually covered to keep out dust, and a pounce-pot, can be found dating from the end of the sixteenth century and became more fashionable throughout the seventeenth; by the eighteenth century the standish was the usual form of ink container for the gentleman's desk. Some incorporated a wafer-box, or a shot-container for cleaning the pen, others a taperstick or perhaps a bell to summon a servant. A study of English silver standishes reflects the changing styles in the decorative arts in general, from the chinoiserie of the Charles II period through the baroque and rococo styles to the neo-classicism of the late

eighteenth century.(228 to 234) Similar forms are also found in ceramics.(235, 236) Early base metal standishes in brass and gun metal are now less common, more probably because of the recycling of damaged goods which has always been a feature of the brazier's trade, and because of the munitions drives of two world wars, rather than because few were made. Such inkstands often reflect the forms of their counterparts in silver.

One of the more frequently encountered designs is that known as a 'Treasury' inkstand, so-called because the pewter inkstands used in that government department in the late seventeenth century were of this form, although earlier domestic examples in silver are known. As well as pewter, tinned iron inkstands of this type are found, some with 'japanned' or with painted decoration, while at least one fine example in wood has survived from the seventeenth century.(237 to 240)

Other pewter inkstands include the box type favoured in Ireland,(241) a type also found, but rarely, in English silver.(242) Other combinations of pewter inkwell, pounce-pot and quill-holder are found on the Continent.(243) Perhaps the simplest and most popular type of pewter inkwell is that of plain capstan form, with or without a lid, having quill holes around the shoulder,(244, 245) which are also found in ceramics.(246, 247) Similar inkwells were also made of lobed, oval and square forms, on the same basic design.(248 to 250) Wooden inkwells of capstan or other forms usually had glass liners,(251 to 253) and in spite of their waterproof nature, even porcelain inkwells were sometimes similarly protected. In an account for a 'China Ink Tray. Green Ground Birds Gold Traced embossed Flowers' supplied by the Rockingham Works to Wentworth House, home of the Earl Fitzwilliam, in 1839, the price of twelve guineas included '2 China Inks with Glass linings'.[11]

In the early nineteenth century, inkwells, in common with most other useful artefacts, attracted the attentions of some of the inventive minds which typify the period. The two enemies of ink, which each reduce its liquidity and render it useless, are evaporation and dust. An inkwell which is totally enclosed, with a pump to raise a small quantity of ink for immediate use, is one solution to the problem. Such an invention, the brainchild of one David Edwards, was patented in 1825 and was immediately taken up by others, presumably by licence.(254) The ink was stored inside the ink-well, which contained horsehair, wool or other absorbent material, and was forced by screw pressure up a tube into a cup when required.[12] Variations on the same theme were made by the firm of James Perry and advertised in the *Athenaeum* in August, 1839, at which time the Edwards patent would not yet have expired.(255) Although Perry advertised them as 'Patent Perryian Filter Inkstands', no such British patent in his name appears to have been granted.

Another type of inkwell with a large capacity of ink which allowed only a small surface area to be exposed to the atmosphere was that based on the syphon principle, also used for bird waterers. In this type, the cistern of the inkwell has only one opening, in the form of a small open spout at its base; it is turned upside down and filled through this spout and then re-inverted, creating a vacuum at the top of the cistern which allows only a small amount of ink into the spout for use.[13] Commercial ink bottles continue to be made on this principle.

Souvenir inkwells in porcelain were already being made in the mid-eighteenth century; several examples from the Bow factory are known, inscribed 'MADE AT NEW CANTON' and dated 1750 or 1751.(246) These may have been intended as advertising gifts to visitors to

the factory. An inkwell with chinoiserie figure decoration from the Worcester factory is of similar form, though somewhat taller, and dates from about 1760.(247) Towards the end of the century the Lowestoft factory produced many different souvenirs with enamelled neo-classical borders of floral sprays or swags, and the words 'A Trifle from LOWESTOFT'; the same factory also produced 'Trifles' from other towns including Bungay and Holt. A Lowestoft inkwell of similar form to that from Bow, inscribed 'A Trifle from WANGFORD', is recorded, as is a pounce-pot, 'A Trifle from LOWESTOFT'.[14]

Inkwells were also made to commemorate historical events or as political propaganda, as in the case of Wilberforce's campaign to abolish slavery. Novelty shapes are also found in the inkwells of the late eighteenth and early nine-teenth centuries,(256) but it was the Victorians' love of novelty which produced a myriad of such 'form' inkwells. One such interesting, if somewhat bizarre, inkwell was that in the form of a phrenological head, one of the many arte-facts produced to meet the demand created by the lecture tours of phrenologists like Fowler and Bridges in the mid-nineteenth century.(257) The huge variety of novelty and other inkwells of the Victorian age has been well-documented elsewhere and is perhaps outside the scope of this work.[15]

VIII

The Quill Fountain-pen

The image of a fountain, with its jets and cascades of water, is not perhaps one with which we would associate an efficient pen of the type we have come to know as a fountain-pen. The term seems to have been first used to describe a pen containing its own ink supply during the final quarter of the seventeenth century, when 'fountain' was commonly used to describe a spring, whose steady trickle of water is, perhaps, more akin to the controlled flow of ink necessary for a pen. The trade-card of a London cutler and general merchant of this period, in the Heal Collection, offers, as one item in a wide range of merchandise, 'Fountain-Pens', without amplification, suggesting, perhaps, that the term was already well-established by this time.(258)

Whenever the term 'fountain-pen' was adopted, the invention of a pen which contained its own ink-supply is of much greater antiquity. The first written record is to be found as early as the tenth century. It appears in a manuscript book entitled *Kitab al-Majalis wa'l Musa'irat*, 'the Book of Assemblies and Discussions', written between 969 and 975 AD by al-Qadi al-Nuᶜman ibn Muhammad, the chief judge of the Caliph Mu'izz who established the Fatimid dynasty in Egypt in 969 AD.[1] The passage was first noticed and reported by an Egyptian scholar, Hassan El-Basha Mamoud, in 1951, whose free translation leaves no doubt that it refers to a true fountain-pen:

> When Mu'izz mentioned the pen he described its merits and regarded it as the symbol of the secret of knowledge; he then said he would like to make a pen which would write without the need of an ink-pot.
>
> Such a pen, said the Caliph, would be self-supplying and have the ink inside. One could write what one wanted with it but as soon as one relinquished it the ink would disappear and the pen

would become dry. The writer could keep such a pen in his sleeve without fearing any mark or filtration of the ink for the ink would filter only when the pen wrote. It would certainly be a wonderful instrument and one without precedent.

In a few days the craftsman to whom the pen had been described brought a model made of gold. After filling it with ink, he was able to write with it. But as more ink came out than was needed, the craftsman was ordered to alter it. Finally the pen was brought back repaired. It was turned over in the hand and tilted in all directions and no ink appeared. But as soon as he took it and began to write, he wrote the best hand for as long as he wished and when he took the pen away from the paper the ink vanished. Thus I beheld a wonderful work the like of which I had never thought to see.[2]

This gold fountain-pen fulfilled all the requirements of a modern fountain-pen. It was self-supplying, did not leak, and wrote immediately on contact with the writing surface. The achievement of these qualities is no mean feat, and many of the early European attempts to produce a self-supplying pen failed to overcome the problem of a balance between the tendency to leak and the need for a steady flow of ink when required. In one of his series of lectures to the Society of Arts in 1905, James P. Maginnis discussed this question:

> It is the feed which is in great part responsible for the proper writing of the pen. When a filled pen is held point downwards, the ink it contains is acted on by a variety of forces, among which may be reckoned gravity, inertia, capillary attraction, air pressure, friction, and the viscosity of the liquid, as well as several minor forces. If the pen is properly made, these forces are in a state of equilibrium, and the ink does not run out of the reservoir. As soon, however, as the point touches a surface it is capable of wetting, the action of the capillary attraction is altered, with the result that the ink is enabled to flow from the reservoir, and that the pen writes.[3]

A very simple method of producing a pen

with its own supply of ink was to make a reservoir by taking the barrel of a quill with its tip intact; after piercing a small hole in this closed end, the barrel was then filled with ink and the open end sealed with a plug of sealing wax or a small cork. By inserting this reservoir into a well-fitting second quill cut as a pen so that this hole was positioned just above the end of the slit of the pen, a simple fountain-pen was produced. A steady supply of ink to the nib was obtained by squeezing the pen gently. This type of pen is described and illustrated in his *Deliciae Physic-Mathematicae*, by Daniel Schwenter, published in Zurich in 1651[4]; an earlier edition published in Nürnberg in 1636 is recorded.[5]

The first mention in English of a fountain-pen, although he does not use that term, is probably that of Samuel Pepys in his diary for 5th August, 1663:

> This evening came a letter about business from Mr Coventry, and with it a silver pen he promised me to carry inke in, which is very necessary.

Four days later, he writes:

> This day I begun to use the silver pen Mr Coventry did give me.

Pepys obviously felt such a pen to be a great boon to him, although we are not told whether it was this pen or perhaps another form of 'pen and ink' which is referred to in the diary on 28th November, 1665:

> Up before day and Cocke and I took a hackney coach appointed with four horses to take us up and so carried us over London Bridge. But there, thinking of some business, I did light at the foot of the bridge, and by the help of a candle at a stall, where some pavers were at work, I wrote a letter to Mr. Hater, and never knew so great an instance of the usefulness of carrying pen and ink and wax about me; so we, the way being very bad, to Nonesuch.

The first metal fountain-pen of which we have a contemporary illustration appears in *The Construction and Principal Uses of Mathematical Instruments. Translated from the French of M. Bion, Chief Instrument-Maker to the French King . . . . . . to which are added . . . . . . Those invented or improved by the English*. This translation, by Edmund Stone, was first published in 1723.[6] A second edition followed in 1758 using the same illustration, and it is indicative of the slow progress made in the development of the fountain-pen during this period that a virtually identical plate appears in the *Diction-ary of Arts and Sciences*, Second Edition, published in 1764, almost half a century after Monsieur Bion's death in 1715.[7](259)

This pen could be constructed either of silver or of brass and consisted of a barrel with a screw-on cover at one end, the other end attached to a short tube of smaller diameter to provide a 'feed' over which a quill barrel nib could be fitted; the inside of this end had a screw thread to receive a similarly threaded plug contained in the nib cap. The ink was poured into the barrel at the wide end using a funnel, and held in by vacuum when the cover was replaced, on the principle of a pipette. In the pocket, leakage from the other end was further prevented by the plug in the screw-on cap, which passed within the nib to seal the feed. To use the pen, the nib cap was unscrewed and to allow a flow of ink a small amount of air was allowed into the other end by slightly loosening the cover, 'and the pen a little shaken, to make the ink run more freely'. Needless to say, this primitive open feed would flood readily if the air pressure inside the pen equalled that outside and to help overcome this problem a loose tapering brass plug was sometimes introduced into the barrel to reduce the openness of the feed, with the disadvantage of reducing the pen's ink capacity at the same time.

The earliest recorded example of an actual fountain-pen, which is basically of Bion's design, is made of brass and is of superb quality. It is inscribed with the name of its original owner William Line and dated 1702. The cap has an internal threaded pin which passes through the quill barrel nib and screws into the feed to seal the pen for the pocket. The seal terminal is engraved with a lion rampant, a rebus of the owner's name, and encloses a cork which seals the ink reservoir.**(Colour plate VI(i))**

Two other fountain-pens made on Bion's principle, in the author's collection, are both of similar tapered form, with intaglio seals on their covers (a refinement noted by Stone in his edition of 1758) from the design of which, these pens may be dated to the mid-eighteenth century. One is of plain turned brass, the other of brass with a decorative coating of 'combed' black and vermilion hard wax; the latter example still retains its stamped *cuir bouilli* case.**(260 and Colour plate VI(ii)a and b))**

Similar pens were made in silver and gold. A fine silver example, in the collection of the late William Bishop, has a heliotrope seal terminal engraved with a bird, and like Bion's pen, it incorporates a *porte-crayon*.(261) Another of similar design in the author's collection retains its original black ray-skin slip case.(**Colour plate VI(ii)c**) It is likely that the fountain-pen supplied by London silversmiths Wickes and Wakelin to Asheton Curzon in 1757 at a cost of £2 10s 0d was of this basic design. A gold fountain-pen was purchased by one Mr Colebrooke from the same firm in January, 1758, for the same sum.[8] Perhaps the pen referred to by Fanny Burney (Madame D'Arblay) in her Diary for Tuesday, 18th August, 1789, was also of this type:

> This day the Royals were at a grand naval review, I spent the time very serenely in my favourite wood, which abound in seats of all sorts; and there I took a fountain pen and wrote in my rough journal for copying to my dear Sorelle.

In Germany, in 1781, a Leipzig mechanic is reported to have made a very similar fountain-pen.[9]

During the early nineteenth century, there were many ingenious inventions and improvements to the fountain-pen and a spate of patents, the first of which was that granted to Frederick Bartholemew Fölsch of Oxford Street, London, in May, 1809, whose pen had a spring-loaded plunger with which the flow of ink from the barrel through the feed could be increased as required.[10] Another innovation in his design was the use of a small hole in the hollow socket of his metal nib 'to admit the air, and to adjust the quantity of ink it will bear', and instead of the usual slit, the nib had a groove which 'guides the ink to a point'.(262)

Joseph Bramah's patent of September, 1809, more important for its quill-cutting aspects, perhaps, (see Chapter IV), includes a simple form of fountain-pen. For use with his quill pens, instead of an ordinary pen stick, Bramah proposed a hollow tapering tube of silver or other suitable metal with a small hole near the end which allowed ink to be let down into the mouth of the pen; the tube was filled with ink through its upper open end, which was then stoppered with a cork or cover, and being airtight, no ink would then flow out through the feed. In order to allow such an ink-flow at will, the walls of Bramah's tube were made thin enough to be compressed by finger pressure to squeeze a drop or two of ink at a time into the barrel of the pen nib above the slit; alternatively a screw plunger could be fitted.[11] As we have seen, the squeezing principle had been used by Daniel Schwenter as early as 1636, the piston by Fölsch earlier in 1809, and the airtight cover with its 'pipette' control added nothing to Bion's invention.

Bramah's real contribution to the development of the fountain-pen lies in his introduction of a cork stopper into the feed end of his hollow tube, extending to a point just above the slit of the nib; into this cork he cut 'a small groove, not larger in dimensions than the smallest pinhole, longitudinally along the surface of the stopper', thus creating a feed controlled by capillary attraction, a type of feed which was, in a more sophisticated form, to mark the turning point in the success of the fountain-pen, in Waterman's fountain-pens in the 1880s An example of Bramah's fountain-pen does not yet appear to be recorded.

The next patent was that of John Scheffer, in 1819.[12] In this pen the ink was contained in a section of quill barrel covered with sheep gut, within an external metal case. The ink-flow was controlled by pressing a button which in turn exerted pressure on the reservoir and squeezed ink into a feed-cock which could be closed by the operation of a small lever to render the pen leakproof for the pocket. The pen was designed for use with either a metal or quill nib, with a cap which could only be replaced when the feed-cock lever was in the closed position. (263) This type of pen was advertised by one J. H. Farthing in *Robson's London Commercial Directory* of 1826/7, as Scheffer's Patent Penograph or Writing Instrument. A virtually identical advertisement of the same period names W. Robson as manufacturer.(264) A pen conforming exactly to the Scheffer design, in a silver case hallmarked London, 1823, maker W. R., is also impressed 'W. ROBSON & CO, PATENTEES, LONDON, 2945'.(**265a and Colour plate VI(ii)d**) It is also recorded, however, that Scheffer's Penograph pens were manufactured by Messrs Mordan and Co, in 1843,[13] and they are illustrated in an early Mordan advertisement.[14] It would appear that a number of licences may have been granted under Scheffer's patent, or perhaps the patent rights changed hands a number of times during this period.

In December, 1819, James Henry Lewis, an itinerant writing master of Ebley in Gloucestershire, who gave writing classes in London from time to time, was granted a patent for

An improvement on, substitute for or addition to; pens as usually employed in the art of writing, which I determine caligraphic fountain pens.[15]

In principle, Lewis's pen differed little from Bramah's, previously described, comprising a quill barrel in the bottom of which a small puncture was made. Into the upper end was placed a short metal tube to preserve its cylindrical form. This formed the reservoir of the pen, the upper end of which was then encased in another short metal tube with a rim, to which was fitted a cover. A similar tube, its lower end designed to accept a nib, slipped over the lower part of the reservoir to complete the pen. When the pen was filled with ink and its cover replaced, the pressure of finger and thumb caused a supply of ink to flow to the nib, which could be further regulated, if required, by placing a small piece of sponge in the bottom of the reservoir.

Lewis's pen was designed for use with a variety of steel nibs, termed 'The Elastic Everlasting Points'. By 1826, when he published a treatise on pen-cutting and the art of writing, Lewis's pens, a variety of which he illustrated in an engraved plate,(267) had enjoyed some success:

> many thousands of them have been made use of in various parts of the Kingdom, and have given universal satisfaction.[16]

An actual example of Lewis's Patent Pen does not appear to be recorded, but the principle was adapted in the late nineteenth century in a primitive fountain-pen marketed as 'The Little Imp Fountain Pen'; this used a glass reservoir tube, closed at the top end while at the other end there was a rubber plug through which passed a short piece of quill barrel, its end intact but pierced on each side about 5 mm along its length. This provided the feed to the steel nib, the flow of ink assisted by a piece of string acting as a wick between the glass tube and the quill barrel. The nib itself was fitted to the end of the steel outer casing, with a slip-on cap.(268)

William Johnston was granted a patent in 1826 for a fountain-pen with a stop-cock between the ink reservoir and the nib, operated by a finger lever, a principle which, as we have seen, was already employed in Scheffer's

Patent Penograph.[17] The following year, a patent was granted to George Poulton for a 'self-supplying pen' which comprised a 'pen, tube or reservoir with a weight within it which presses the ink into the pen by its own gravity when in use', and a shield or cover to protect the pen from injury when not in use. The flow of ink from the tube into the pen or nib-section was to be controlled by a valve.[18]

A much more significant development was the first self-filling fountain-pen, patented by John Jacob Parker in 1832.[19] Previous fountain-pens had been filled with a funnel; Parker's pen is filled by immersing the nib in ink and turning the end of the case to raise an internal piston and draw ink in to fill the resulting vacuum, a method still used in some modern fountain-pens.(266) The tube of the pen was to be lined with glass or gold to overcome the problems caused by corrosive inks, and the cap had an interior wire which entered and sealed the feed when it was replaced after use. Examples of Parker's pen are found in hallmarked silver cases.(265b and Colour plate VI(ii)e) Although Parker was the first to patent the self-filling fountain-pen, it is recorded that a precisely similar device had been proposed a long time previously by one Mr W. Baddeley, which was reported in the *Mechanic's Magazine*.[20]

During the remainder of the nineteenth century many patents were granted for fountain-pens, mainly for improvements in the feed mechanism. These, which used metal nibs, were illustrated and discussed in detail by Maginnis in his 1905 lecture.[21] It has often been said that public acceptance of the fountain-pen, truly efficient, reliable and leakproof, stems from the invention and mass-marketing of his 'Ideal' pen by Lewis Edson Waterman in 1884.(269) Although this may be so, it was, as we have seen, by no means the beginning of the story; the fountain-pen already had a long history. Undoubtedly, one of the factors which enabled the success of Waterman's pens was the development of the iridium-pointed gold nib, an English invention, which, as we shall see in the next chapter, was to be most successfully exploited in America.

IX

Metallic Pens

Largely because of its natural flexibility, a well-cut quill pen is an extremely sympathetic writing instrument but, as we have seen, it does require frequent reshaping as its edge becomes dulled with wear during use, a task which seems to have caused considerable difficulty to many people. The reed pen is even less durable than the quill and also required frequent mending to maintain its efficiency. It was natural, therefore, that the development of a pen which did not easily wear out would be a great prize to its inventor, and the search for such a pen has lead through the ages to the use, for the making of pens, of several different metals, first in imitation of the reed pen and later of the quill.

There are references in the Old Testament to 'pens' of iron, but from their contexts, it seems reasonable to assume that these were either styli or gravers.[1] The Romans certainly had bronze pens, some of which, perhaps significantly, seem to follow more closely the tapering form of the quill than that of the reed. Such a pen, found in London in 1864, was reported to have a considerable degree of flexibility. Another, which came to light during the excavation of Pompeii and therefore pre-dating the destruction of that place by the eruption of Vesuvius in 79 AD, is now in the Naples Museum. It is illustrated in the museum's catalogue of 1882, and resembles a reed pen.[2] Several bronze pens, clearly of quill form, with slit nibs, are in the Museum of London. These have long been ascribed to the Roman period which dating has more recently been called into question. It is now thought that they may date from the late medieval period.(270)

An entirely different form of metal pen, dating from the fourteenth century, two examples of which are also in the London Museum, has a four-finned point, very reminiscent of the glass pens of the nineteenth and twentieth centuries, a surprisingly efficient alternative to the slit as a method of harnessing surface tension to provide a controlled flow of ink.(271, 272)

A colophon to a book printed in 1465 by John Fust and Peter Schoeiffer, former partner and apprentice of Gutenberg, the inventor of moveable type, informs the reader that

> This work is fashioned and by diligence finished for the service of God, not with ink nor with brazen reed, but with a certain invention of printing or reproducing . . .[3]

Pens were also made from a variety of other metals as is clear from an account by John Neudörffer, (1497-1563), published in 1544, which has been translated:

> Now the things from which one makes pens, and with which one writes, are iron and copper tube, also copper and brass thin sheet.[4]

In 1691, the poet Jean de la Fontaine wrote to Sister Elizabeth Agnes de Feron:

> If I did not fear to be importunate, I would ask you if you still make copper pens, and in that case I would ask the Reverend Mother to give me some.

That he received his pens is clear from a subsequent letter of thanks to the Mother Superior.[5]

Brass pens are found in many Sheffield-made brass penners of the late eighteenth century.(207) These pens are particularly lacking in flexibility and extremely difficult to write with. Even those who made them were of the same opinion. Referring many years later to these very brass pens and their accompanying ink-pots, one writer who had 'himself made hundreds of dozens of them, which, however, he never used nor steel ones either, as long as he

44

could get a goose quill, good, bad or indifferent', made this very clear.[6]

It was, however, in the development of the steel pen and the gold pen that those major advances were to take place which would eventually supersede the quill pen, when the problems of flexibility in the durable steel pen, and of durability in the flexible but easily worn gold pen, had been overcome. The quest for a truly flexible and hard-wearing alternative to the quill pen was to gather momentum and to reach fruition in the early years of the nineteenth century, in that climate of inventiveness and interaction between lively minds which typifies this period, but both steel pens and those of precious metals have much longer histories, which are worth considering in some detail.

The credit for the invention of the steel pen has been variously claimed for Germany in the person of one Johann Janssen, a magistrate of Aix-la-Chapelle, in 1748, for France, where in 1750 a mechanic, Arnoux, is said to have made steel pens, and for America, where steel pens were produced by a New York jeweller, Peregrine Williamson, circa 1800.[7] The truth of the matter is that steel pens existed at least two centuries earlier; in his writing manual *Arte Subtilissima*, first published in 1548, Juan de Yciar, the Spanish writing master, discussing the Blackletter hand, has this to say:

> This lettering is usually written with a pen of brass or iron or steel. These are alright for those who are used to them, but best of all, for any letters for which it is big enough, is a vulture quill since it weighs less and is smoother.[8]

Steel pens were being produced in France in the late seventeenth century; writing from Paris to her brother Lord Hatton in England in 1680, Mary Hatton suggested to him that if they were not already available there, she thought he ought to have some and would send them to him.[9] In his autobiography, the Hon Roger North, quoting from a letter written to his sister Mrs Foley in 1700, writes:

> You will hardly tell by what you see that I write with a steel pen. It is a device come out of France of which the original was very good, and wrote very well; but this is a copy, ill made. When they get the knack of making them exactly, I do not doubt but the government of the goose quill is near an end, for none that can have them will use others.[10]

It was to prove more than a century before a steel pen which could threaten the supremacy of the quill was to appear.

In England, in 1723, the diarist John Byrom, in a letter to his sister Phoebe, despaired of ever finding a steel pen, which he required when writing shorthand.[11]

The first recorded maker of steel pens in England seems to have been Samuel Harrison, a split-ring maker of Birmingham, circa 1780. Sir Josiah Mason, writing to Mr Sam. Timmins, some time before 1875, stated that 'The first making of steel pens that I know of was about the year 1780, by my late friend Mr Harrison, for Dr Priestley', a statement repeated publicly at a meeting after the laying of the foundation stone of the Mason College, in 1875, and supported by an item in the inventory of property destroyed at Fairhill, the residence of Dr Priestley in Stratford Road, Birmingham, during the Church and King Riots, in 1791:

> A steel pen in a silver case; a ditto silver case and metal pen, value 10s.[12]

These early steel pens were made from lengths of tube hammered out of sheet steel, the join providing the slit of the pen, the profile of the nib formed by filing away the underside of the barrel. Somewhat later, a rough pen-shaped blank was punched out of thin sheet steel and rounded into barrel form. The slit was made by marking the inside of the nib with a sharp chisel and by 'tabbering' this mark with a small hammer which caused the metal to crack, after which the pen was tempered, hardened and ground to its final precise form.

Steel barrel pens of this type were first manufactured on a commercial scale by Jacob Wise, in London, circa 1803. An account written some thirty-five years later states:

> . . . Mr Wise constructed barrel pens of steel, mounted in a bone case for convenience of carrying in the pocket. These pens were very dear, and produced to their inventor but a scanty income. For many years, however, Wise's pens were the only steel pens that could be had, and by means of great activity in pushing a sale of them, they were to be had at almost every stationer's shop in the Kingdom.[13]

Jacob Wise, Manufacturer of Elastic Steel Writing Pens, was working at Newington Crescent, Ball's Road, in 1805, and at No 7 in the same street, in 1811.[14] By 1822, John Wise had succeeded him in the same premises, where he continued until 1828/9.[15] In spite of quarter of a century of production, few examples of the

Wises' pens appear to have survived. One such pen, in a turned bone case stamped 'J. WISE' has a screw-on cap and a blued steel barrel nib with slits in the shoulders for increased flexibility.(273) A similar but anonymous pen, the case provided with a thread at both ends so that the cap may be attached during use, is impressed 'IMPROVED ELASTIC STEEL', a description adopted by Wise and by later makers.(274) Wise's pens were said by one anonymous author to possess 'but in a very remote degree the requisite properties of a writing instrument.'[16]

His work is nevertheless of considerable significance in having pioneered the manufacture on a commercial scale of steel pens; his pens were also the first 'three-slit' pens, a form which was to be extremely popular with Perry and other later manufacturers.

A contemporary maker of steel pens was Daniel Fellow, a journeyman blacksmith of Sedgeley, near Wolverhampton. In 1869, a number of correspondents to the 'Local Notes and Queries' column of the *Birmingham Weekly Post* recalled his activities from about 1800 until 1822, one writer expressing his view that Fellow was making steel pens as early as 1793. In fact, he was almost certainly making such pens before 1790. A recently discovered printed advertising broadsheet published by Fellow himself before 28th June, 1805, the date inscribed in ink upon it in a contemporary hand, claims that he was 'The Original Inventor of Steel Pens'; he further stated that he had been making them for more than fifteen years, this in response to a similar claim by one of his erstwhile employees, a wood-turner whose name is unfortunately not given.(275)

By 1806, his apprentice Thomas Sheldon was also making pens for Fellow, and one gentleman for whom Sheldon made two pens in 1822 recalled that the latter told him that Mr Gillott started making steel pens after seeing those of Sheldon. The business continued, selling 'considerable quantities' of pens through the Birmingham stationers Beilby and Knott, from 1818 to 1828, but was eventually unable to compete with the industrially-produced pens of Mitchell and Gillott. In 1815, the price of Sheldon's pens was eighteen shillings a dozen, with a ten per cent discount for cash. A firm of steel toy makers, B. Smith and Co, of St Mary's Square, Birmingham, in a catalogue illustrated with engravings of their wares, offered these pens at thirty shillings per dozen, and those 'in a bone handle, the top of which screwed off, for carrying in the pocket, at thirty-six shillings per dozen'.

Several other makers of hand-made steel pens are recorded at about this time in Birmingham, amongst whom were John Edwards of 40 Hill Street, a maker of 'Elastic Steel Pens' which were 'warranted to write exceedingly fine and free', in 1823, and a maker called Spittle living at Chequers' Row, Bath Row, who in 1824 was making barrel pens to fit on a quill, at one shilling each.[17]

The first steel pen patent was granted to Bryan Donkin, an engineer whose firm survives to this day. Donkin, born in 1768, was a man of his times, with a wide range of interests. He started his working life as a paper-maker and his inventive mind was soon engaged in the improvement of existing technology in that field. Among his other inventions were a system of canning foods, a copying press and security printing using compound blocks.[18] Unlike the steel pens of his contemporaries, which were hammered into their barrel form using the techniques of the blacksmith, Donkin's pen exhibits the skills of the designer and engineer. To make the pen, two thin sheets of steel or other suitable metal, each shaped to form half the nib, were brazed together at an obtuse angle forming a V-section, which was then provided with a brass tube into which it could be made to partially retract to reduce flexibility.(276) The pens were sold at three shillings and sixpence each with replacement nibs at one shilling, but although they were of undoubted quality, it appears that they failed to make much impact on the market. A later writer recalled that 'the price was high, and the demand inconsiderable'.[19] An example of Donkin's patent pen may be seen in the Science Museum in London.(277)

The steel pens so far considered were made by hand in small workshops and in relatively small numbers, and although made in imitation of it, provided no real alternative to the quill pen. It is not surprising that steel pens at half-a-crown or three shillings and sixpence each should have found little popularity considering that the former sum would purchase a dozen of the best quality and up to 250 of the lowest quality quill pens at that time. It was the application of steam power to the production of the steel pen which was to lead to the vast industry which developed from these small beginnings, in the second quarter of the century, by men who became household names: John Mitchell, James Perry, Joseph Gillott and Josiah Mason.

By 1838, mass-produced steel pens could be had at fourpence per gross, a real alternative to the quill pen rather than a mere imitation of it, and from this time the decline of the quill pen was inevitable. The other main factor in the eventual demise of the quill pen was clearly the fountain-pen, with its virtually everlasting gold nib, and it is to the history of the gold pen which we must now turn.

Gold, and to a lesser degree silver, are both suitable for the making of pens so far as flexibility is concerned, though their relative softness and consequent susceptibility to wear is a serious drawback which was not to be completely overcome until the 1830s. We have seen in the previous chapter that there is an instance of the use of gold to make a pen in tenth century Egypt; in Europe the earliest mention of a pen which was probably of gold appears in the fourteenth century in William Langland's *The Vision of William concerning Piers the Plowman*:

This was the text truly I took good gome
The glose gloriously was writ with a gilt pen.

In 1558, in an *Inventory of the Jewels, Wardrobe and Furniture* of the Emperor Charles V at Yuste, taken after his death on 22nd September, there is an entry:

Item – A Notebook [*Libro de memorias*] with its gold pen.[20]

Perhaps the earliest surviving pens of precious metals are those contained in the handles of a number of South German silver-gilt spoons and forks, dating from circa 1580-90. The pens screw out of the shanks of these pieces of fine art cutlery, and they themselves contain folding tooth- and ear-picks. As well as the Waddeson examples in the British Museum,(278) there are similar spoons in German museum and private collections.[21]

In the Statutes of Tonbridge School, Kent, dated the fifth year of the reign of Queen Elizabeth I (1563), is the following regulation for the award of prizes for the annual disputations:

And I will that the first allowed [the winner of the first prize] have a pen of silver, whole of guilt [gilt], the price two shillings and sixpence; the second a pen of silver, parcel guilt, of the value of two shil-

lings; the third a pen of silver of twenty pence for their rewards.[22]

This tradition, carried out on Skinners' Day, on which the school's founders and governors, the Skinners' Company, visited the school, continued into the nineteenth century. Examples of Tonbridge School prize pens, in silver, for the years 1869 and 1871 are recorded.[23] These pens were in the form of natural quills, some with the nibs fashioned as an integral part of the barrel, later examples having Bramah's patent holders for use with a quill nib. A fine example, parcel-gilt, engraved *'Prize at Tonbridge School, July, 1838'*, still retains its original wine morocco leather case.(279) Other schools gave similar prizes.(280, 281)

Both gold and silver pens, sometimes with ivory holders, are found in penners and portable writing étuis of the eighteenth century.(194 to 196, 212) Since many of the same penners contain a pen-knife, it may be presumed that the metal pen would be used as a convenience rather than for protracted writing, or for those occasions when a quill was not readily available. On the whole, these pens are flexible enough to write very efficiently. Mention of such a pen appears in a passage by Steele, in *The Spectator* of 7th October, 1712, describing the conspicuous manner in which a certain lady conducted herself in church:

For she fixed her eyes on the preacher and as he said anything she approved, with one of Charles Mather's fine tablets, she set down the sentence, at once showing her fine hand, the gold pen, her readiness in writing and her judgement in choosing what to write.[24]

For serious writing, however, and for everyday purposes, a more durable pen was required. One solution to the problem was that of William Hyde Wollaston (1766-1828), whose researches from about 1800, in partnership with Smithson Tennant, led eventually to the production of malleable platinum. A by-product of this research was the discovery of the four metallic elements osmium, iridium, rhodium and palladium, all of which were known to Wollaston by 1804.[25] His continued research led eventually to an alloy suitable for pen tips, consisting of rhodium and tin in the proportions of four to one, which was extremely hard. From about 1822 to 1825, according to Wollaston's notebook, now in the Science Museum, enough of the alloy was produced for about 13,000 tips, which as two were required for each pen, would allow the production of 6,500 pens. A London optician and instrument-maker, T. C. Robinson, purchased these rhodium-tin alloy pen tips from Wollaston, and by fusing them to gold nibs produced flexible pens with very hard and durable points. A pen made of silver with rhodium alloy points, which probably pre-dates those made by Robinson, is still in the possession of the Wollaston family, together with an old undated paper on one side of which is written:

> This was I believe the first Rhodium pen ever made; it was given to General Sir William Codrington when he was a boy living with his father at 43 Charles St., Berkeley Square. – by Doctor Wollaston – who I believe made the pen himself,

and on the reverse,

> Dr. Wollaston's Rhodium pen in this case, which went through the Crimea campaign with W. C.

A letter, also in the Wollaston family's possession, to William Codrington from his father, and dated 5th May, 1822, begins:

> The accompanying pen is Dr. Wollaston's present to you, the nib being a bit of his own metal, Rhodium.[26]

A drawing in the author's possession, made in 1885, from an unknown source, by Frank Crosbie, eventual successor to the firm of Francis Mordan & Co, probably the largest producers of gold pens in Britain during the second half of the nineteenth century, shows the form of Dr Wollaston's Rhodium Pen in 1823.[27] It was formed of two flat pieces of gold soldered together to form a nib of V-shaped section, much in the manner of Donkin's steel pen.(282)

This form of nib was also used by William P. Doughty, a watchmaker who turned his hand to making ruby-pointed gold pens in about 1822.(283) In these pens the tips of the nib were small rubies cut by the lapidary into precise triangular prisms and cemented into small pockets of similar form fashioned in such a way that the tips of the rubies protruded to form the writing points.(284) Doughty first appears in *Kent's London Directory* for 1819, where his address is given as 10 Great Ormond Street, where he stayed until the 1830s when he moved to the Strand, first to No 19 and by 1835 to No 431. A letter to the Editor of the *Mechanic's Magazine* in 1825, asking if anyone could supply Mr Doughty's address elicited the reply that 'Mr Doughty, inventor and manufacturer of Ruby-

pointed pens is at 10 Great Ormond Street, London'.

One of Doughty's gold pens, however, a document in itself, throws some doubt on the origin of the invention, the back of the nib impressed 'ROSE INVENIT & JEWEL^R/ DOUGHTY FECIT'.(284b) The name Rose does not appear to be mentioned in contemporary accounts of Doughty's pens; it seems likely that he was the lapidary employed by Doughty to provide his ruby points, and was possibly the Jn°. Rose whose premises were 427 Strand, in 1826, only two doors from those Doughty himself was to occupy a few years later.[28] It is tempting to think that Doughty may have discovered these vacant premises on one of his business visits to Rose.

An advertisement in the newspaper *John Bull* of 14th November, 1824, after a recital of the merits of Doughty's Perpetual Ruby Pen, goes on to say that

> it is sold, price £2.12s.6d. by Messrs. Bramah, 124 Piccadilly; Mr. Palmer, 2 St. James's-street, Mr. Parkin, 406 Strand; Messrs. Rowe and Waller, 49 Fleet-street; Mr. Dollond, St. Paul's Churchyard; Messrs. Smith and Elder, Fenchurch-st.; Mr. Edwards, 21 King-st. Bloomsbury; Mr. Daniels, 125, Regent-st.; and W. P. Doughty, at the Manufactory, 10, Great Ormond-st.

These were major firms, several of whom enjoyed royal patronage, which is a measure of the quality of Doughty's pens. It is not surprising that they enjoyed considerable success, a fact reflected in an article published in 1838:

> With these pens a person could write as finely as with a crow-quill, or as firmly as with a swan-quill, or the two modes might be combined. These pens possessed considerable elasticity, and by their means an uniform manuscript, unattainable by means of ordinary pens, could be produced. Pens of this construction have been in constant use for upwards of six years, and at the end of that time exhibited no signs of wear, they were as perfect then as ever. In using them, however, care is necessary to preserve the nibs from contact with hard bodies; they require occasional washing with a brush in soap and water. Mr. Doughty states that although they are costly at first, yet, in the end, they will be found economic, on account of their permanency. To prevent injury to the points, in the act of dipping this pen into an ink-stand, Mr. Doughty lines the interior of his elegant ink-stands with India-rubber, or places a bottle of that material within the stand to contain the ink.[29]

These inkwells, at least one of which has survived, are of brass, the hinged lids engraved 'PATENT CAOUTCHOUC INKWELL DOUGHTY FECIT'.[30]

Although Doughty's pens were possibly the most successful to employ ruby points, they were not the only ones. A patent was granted in 1822, to Messrs Hawkins and Mordan, for pens which also relied for their durability on the use of precious stones; small particles of ruby, diamond or other extremely hard substances were embedded under pressure into the tips of nibs of tortoiseshell or horn, which had first been softened by immersion in almost boiling water. The natural elasticity of these materials could be controlled by the attachment of sliding springs, to suit various hands. A variation which also allowed quills to be similarly treated, employed varnishes, resins or sealing-wax as the means of attachment of the particles of precious stones.[31] It would appear that these pens enjoyed little success:

> . . . the particles of diamond were by degrees dragged out of the cement by the paper, and thus caused a feeling of roughness while writing.[32]

Sampson Mordan was, however, advertising 'Every kind of Gold, Silver, and Steel Pens, Rhodium Pens, and Ruby Pens' in 1827.[33] It was Mordan's co-patentee, the highly inventive Hawkins, whose persistence in the pursuit of a truly durable yet flexible pen was to lead to complete success.

John Isaac Hawkins was born on 14th March, 1772, at Taunton, Somersetshire, the son of a watch- and clockmaker. He embarked on a medical training in America, but his inclination for things mechanical soon led him to change his course of study. Among his many inventions were the 'Physiognotrace', a machine for taking likenesses in profile,(285) a very successful copying machine, improvements in the pianoforte, machinery for the refining of sugar, the ever-pointed pencil, and that which concerns us here, the 'everlasting gold pen'.[34]

Hawkins had, from as early as 1804, been seeking a suitably hard material to solder to the tips of a gold nib to produce a permanently durable pen. It was not until about 1833, when the earlier experiments of Dr Wollaston came to his notice that Hawkins began to experiment with the native alloy of osmium and iridium, as he was to recall in later life.[35] Wollaston had sent particles of both rhodium and the osmium-iridium alloy to T. C. Robinson, maker of ruby-pointed pens, to have pens made with points of each metal. As we have seen, the rhodium-pointed pens were made, but Robinson had returned the osmium-iridium which he said was too hard to be ground into shape for the purpose. Hawkins, realising that this property, if the problem of grinding could be overcome, was exactly what he required, set about producing a lathe capable of giving ten thousand revolutions per minute, with which, using a lap impregnated with oil and diamond dust, he succeeded in abrading the iridium and produced his first pen, of silver tipped with iridium points. One of the points quickly became detached and Hawkins made the second pen of gold, which was a total success. His third pen was sold on 26th April, 1834 to Mr Vine, an eminent London merchant whose trade with Russia led to orders for pens for the Czar and others. These early gold pens sold for twelve shillings each, without a holder. Hawkins obtained his supplies of iridium from Mr Johnson of Hatton Garden, whose firm is still in business there, as Johnson Matthey, and as he selected the better material, it became progressively more difficult to obtain iridium of a quality suitable for his purpose.

In August 1835, he sold the business for the sum of £300 and a percentage arising from the sale of pens, by an agreement with the Rev Charles Cleveland, to the latter's brother Aaron Porter Cleveland, whose sole interest was in acquiring the business and the pen-making skills necessary in order to pass the management over to his brother-in-law, Simeon Hyde of New York. Having carried on the London manufactory from 21st January, 1836 until the end of May of that year, Aaron Cleveland returned to New York to establish the business there and to train Hyde's workmen, Levi Brown and George Barney in the secrets of Hawkins's process. Hawkins agreed to run the London concern, allowing Hyde half-a-crown for each pen sold.

It was however in the United States that the making of iridium-pointed gold pens was most successful. In the course of time some of Hyde's workmen, among them Levi Brown, were to leave to start up their own businesses, and by 1849 there were no less than fifteen manufacturers of gold pens in the United States, mostly located in New York, including that of John Foley.[36]

In London, within a few years of the sale of

Hawkins's business in 1835, Francis Mordan (the son of Sampson Mordan, Hawkins's co-patentee of 1822), was involved in the manufactory.[37] The style of the firm became 'Mordan and Hyde' in 1845, and on Hyde's final return to New York in 1848, it would appear that Francis Mordan became the sole owner of the London firm, becoming incorporated as Francis Mordan & Co, in 1869.[38] Francis Mordan's best quality Everlasting Gold Pens sold, in 1892, complete with ivory handles, in morocco cases, at prices ranging from ten shillings and sixpence for the Ladies' Gold Pen to two pounds two shillings for the Magnum Bonum Gold Pen, and were guaranteed for ever against failure in normal usage.(286) Second quality pens sold for about half these prices and third quality for about five shillings each.

Hawkins's achievement in producing the first iridium-pointed gold pen was to have its most marked effect some half a century after the event, since without it, Lewis Edson Waterman's development of the first truly efficient pocket fountain-pen, patented by him in 1884, would not have been possible. It was the mass-produced fountain-pen, widely available at affordable prices, which perhaps more than the steel pen was to bring about the final demise of the quill pen as a popular writing instrument.

X

Pencils & Porte-crayons

The black-lead pencil with which we are all familiar today contains no lead but it is in this misnomer that we can find a clue to its origins. The Roman scribe's *plumbum*, a disc of true metallic lead, was used to rule his guide-lines on papyrus. The medieval scribe ruled his guide lines across his parchment either with a simple stylus, probably of bone, which incised a fine groove on one side of the skin and a corresponding raised line on the other, or with a fine stylus of lead, which produced a light grey line. In either case the parchment was first marked out, several sheets at a time, with a series of pinpricks down each side, using a bone-handled pricker with an iron point.(287) (In the offices of eighteenth- and nineteenth-century scriveners, this marking out was done with a parchment runner, a steel-spiked brass wheel.(288))

Evidence of the use of metallic lead pencils in the medieval period, both for ruling guide-lines and for preparatory sketching-in prior to the illumination of initial letters, is to be found in manuscripts of the period.[1] By the fourteenth century, artists were using fine pencils of lead, tin or silver to produce the delicate drawings now known as 'silverpoint'.

During the second quarter of the nineteenth century metallic pencils based on this principle enjoyed a brief vogue for use with pocket books. These pencils usually had turned bone, ivory or wooden handles and short conical points made of an alloy of tin, antimony and lead, which left an indelible grey mark when used with a specially coated paper. The books were sold as Harwood's Improved Patent Memorandum Books, although no patent appears to have been taken out. Harwoods advertised them in *Pigot's London Directory* for 1832 and later examples are found manufactured by A.

Cowan and Sons of Cannon Street, London, under the Harwood name; Henry Penny produced very similar books.(289) Handy notebooks of this type may be seen as the successors to the wax-covered wooden tablets of the Romans on which the ephemeral jottings of the day could be inscribed with a metal stylus, or the writing tablets which served the same purpose throughout the medieval period.(290)

It is not surprising that when, in the sixteenth century, a new material was discovered which had a natural metallic lustre and which wrote like lead but with a stronger black line, it should be called *plumbago* and more commonly, 'black-lead'. Although this latter term is still in common use today, the true nature of plumbago as an allatropic form of pure carbon was demonstrated as long ago as 1779, by K. W. Scheele, whose chemical analysis showed there to be no lead present. A decade later, A. G. Werner suggested the name *graphite* from the Greek word 'to write'.[2]

The word 'pencil', too, owes its origin to an ancient writing implement. It has been shown that the serifs of Roman inscriptional letters owe their form to their having been painted in with a square-ended brush prior to carving;[3] such a brush was called a *penicillus* or 'little tail'.

A large and extremely pure deposit of plumbago, also known locally as 'black cawke' or 'wadd', was discovered at Seathwaite in Borrowdale, a few miles from Keswick, Cumberland, in the sixteenth century; it is held locally that the discovery of this 'grand pipe' of plumbago was made by a local shepherd who noticed the shining deposit at the roots of a tree felled by a violent storm, and there is a tradition that the first use made of the wadd was as a means of marking sheep. The precise date of the discovery is uncertain; various writers have suggested dates from 1554 onwards, but it would appear from a Rental for the year 1540-41, of Furness Abbey (whose possessions included the Manor of Borrowdale), which lists 'a quarry of Calkstone alias Shepe Oodde' (wadd), which could only be the Seathwaite mine, that mining was already taking place by that date. There is no record of the monks themselves carrying out any such mining, and it is likely that the site was in the possession of a manorial tenant, using local labour. During the years following the dissolution of the monasteries, such industrial activity, which had provided employment for a large proportion of the inhabitants of the dales, virtually disappeared. It was to be revived by the advent of both expertise and capital from Germany, mainly from Augsburg.[4] The Mines Royal Company was formed by charter granted by Queen Elizabeth I to Thomas Thurland, Master of the Savoy, and Daniel Hechstetter of Augsburg, in 1561; the detailed accounts of its mining operations in Cumberland, which for the years 1564 to 1577 are still extant, make no mention of wadd mining. It seems unlikely, therefore, that the Germans took any part in the Borrowdale wadd mining before this time, and it appears that the only evidence for their involvement after 1577 is the fact that one of the old workings is traditionally known as the 'German's Vein'.[5]

It is possible that even in these very early days plumbago-mining was carried out only on an intermittent basis as the demand for the new mineral increased as uses were found for it; during its later and more active history, the mine was worked only at intervals of about five or seven years, to avoid the supply exceeding demand.

Local tradition maintains that pencil-making at Keswick dates from the reign of Elizabeth I, but there seems to be no hard evidence of the making of pencils there on a commercial scale until much later. The plumbago from the Seathwaite mines was of a very high quality; it was extremely pure and free from grit, and was therefore very suitable for pencil-making.(291) The poorer quality material was also to find many uses: as an excellent lubricant, in the making of moulds for the casting of cannon balls, for the rust-proofing of iron and steel generally, as a 'glaze' which which to line and harden crucibles, and even for medicinal pur-

poses.[6] Until quite recently, its use as a black-lead polish to preserve domestic iron stoves and grates from rusting was almost universal.

The high quality of the Borrowdale wadd was such as to command extremely high prices, and the mines were operated only at intervals to allow the mining of sufficient to meet the foreseeable demand, after which they were sealed until a further supply was necessary. Such careful husbandry no doubt sustained a high level of prices and maintained a continuous supply of raw material for the pencil-manufacturers for some three centuries, until the deposits were finally exhausted, probably around 1865, although the exact date of the final closure of the mines is not recorded. The high value of the wadd resulted in handsome profits for the owners. In 1769, the best plumbago was worth 30s a pound, and in 1803, a deposit was discovered which yielded over 31 tons, worth, at that price, £105,000. By 1838, when the mines were beginning to run out, the value had risen to 45s a pound, with an annual consumption of between £3000 and £4000.[7] Naturally, such potential returns attracted the attentions of thieves and smugglers; up to £1000 worth of plumbago is thought to have been stolen annually by a gang which, in 1751, attacked the mine steward's house, built over the mine entrance, resulting in legislation in 1752 making it a felony 'to break into any mine or wadd-hole of wadd or black-cawke, commonly called black-lead, or to steal from thence . . .'

Needing only to be washed and sorted, the plumbago could be sawn directly into slices and thence into rods; as early as the end of the sixteenth century, it was being exported to the Continent, where it found particular favour with Dutch and Flemish merchants as a raw material for the making of simple crayons which became known as *crayons d'Angleterre*.[8] That same property which makes plumbago so suitable as a writing material, its readiness to impart black marks to everything it touches, including fingers, no doubt quickly lead to the adoption of some form of holder, or perhaps a binding of string. Later, metal holders known as *porte-crayons* were devised, and examples are found in steel and brass, or even in silver.(292, 293) Double-ended *porte-crayons* were often used for drawing, with both black and white crayons, over a considerable period, from the seventeenth to the nineteenth century.(294)

The earliest recorded mention of the use of a

52

wooden holder for a pencil, which may have used Borrowdale plumbago, although the author referred to it as 'English antimony', is to be found in a treatise on fossils, by Konrad von Gesner of Zurich, published in 1565.[9] A certain reference to a wooden-cased graphite pencil is that of Sir John Pettus in his *Fieta Minor*, published in London in 1686.[10] Referring to black-lead, he writes:

> of late it is curiously formed into cases of deal or cedar and so sold as dry pencils, something more useful than pen and ink.

An even earlier reference to 'a pensil of black lead' was made by J. Brinsley in 1612, though we are not told whether or not the pencil in question was encased in wood. J. Dupont, in about 1660, refers to a 'black lead pen'.[11]

Although it is traditional in the Keswick area that the pencil industry dates back to the time of the opening of the wadd mines in the sixteenth century and it is likely that pencils of a sort were made there on a small scale from then on, there appears to have been little pencil-making on a commercial basis until about the turn of the eighteenth/nineteenth centuries. Indeed, the earliest record so far discovered of black-lead pencil-making in Cumberland is not at Keswick at all, but at Whitehaven, in 1775. An advertisement in the local newspaper reads as follows:

BLACK LEAD PENCILS
THIS is to inform the Public, That the genuine BLACK-LEAD PENCILS made by William Kitchen, Cabinet and Pencil Maker, in Hartley Street, Whitehaven, are sold Wholesale and Retail by the said William Kitchen and by John Ware and Son, on reasonable Terms; the Particulars of which may be known by applying as above. – All pencils disposed of by them, to Stationers, Booksellers, Shopkeepers, Gentlemen and Others, will be warranted GOOD; the Common Pencils of 7 inches having 5 inches of Lead in each, without Deception; and the others in Proportion[12]

The tools and skills of the cabinet-maker are ideally suited to the making of pencils by hand, and it is unlikely that William Kitchen was the only member of his trade to see the potential in this sideline. His advertisement also throws light on the way in which pencils were made at that time.

The wood almost universally used for pencils is the Virginian Cedar (*Juniperus Virginiana*), which is also known as Scented Cedar or Pencil Cedar. The logs were first reduced to slats of

pencil length and grooves of square section were cut lengthwise using a plough plane, leaving the last inch or two ungrooved; into these grooves were slotted pre-sawn slices or 'scantlings' of graphite of the same thickness, and perhaps from one to three inches in length, depending on the size of the nodule of raw material from which they were cut. This was then scored and broken off flush with the surface of the wood, and the process repeated until the entire groove had been filled. A thinner slat of cedar was glued firmly to the first and the slats sawn into individual pencils which were then rounded and finished.

Because the groove into which the hand-sawn 'lead' was fitted was cut by hand, it was possible to conserve the valuable black-lead by terminating the groove an inch or two from the end of the pencil, since it was unnecessary to have any 'lead' in that portion which would be thrown away at the end of the pencil's useful life. Naturally, the 'blind' end of such pencils laid the trade open to abuse either by the insertion of very short leads, or by the use of poor quality compositions of graphite dust mixed with various binding agents to fill all but the end which would be first sharpened; hence the need for Kitchen's warranty of the quality of his pencils. Pencils with square leads and one blind end were still being made in the third quarter of the nineteenth century.

The earliest mention previously noted of a pencil-maker in Keswick is that of John Foulk who is described as such in the parish registers of Crosthwaite Church on 23rd April, 1814.[13] However, three names appear in *Jollie's Directory of Cumberland, Part II*, published in 1811, under the heading 'Persons in Business' at Keswick:

Airey, John	– Pencil maker, Librarian
Banks, Jacob	– Pencil Maker
Laydeman, John	– Pencil Maker and Woollen Manufacturer

The first of these was still in business in 1847 and a pencil impressed with the name of his successor, 'JOSEPH USHER LATE AIREY' may be seen in the Fitz Park Museum, Keswick.

John Ladyman was one of the acknowledged sources of information concerning the Seathwaite wadd mines in Hutchinson's *History of the County of Cumberland and Some Places Adjacent*, published in 1793/4. In 1817, he gave up the woollen trade to devote himself to full-time pencil-making.

Jacob Banks retired before November, 1824, when in his will he is described as 'late Black lead Pencil Maker'.[14] The name Banks is one which features large in the history of the wadd mines and in the later pencil manufactories. Henry Banks, Esq, MP was co-owner of the mine in 1614; by 1622 Sir John Banks was in possession of the Banks's share.[15] In 1710, when William Nicholson, Bishop of Carlisle, described his visit to the mine which had been newly re-opened after a period of closure of some thirty-two years, it was in the co-ownership of 'Mr Shepherd and Mr Banks'.[16] Such a long pause in the operation of the mine may be accounted for by the fact that as late as 1657, the mineral's primary use may have been for medicinal purposes; in an exhaustive list of over a thousand items imported during the Commonwealth, which includes writing materials such as paper, parchment and quill pens, 'black-lead' appears only under the general heading of 'drugs'.[17] This medicinal use was, in 1704:

> . . . a present remedy for the colic; it easeth the pain of gravel, stone and strangury; and for these and the like uses, it is much bought up by apothecaries and physicians. The manner of the country people's using it is thus: first they beat it small into meal, and then take as much of it, in white wine or ale, as will lie upon a sixpence, or more if the distemper require it.[18]

In 1759, the mine was still in the joint ownership of the Banks and Shepherd families in the persons of Mr Banks of Corfe Castle and Mr Shepherd of Boonwood, Cumberland, the latter granting a lease of 'his half of the mine to several gentlemen, chiefly resident in London'.[19] By 1796,

> Mr. Hy. Banks, M.P. for Corfe in Dorsetshire has one half of this Mine, the remaining half is divided into 8 shares of which Sir Jos. Banks has one. . .[20]

It is perhaps more than coincidence that one of the three earliest recorded pencil-makers in Keswick was also named Banks. By his will, proved in 1830, Jacob Banks left only £200 to his son, also Jacob, having probably passed on the pencil-making business to him on his retirement prior to 3rd October, 1824, the date of its writing. Jacob Banks, the elder, also left property which was in the possession of Joseph Banks, who in 1832 was to found the firm of Joseph Banks and Company, in an old woollen mill on the River Greta at Keswick.(295) The business flourished, and at the Great Exhibition

of 1851 was awarded a 1st Class Medal. By 1854, the factory was producing some 5-6,000,000 pencils annually; an account of pencil-making at Keswick, largely based on the activities of Banks and Company, was published in *The Illustrated Magazine of Art* in that year.[21] The Greta Pencil Works was also honoured, in 1857, by a visit from Edward, Prince of Wales, a visit of which Joseph Banks was naturally extremely proud, using it widely in his subsequent advertising. A further Prize Medal was awarded to the firm at the International Exhibition of 1862 in London.

A pencil in the Cumberland Pencil Company's Museum at Keswick, probably dating from the 1840s, is stamped 'BANKS FOSTER & CO Manufacturers, Keswick, Cumberland'; if this was a partnership with Joseph Banks, it must have been short-lived, appearing in only one directory, in 1847.[22] Another pencil, of mid-nineteenth-century date, in the same collection, is impressed 'W. FOSTER SON & CO'.

Joseph Banks died in 1860, leaving his entire estate to his widow Ann for her lifetime, after which it was to be sold for the benefit of his children.[23] The will makes no mention of any specific property, but clearly did not include a controlling interest in the firm of Banks and Company, which carried on under different management, between whom and Ann Banks there was certainly no love lost.[24] She secured the services of 'the working manufacturer who gained for the late firm the Exhibition Prize Medal', and by 1869 she was trading successfully in competition with Banks and Company as 'ANN BANKS, BLACK LEAD PENCIL MANUFACTURER, KESWICK PENCIL WORKS, (Only BANKS in the Trade)'.

She also had a London Warehouse, and made free with the medal-winning successes of her late husband's firm in her own advertising, and by implication suggested that she and not Banks and Company was the true successor of the original firm established in 1832.(296) She was without doubt an able and innovative businesswoman, introducing new machinery and methods, which according to a report in the *Carlisle Journal* gave 'fresh stimulus to Keswick's pencil trade'.[25] The products of her factory were of very high quality.(297) Although she was to die in 1871, the firm, in Main Street, Keswick, was still in business as a limited company at least until about 1894, when under the title of Mrs Ann Banks Ltd, it was listed in *Kelly's Directory*; it would appear that the Cumberland Pencil Company took over the Main Street works before 1910.

The original firm of Banks and Company continued at the Greta Pencil Works. Thomas Keenliside was its manager in 1883, and Henry Birkbeck, who was manager in 1901, became the owner in 1906, to be succeeded by his son Simon, who retired in 1921.[26] The business was sold as a going concern to H. J. Billinge, a Manchester businessman, who continued to make pencils, employing about thirty workers, until the factory was virtually gutted by a disastrous fire in December, 1941, ending a continuous history of pencil-making at the Greta Pencil Works starting in 1832.[27]

Another leading firm of pencil-manufacturers in late Victorian Keswick was that of Hogarth and Hayes of the Southey Hill Pencil Works, whose building still stands and adjoins the modern Cumberland Pencil Company's works. They also made a wide range of cedar novelty goods, often transfer-printed with Lakeland views, which may be distinguished from the similar Mauchline ware, made of sycamore, by their darker colour. Richard Hogarth died in 1905, leaving the Southey Hill works and another at Stair, near Keswick, to his son George, who himself died in 1912.[28]

In addition to those already discussed pencils are found impressed: 'COUPLAND MANUFACTURER KESWICK CUMBERLAND', 'CROSTHWAITE AND LANCASTER MANUFACTURERS KESWICK' and 'ROBERT WILSON GRETA BRIDGE KESWICK CUMBERLAND'. There are several Cumberland directories which contain clues to the dates of operations of these makers, notably *Jollie's* (1811), *Parson and White's* (1829), *Pigot's* (1834), *Mannix and Whellan's* (1847), *Slater's* (1869), and *Bulmer's* (1883 and 1884).

In 1829, there were five pencil-makers listed for Keswick, including Gates and Coupland; by 1834, the firm was 'Robert Coupland (Late Gates and Coupland)', and by 1847, Robert Coupland is also listed as a bobbin-maker.

Along with John Ladyman, one of the sources of information about the Borrowdale wadd mines acknowledged by William Hutchinson in his *History of Cumberland*, published in 1793/4, was a Mr Crosthwaite, who may have been the D. Crosthwaite who is listed as a Keswick bookseller in 1811. The only directory entry for a pencil-maker of this name is that of 1847, as 'Crosthwaites, Lancaster and Company'.

Robert Wilson is first listed in 1869 as a pencil-maker at Braithwaite, near Keswick, where the firm was still operating in 1883 as 'R. Wilson and Co', under the management of William Keenliside, a relative of Thomas Keenliside who, as we have seen, was manager of Banks and Company's Greta Works at that time, suggesting a possible connection between the two firms. The Wilson pencil mentioned above, which is in the Fitz Park Museum, Keswick, and a document in itself, would tend to suggest that it was Ann Banks, rather than Banks and Company, who took over Wilson's other works at Greta Bridge, his address at the time of its manufacture, as this was the site of her Main Street, Keswick factory. The Braithwaite factory, by then known as the Coledale Pencil Mill, was destroyed by fire before 1899.[29]

Another manufacturer worthy of note was Abraham Wren whose business was established by 1847; in 1858, his factory was known as 'Wrensville'.[30] According to one writer, Hogarth and Hayes took over Wren's firm in 1886.[31] If so, it may be that 'Wrensville' was at Southey Hill, the site of the Hogarth and Hayes factory during the final phase of their history; in 1869, they had a pencil works on the Penrith Road.

There are other Keswick pencil-makers to be found in the directories, whose activities seem to have been shortlived, and other apparent makers' names impressed on pencils which are actually those of stationers in the town, one of whom was 'GRISDALE, 16 LAKE ROAD KESWICK', early this century.

One reason for the apparent dearth of early pencil-makers in Keswick, so near to the source of the essential raw material, is perhaps provided by *The Saturday Magazine* of 21st July, 1832:

> When taken out of the [Borrowdale] mine, the wad is sorted according to its various qualities, and the best sent to London, where it is sold to the dealers once a month. The pencil-makers of Keswick receive their supply from the metropolis, as the proprietors of the article will not allow any to be sold until it has been deposited in their own warehouse.

The valuable graphite was transported under armed guard; in his *Magna Brittania*, published in 1816, Lyson describes the procedure:

> When the mine is opened, a sufficient quantity is procured to answer the demand for several years;

the black lead of the best quality is packed in barrels and sent to London by the waggon, the proprietor of which is bound in a considerable sum for its safe delivery. It is then deposited in the cellars under the Unitarian Chapel in Essex Street; and on the first Monday in every month there is a sale of it in an upper room of a public-house in the neighbourhood. The pencil-makers attend, and selecting pieces of the best quality, purchase according to their respective wants. The coarser sort is then sold for other purposes. About three thousand pounds worth of the black lead is sold in a year; the price of the finest quality is 35s. per lb.; of the coarser 120£. per ton.[32]

Although Keswick was to become the main centre of British pencil manufacturing in the mid-nineteenth century, it is to London, the commercial destination of the Borrowdale graphite, that we must look for the earlier manufacturers of note. In an article on pencil-makers, written in 1843, we find:

> The lead itself, or plumbago is a dark shining mineral . . . . . Its value is regulated by its evenness and solidity, qualities which are bettered by age, and which some makers extend to indefinite periods. Formerly, Mr. John Middleton was the most celebrated maker in this respect; but at present Messrs. Brookman and Langdon manufacture the most desirable surveyor's pencils; and these necessarily command astonishingly high prices.[33]

It is probable that the John Middleton mentioned is he who is listed, without mention of his trade, as of Vine Street, London, in 1777; John Middleton, 'black lead pencil manufacturer', was listed at Vine Street in 1784, and at 24 Vine Street the following year.[34] Between 1817 and 1826 he moved to 9 Charlotte Street, Rathbone Place, and by 1834 his firm, now John Middleton & Co, was at 90 Newman Street, moving to 55 Berner's Street, Oxford Street by 1840.[35] A portrait of John Middleton, in oils, painted about 1770, shows him holding a bundle of cedar pencils.(Colour plate V(i)) On its reverse is an inscription, written in 1883, suggesting a possible Keswick connection:

> This portrait of Mr. Middleton, the father or grandfather of my brother-in-law John Middleton, I give to my son Canon T. K. Richmond. Painted on cedarwood no doubt supplied by the old pencil-maker himself.

At the funeral of this same Canon Richmond in 1901, at Crosthwaite Church, Keswick, a wreath was sent to the church by a Mrs Middleton of Fawe Park, Keswick.[36] The connection, if any, between this Keswick family and John Middleton has so far eluded discovery.

John Middleton achieved recognition as the supplier of pencils to King George III and as a leading wholesaler, as his trade cards show.(298) By 1822-23, *Pigot's London Directory* was listing no less than sixteen Black Lead Pencil Makers, including Middleton and Brookman and Langdon, the latter at 28 Great Russell Street, Bloomsbury.(299)

We have seen that the best quality graphite was reserved for the making of pencils and the supply carefully monitored so as not to exceed the demand. Nevertheless, as the demand increased, the Borrowdale mines which had previously been opened only at intervals of a few years, were later worked for several weeks each year. The graphite deposits inevitably ran out in the mid-nineteenth century, although stocks of the pure mineral, accumulated much earlier, were still being used at Keswick, at the end of the century. The poorer grades of graphite, which had lacked the quality necessary for sawing directly into pencil leads had originally been used only for other purposes, but in the early nineteenth century several ingenious solutions to the problem of making use of this low quality material for the making of pencils were to emerge.

From about 1662, in Nürnberg, experiments had taken place in the making of pencils using the poor grade plumbago which was available from mines in Bohemia. The powdered black-lead was bound with various substances including gum, resin, sulphur, antimony and isinglass, to produce a usable alternative to the pure black-lead crayon. It was probably something similar to these German 'white lead sticks' which were produced by Kaspar Faber, who started pencil making in Nürnberg in 1761, a business which continues to the present time, as Faber-Castell.[37]

In 1790, Nicholas Jacques Conté in Paris, and Josef Hardtmuth in Vienna, each independently discovered a method of producing satisfactory pencil leads by mixing finely powdered graphite with china clay and firing it to red heat in a kiln, which, depending on the proportions of the materials used, produced leads of varying degrees of hardness.[38] It is this method which is still used by pencil-manufacturers today.

In England, in 1843, a process for the consolidation of powdered graphite into a homogeneous block under great pressure and *in vacuo*, which could then be sawn into leads in the normal way, was patented by William Brockendon, FRS,[39] and remarkably, such a block has survived intact.(300) A somewhat similar process which achieved a similar consolidation of graphite dust, using a cylinder and ram which produced a pressure of some five tons per square inch, while the whole apparatus was heated to red heat, had been developed a few years earlier by another Fellow of the Royal Society, Sir Henry Bessemer.[40] Leads produced in this way were marketed as 'Fireproof' as a safeguard against cheap imitations made by mixing graphite refuse with sulphur; the test was to hold the leads in a candle flame, the 'false' leads burning with a blueish flame while the pure black-lead was unaffected.

Sampson Mordan, the co-patentee of the propelling pencil in 1822, adopted Brockendon's process, as one of his advertisements shows.[41] An earlier Mordan advertisement of 1827, only five years after the grant of his patent for the ever-pointed pencil, lists his 'Black Lead Points', in five different sizes and degrees of hardness, marked VH, H, M, S, and VS. The nozzles of the patent pencils themselves were marked according to which size and hardness of lead they were intended for.[42] The black-lead was said to be of the finest quality and prepared by 'an entirely new chemical process', which must have been similar to that of Conté or Hardtmuth. An account of the reduction of sawn leads into the cylindrical form necessary for Mordan's ever-pointed pencils is given in the *Saturday Magazine*.[43] The leads were reduced gradually by being forced first through an octagonal hole in a plate of ruby, then through a similar but slightly smaller sixteen-sided hole and finally through a circular hole of the correct dimension. These leads, each individually housed in a fine glass tube, were sold in morocco cases gilt-stamped with the degree of hardness, which were advertised in *Pigot's London Directory* for 1832, and later in similar paper cases.(301) Similarly packaged leads were also made by Messrs Carter and Bromley.

The co-inventor and co-patentee with Mordan of this first-patented propelling pencil, was John Isaac Hawkins, whom we have already met as the inventor of the iridium-pointed gold pen. (Chapter IX). Hawkins sold his half interest in the patent less than a year later, in October, 1823, to Mordan, who promptly resold this moiety interest to a successful stationer,

Gabriel Riddle.[44] Mordan thus acquired a partner who could complement his own skill as a machinist with the necessary capital for a successful business. Riddle's son, William Riddle, in a letter to *The Builder* of 3rd August, 1861, was to claim 'my father's money founded the firm of S. Mordan & Co'.[45] Mordan and Co's early propelling pencils were hallmarked using the makers' mark SM.GR and the legend 'S. MORDAN & COs PATENT'.(302a) The partnership was later dissolved in 1837, Mordan retaining the manufactory at 22 Castle Street, Finsbury and Riddle immediately setting up a new manufactory at 172 Blackfriars Road, after which both Sampson Mordan and Gabriel Riddle each advertised energetically and competitively his own high quality propelling pencils. Pencils are found, dating from about this time, marked 'S. MORDAN & Co MAKERS' and 'PATENT. G. RIDDLE. MAKER'.(302b)

William Riddle himself was the inventor and patentee of an ingenious form of propelling pencil which took several leads throughout its length so that when one was exhausted the next was already in position.[46] The wooden outer case was incised with an helical groove in which travelled a similarly grooved brass collar attached through a slit to the propelling mechanism behind the leads. William Riddle does not seem to have exploited his invention to the full and disposed of his interest in the patent to William Lund, a wood- and ivory-turner and son of Thomas Lund, of 57 Cornhill, London. (See Chapter IV). An early version of this type of pencil, made of cedar with an ivory cap and nozzle, is impressed 'W. RIDDLE'S PATENT MADE EXCLUSIVELY BY W. LUND LONDON', while later, shorter examples turned in ivory with mounts of nickel, silver or gold are found, marked only 'LUND PATENTEE, LONDON'.(303)

William Riddle's propelling pencil was an ingenious improvement on the simple 'Stop Sliding Pencils', first patented in 1783.[47] These were made by several makers in the late eighteenth century.(304, 305) The lead was simply pushed out as required by a sliding 'stop' which travelled in a dovetail slot cut in one side of the cedar pencil. Pencils using a very similar principle, patented in New York by J. G. Dodd, were manufactured in modern times by the American Pencil Company.(306)

Although Hawkins and Mordan were the

first to be granted a patent for a truly mechanical propelling pencil, they were not apparently the first to manufacture such pencils. Joseph Willmore of Birmingham, a 'Silversmith and Dealer in Trinkets', in a case brought against him by Mordan and Riddle for alleged infringements of their patent, was able to satisfy the court that Mordan's 'invented improvements on pencil holders or port crayons for the purposes of facilitating writing and drawing by rendering the frequent cutting or mending of the points unnecessary had long been known and practised by machinists and manufacturers in London, Birmingham and various other parts of England', and that there had been no infringement of Mordan and Riddle's patent rights.[48]

Black-lead pencils are now manufactured by automated processes; powdered graphite for the leads, which are made by extrusion using the Conté principle, has in recent years been imported mainly from Mexico and to a lesser extent from Ceylon (now Sri Lanka), Korea and Siberia, the cedar wood for the casings almost exclusively from Virginia, Tennessee and Alabama, in the USA.

No doubt one of the earliest tools used by man to make meaningful marks was a simple piece of pointed stone with which to inscribe another stone, and no description of pencil-making would be complete without a brief mention of the slate pencil. Used by countless generations of schoolchildren, it had the great advantages of both durability and cheapness. The writing produced by a slate pencil on a smooth flat slate is distinct yet easily erased.(307)

Slate pencils were also used with thin sheets of slate in gentlemens' leather pocket books; an advertisement by the proprietors of the Whitehaven newspaper *The Cumberland Pac-*

quet in 1774, listed among a wide range of stationery available in their shop 'Liverpool Pocket Books of different Sizes, with or without Slate Books'. A surviving example of such a pocket book, in green morocco leather stamped with the name of its owner and dated 1777, and having the printed label of its Liverpool maker, still retains its iron-cased slate pencil in a slender pocket provided for the purpose, although its slate book is no longer present.(308) Similar notebooks, sometimes in conjunction with printed almanacs, were popular from the seventeenth century onwards.(309)

A correspondent to *Notes and Queries*, in 1943, drew attention to even earlier 'Tablet Books', mentioned on seventeen occasions by Shakespeare; these were small leather-covered books with leaves of asses' skin, to the fore edges of which were affixed four small rings in pairs, through which passed, when not in use, the accompanying metal writing stylus.[49]

The cylindrical form of slate pencils was achieved by forcing a length of slate of square section through a series of reducing tubes, on the same principle as the shaping of black-leads already described. A machine for this purpose was devised by a Cumbrian, J. Brockbank, in 1811.(310) Up to this time most slate pencils were imported from the Continent and were known as 'Dutch Pencils'. Taking advantage of an abundant supply of suitable slate and the 'great and constant demand for such pencils in every village in the kingdom', Brockbank invented a hand-operated machine, by which he produced short and long pencils to sell at five and ten shillings a thousand. He was able to produce about twelve hundred pencils daily, and his success led him to install a water-powered version of his machine.[50] Slate pencils were used in schools well into the twentieth century.

XI

Seals & Sealing

The use of seals for the authentication of documents is an extremely ancient practice; seals of cylindrical form which left their impressions when rolled across the surface of clay tablets, were in use in Mesopotamia by the fourth millennium BC, and evidence exists of the use of simple stamps for sealing, during the previous millennium.[1] In the Old Testament, there are several references to seals. Judah had a signet (Genesis, Ch XXXVIII, v 18), and that of King Ahasuerus, used to seal and authenticate letters containing his orders for the destruction of the Jews, was in the form of a signet ring (Esther, Ch III, v 12).

The other main function of a seal, from which the name derives, is to ensure that the contents of the object on which it is applied cannot be tampered with without the fact becoming self-evident; from ancient times seals have been used for this purpose not only on documents but on boxes, doors, storage jars and the like. A more modern and somewhat bizarre extension of this practice was reported in *The Times* of 2nd March, 1868, in a report on the Great Tibetan Road from Llasa to Gartokh, by one Captain Montgomerie:

> . . . the couriers go continuously, stopping neither night nor day, except to eat and change horses, and, after an 800 miles' ride, are haggard and worn. . .To make sure that they shall not take off their clothes they are sealed over the breast, and none may break the seal save him to whom the messenger is sent.[2]

It is perhaps worth noting at this point that the term 'seal' is commonly used both for the impression and for the device which makes it, more correctly the 'matrix', a term which will be used in this work, however, only where confusion might otherwise arise.

In addition to a type of clay, their *'terra sigillaris'* or sealing earth, the Romans also used wax for sealing. Cicero, in a dispute over two documents, each of which purported to have come from Asia, is said to have proved the authenticity of the genuine one by the fact that it was sealed with sealing earth as was customary in Asia, while the forgery was sealed with wax, a practice adopted only by the nations of the West at that time.[3]

Although in the ensuing centuries other methods of sealing were used, such as metal *bullae,*(311) which were discs of lead or even gold, and *maltha*, a composition of pitch and wax, by the eleventh century wax had been generally adopted throughout Europe as the main material for seals. Perhaps the earliest surviving English wax seal is that of Offa, King of Mercia, on a charter of 790, in a grant to the Abbey of Saint Denys, but it is not until after the Norman Conquest, when seals became obligatory on legal documents, that their survival in large numbers was ensured.[4] True sealing-wax, used for all medieval seals in England, consisted of about two-thirds beeswax and one third resin; it was mainly used either in its natural state or coloured, red by the use of vermilion or green using verdigris.[5]

Sealing-wax as we know it today is not wax at all; its main constituent is shellac which was first imported from the East in the sixteenth century, from which time this type of sealing-wax has been widely used. It is the shellac which imparts to modern sealing-wax its hard, brittle and glossy character. An early nineteenth century account gives this recipe: two parts of shellac and one of vermilion all in a powdered state were melted over slow heat and poured into plain or ornamental moulds, or rolled into sticks which were then given a final gloss by further momentary exposure to heat. Sealing-wax made from shellac was in use as early as August, 1554, the date of a letter bearing such a seal.[6] A stick of red sealing-wax, which may be of this type, forms part of the writing paraphernalia of the merchant Georg Gisze in Holbein's portrait of 1532. **(Colour plate I)**

In the nineteenth century, as well as in the more usual sticks, sealing-wax could also be bought in the form of small spherical or button-shaped pieces, each suitable for a single sealing. These often formed part of the contents of sealing sets which contained a small brass ladle, a miniature brass taperstick and tapers, over which the sealing wax would be melted, and a metal matrix bearing the owner's initial or monogram. A refinement of this was an invention of Isaac Davis patented in 1841, which consisted of very small sticks of sealing-wax, each large enough for one sealing, the ends of which were coated with a 'detonating or combustible material', which could be ignited by friction.[7] **(Colour plate V(iv))**

The chief use of seals in medieval times was to authenticate; at a time when few could read or write the seal took the place of a signature. As literacy increased, signatures were used side-by-side with seals, and as they assumed greater importance as the means of ensuring authenticity, the need for individual seals became less crucial. There are many examples in later times where several signatories to the same document shared the use of the same seal, and the seals on modern legal documents are often no more than purely formal stuck-on discs of red paper. Legal, administrative and company seals are often impressed by machine directly on to the paper of the document.

Although 'sealing to close' was, as we have seen, a much earlier practice, by the seventeenth century the use of a personal seal to close a folded letter was commonplace and continued into the nineteenth century until it was made redundant by the advent of the gummed envelope, at about the time of the introduction of the postage stamp in 1840. Even so, old habits die hard, and the first envelopes often had imitation seals embossed on the gummed flap.**(312)**

Any study of sealing in medieval Europe must first be concerned with royal or state seals, in England the Great Seals, which from the eleventh century depicted the sovereign enthroned on one side and on horseback on the other, a tradition carried through to modern times, with only one or two exceptions.**(313)** Lesser Royal seals of a smaller and more personal nature, which were not under the control of the Chancery, were also used. The Privy Seal, introduced in the early thirteenth century, was in the custody of the Clerks of the King's Chamber, and gained in importance until, during the following century, the keeper of the Privy Seal ranked as the third Minister of State. By 1400, under Edward II, a 'secret' seal known as the 'signet' was also in use, in the charge of the King's *Secret*ary.

Most matrices were circular, although examples exist of triangular and of shield forms. Their designs usually reflected the nature of the institutions or the standing of the persons to whom they belonged. Baronial seals often bore an equestrian portrait of the knight in armour and episcopal seals, always of vesica or pointed-oval form, usually depicted a standing portrait of the bishop.**(314, 315)** A sheriff's custody of the Royal castle in his county might result in the use of this motif for his seal while a College might use a portrait of its founder, as, for instance, in the case of New College, Oxford, whose silver seal matrix of circa 1386 depicts the Founder seated above the four Patron Saints of the College. In the case of lesser private seals, whose use by the thirteenth century was not uncommon, armorials, merchants' marks or the tools of the owners' trades were often used. By the fourteenth century, simple matrices could be purchased ready-made.

The matrices themselves were often made of silver, as in the case of the Great Seals, or more commonly in latten, a type of bronze, although examples do exist in other metals, ivory, jet or even wood. For double-sided seals, two interlocking matrices were necessary. Single-sided matrices often had a lug on the reverse, pierced for suspension from a cord or chain,**(316)** which gradually developed into the more elaborate structures of later seal handles of the type seen hanging from a shelf in Holbein's portrait of Georg Gisze.**(Colour plate I)** The size of the seal, in medieval times, from about three inches in diameter in the case of the Great Seals, down to one and a half inches or less for private seals, reflected the importance of its owner. Modern Great Seals measure six inches in diameter.

Most medieval seals were engraved with a legend, the styles of whose lettering can help in providing an approximate chronology, although considerable overlapping of styles occured and the practice of handing on seals unaltered from father to son necessitates the exercise of caution in such dating. In very broad terms, legends are found in an almost pure but primitive Roman during the eleventh and twelfth centuries, in Lombardic during the thirteenth and early fourteenth centuries, in Blackletter during the late fourteenth and fifteenth centuries, reverting to classical Roman in the sixteenth.

The attachment of the seal to a document was by one of two methods. The seal could be appended on cords or strips of vellum passed through slits in the document, or in some cases strips cut in the body of the document itself; alternatively it could be applied directly to the document, which from the sixteenth century became increasingly the more usual practice.[8] Wax seals from the later medieval period onwards were often protected from accidental detachment by being sewn into tight-fitting covers of cloth or parchment, which although the seal was still susceptible to damage, did preserve the fragments. A better means of protection was the use of a box of wicker, wood, bone or ivory, silver or base metal, known as a 'skippet', the derivation of which is literally 'little skip', a small basket.(317) Modern Great Seals are housed in black-japanned tinned-iron skippets, as may be the seals of lesser institutions.(318)

From the sixteenth century, seal matrices exhibit great variety both of design and in the materials used to make them. The use of hardstones, common in antiquity but seldom used during the medieval period, became commonplace, and steel was also a favourite material. The matrix, from this time onwards, is often attached to a handle of wood, ivory, precious metal or hardstone in a form we now refer to as a desk seal, or has a metal mount for suspension, a type now often called a fob seal, from its later association with the Regency fob-watch as an article of personal adornment.(Colour plate V(iii))

Post-medieval personal seals are usually armorial or engraved with the owner's initials in a decorative monogram or cypher.(319 to 331) One variety of this type of seal was made in stoneware of the black basalt type, notably by Wedgwood and Bentley, during the late eighteenth century.(328f) Similar seals were produced by other potters and sold by their

agents throughout the country. In his advertisement of the 'black basaltes' seals of Samuel Greenwood of Burslem, William Penny, a Brazier and Tinman of Whitehaven, in 1778, presents us with something of a puzzle regarding the method of engraving of the cyphers. Although they were 'so hard as to cut Glass, and no file can touch them', he was able to produce 'Any person's name in a Cypher, either for Watch or Counting-House Seals at 2s each, Elegantly Engraved, in the Etruscan Black Basaltes Stone, and ready to be delivered out in Five Minutes time.'(332)

When seals were cut it was customary for the engraver to supply with the finished intaglio, a specimen of an impression from it. In the late eighteenth century these were of conical form in gesso, a type of hard plaster composition, while in the nineteenth century a red sealing-wax impression, in a turned *lignum vitae* box bearing the seal engraver's trade label in its screw-on lid, was more usual.(333, 334)

Seal matrices were often incorporated on the terminals of other items of writing equipment such as pens, pencils or pen-cases, and particularly of sealing-wax boxes which were perhaps most popular, and known as *boits du ciré* in France and Switzerland, although English examples are found.(335)

An essential accessory in the business of sealing was a convenient means of melting the sealing-wax. From the early eighteenth century, tapersticks in the form of miniature candlesticks are found in silver and base metals, following the styles of their larger fellows, and in some cases forming part of a standish. Less common is the cylindrical bougie-box which contained a coil of tallow taper, the lighted end of which was held by the sliding cover of a hole through the lid.(336) The bougie-box owes its name to a species of white wax which was exported to France and throughout Europe from the Algerian port of that name. Various types of silver taper-holder, now commonly referred to as 'wax-jacks', are found, dating from the seventeenth and eighteenth centuries.(337 to 339) Similar devices were made both in Sheffield Plate and in brass. In the mid-nineteenth century a spring-loaded taper-holder which incorporated a chequered seal end, was manufactured by Thomas Wharton.(340)

Such a chequered seal could certainly be used with sealing-wax, although they are more generally associated with an alternative method of sealing to close, using a moistened adhesive wafer. Wafers were made from a 'batter' of fine wheaten flour, the gluten of which is of an adhesive nature, mixed with white of egg, isinglass and colouring agents such as red-lead, vermilion and smalt. This paste was either spread on sheets of metal and heated under pressure, or applied to both sides of sheets of fine muslin and allowed to dry, again under pressure. When the drying was complete several sheets were placed together and cut into circular wafers using hollow punches. Because some of the colouring agents were poisonous, the refuse cuttings were not wasted, but sold for the purpose of destroying rats and other vermin.[9] Its effect on the user, who may have licked the wafer to moisten it prior to placing it between the folds of a letter to seal it, is not recorded. Coloured isinglass was sometimes used on its own for the making of transparent wafers which were known as French wafers. The use of wafers for sealing was most popular in the late eighteenth and early nineteenth centuries, but the practice dates from considerably earlier. In 1635, one Matthew Cox was granted a patent giving him a monopoly on the making and selling of wafers in England; this, the first recorded English patent for writing materials, complained of the import of inferior and expensive wafer seals, and in the grant Cox was bound to sell his at one penny a hundred.[10]

The Saturday Magazine of 1838 gives an account of an unusual type of sealing wafer, and its method of manufacture:

> A very elegant form of wafers, called medallion wafers, was invented some years ago. The surface of each wafer represents in relief many of those classical and antique devices which we are accustomed to see in ordinary seals, but the effect is more pleasing than in the latter. Medallion wafers are thus prepared:-
>
> A given quantity of very pure glue is dissolved in water, to which a coloured tint has been imparted by tumeric (*sic*), brazil-wood or some other dye. A gem, seal or medallion, is then moistened with a weak solution of gum, in which an opaque white or other material has been dissolved; this coloured gum water is then carefully wiped off the plane projecting parts of the seal, and allowed to remain only in the hollows or other depressions. A small quantity of the coloured glue, in a melted state, is poured over the seal, and the whole is dried by gentle heat. In drying, the glue and gum shrink, and thus become easily separable from the seal. Matters are so arranged that the medallion wafer shall present a thickness not exceeding that of common writing-paper, and it then yields a beautiful copy of the seal; the coloured gum giving the device, and the glue the ground; and when the respective colours are well chosen, the appearance of the wafer is chaste and harmonious. It will readily be supposed that so elegant a wafer is not intended to be hidden by being placed between the folds of a letter: it is, on the contrary, used much in the same way as a common seal of sealing-wax, so far as its position is concerned. The part of the paper to which it is to be applied is wetted slightly, and the back surface of the wafer is placed on the wetted part, to which it immediately adheres, in consequence of the glutinous nature of its ingredients.

A rare survival of a full box of twenty-five mostly different medallion wafers in a variety of colours, by a leading London jeweller, is in the author's collection.(Colour plate VIII)

In the Charles Thomas Collection are examples of wafer seals dating from the first years following the introduction of postage stamps in 1840. Made of pink paper, they are printed in black with mottoes which include 'Thank Rowland Hill for this'. Others have engraved views of 'Loch Lomond' and 'Surgeons' Hall', for example. Another group of Victorian gummed paper and metal foil wafers has embossed mottoes such as 'Respect the Truth' or somewhat wistful exhortations to write including 'Can I prevail' or 'Shall I expect'.(341)

The opening of a letter which had been secured with a wax seal or with a wafer could be achieved simply by tearing it open,(Colour plate I) or by using a paper knife, but it is perhaps worth noting here that by the eighteenth century, a special implement had been invented for that purpose, the seal chisel.(342, 343) Such devices have usually been classified as needlework tools – seam knives or buttonhole cutters. A similar tool does indeed form part of the usually rather crudely made 'drizzling' sets used by those who made a living unpicking the gold and silver bullion work from discarded clothing in the eighteenth century. However, a stationer's catalogue of 1882 illustrates clearly that seal chisels were used by the Victorians.(344) It is therefore perhaps likely that the high quality chisels of similar form and a century earlier, sometimes with hallmarked silver handles, hardly tools for artisans, were also intended for this purpose.

Bibliographical References & Notes

I The History of the Quill Pen

[1] Beckmann, John, Professor of Economics, University of Göttingen, *A History of Inventions, Discoveries and Origins*, published in German, 1797; English translation, undated, nineteenth Century.

[2] A number of printed editions of St Isidore's *Etymologia*, from which this is a quotation, the earliest dating from circa 1470, is listed in the Catalogue of the British Library; Beckmann's reference is *Origines, lib VI, 13, p 132*.

[3] *The Saturday Magazine*, 13th January, 1838, reprinted by Philip Poole, 182 Drury Lane, London, undated, circa 1977.

[4] British Museum, *Ms Cotton Nero D. IV, fol 25v*, illustrated: D'Ancona, P and Aeschlimann, E., *The Art of Illumination*, Phaidon, London, 1969, plate 9.

[5] Vatican Library, *Ms Barberini, Lat 570*, illustrated: Henry, Françoise, *The Book of Kells*, Thames and Hudson, London, 1974, figure 12.

[6] Bovini, Guiseppe, *Églises de Ravenne*, Instituto Geographico de Agostini, Novara, Italy, 1960.

[7] Krautheimer, Richard, *Early Christian and Byzantine Architecture*, Penguin, 1965.

[8] My attention was first drawn to the existence of this mosaic by an original watercolour depiction of the table-top, without identification, in a display of quill pens in the Charles Thomas Collection of Writing Instruments in the Museum of Science and Industry, Birmingham. I am indebted to Mr Oliver Ray of Oxford, who in response to my letter to *Country Life* magazine, 31st October, 1985, after my failure to identify its whereabouts through academic sources, suggested Ravenna as the likely place of origin.

[9] Bonner, Stanley, F., *Education in Ancient Rome*, Methuen, London, 1977, p 129.

[10] Beckmann, John, *op cit*, pp 223-234, quoting: Mehus, L., (Ed), *Ambrosii Traversarii Epistolae*, Florence, 1759, Vol. II, p 566.

[11] *Oxford Dictionary of English Etymology*, Oxford, 1969, p 865.

[12] Jackson, Donald, *The Story of Writing*, Studio Vista/Cassell, London, 1981, Chapter 6.

[13] Osley, A. S., *Scribes and Sources*, Faber and Faber, London, 1980, pp 21 and 44 *et seq*.

[14] Wolpe, Berthold, (Ed), *A Newe Booke of Copies, 1574*, Oxford University Press, London, 1962, p 12, footnote 2.

[15] Osley, A. S., *op cit*, pp 72-73.

[16] Wolpe, Berthold, An essay on *John de Beauchesne*, in Osley's *Scribes and Sources*, (see [13] above), p 228.

[17] Heal, Ambrose, *The English Writing Masters and their Copy Books, 1570-1800*, Cambridge University Press, 1931, and Bonacini, Claudio, *Bibliografia Delle Arti Scrittorie E Della Calligrafia*, Sansoni Antiquariato, Florence, 1953.

[18] Trevelyan, G. M., *Illustrated English Social History*, Penguin Books, 1949, p 52.

[19] *The Saturday Magazine*, as [3] above.

[20] *The Mirror*, 18th April, 1835, p 254.

[21] Pride, B., *The Art of Pen-cutting*, London, 1812, p 9.

[22] *Ibid*, p 12.

[23] *Ibid*, p 11.

[24] *The Saturday Magazine*, as [3] above.

[25] Pride, B., *op cit*, p 17.

[26] *Ibid*, pp 14-16.

[27] Keefe, H. J., *A Century in Print, the Story of Hazells, 1839-1939*, London, Hazell, Watson and Viney, Ltd, 1939, (quoting Mr R. Doran, of Murray Grove, Shoreditch, 'one of the last makers of quill pens left', whose employer still received an occasional order from Lloyds of London, for a thousand pens), and Good, J. M., Gregory, O., and Bosworth, N., *Pantalogia, A New Cyclopaedia*, London, 1813 (under *Quills*).

[28] Woodforde, James, (Ed Beresford, John), *The Diary of a Country Parson*, Oxford University Press, 1978.

[29] Journal of the Writing Equipment Society No 14, 1985.

[30] The Saturday Magazine, as [3] above.

[31] *Pigot's London (Commercial) Directory*, 1822-23.

[32] *Ex Inf:* Mrs J. K. Davies, whose former business premises were those formerly occupied by Thomas Palmer, and who supplied a copy of his portrait, and Mr M. J. Leppard, Hon Curator, East Grinstead Town Museum, to both of whom I am indebted.

[33] Windle's Steel Pen Depot, London Bridge, *Steel Pens*, Thames Press, undated, circa 1857.

[34] Quoted by Greenland, Maureen, *The Practical Pen, 2*, in the Journal of the Writing Equipment Society, No 15, 1986.

[35] Warrell, W., *Scribes, Ancient and Modern*, Lindsey & Co, London, 1889.

[36] *Ex Inf:* 'His Nibs' Philip Poole, of Philip Poole and Company, 182 Drury Lane, London, who received this information from Cooper, Dennison and Walkden, in a letter dated 2nd July, 1975.

[37] Hill, Henry, *The Quill Pen*, one of three lecturettes given

at Stationer's Hall, 13th March, 1925, under the general title of *Pens, Ancient and Modern*, and printed in *Craft Lectures*, London School of Printing and Kindred Trades, London, 1925, pp 73-86.

[38] Watt, Charles, Patent No 4299 of 1818.

[39] This brief resumé of the work of William Southgate is based on original documents from the Walter Southgate Collection, now in the author's collection, and on Southgate, Walter, *That's the way it was. A working class autobiography, 1890-1950*, New Clarion Press, 1982.

[40] I am indebted to C. Cook, Esq, of Lloyds of London, for this information.

II Preparing and Cutting the Quill

[1] Pride, B., *The Art of Pen-Cutting*, London, 1812, p 21.

[2] *Ibid*, p 22.

[3] *The Saturday Magazine*, 13th January, 1838.

[4] Child, Heather (Ed), *The Calligrapher's Handbook*, A. & C. Black, London, 1985. This newly revised edition contains an excellent and fully illustrated account of the curing and cutting of quills, adapted for modern practice, by Donald Jackson, MVO, Scribe to Her Majesty's Crown Office.

[5] Shinton, W. E., *Lectures on an Improved System of Teaching the Art of Writing*, London, 1823.

[6] Osley, A. S., *Scribes and Sources*, Faber, London and Boston, 1980, p 93.

[7] *Ibid*, p 42.

[8] *Ibid*, pp 48 and 60.

[9] *Ibid*, pp 79 and 101.

[10] Fairbank, Alfred, *Augustino da Siena*, the 1568 Edition of his writing book in facsimile, The Merrion Press, London, 1975, p 20.

[11] Osley, A. S., *op cit*, p 222.

[12] *Ibid*, pp 248-249.

[13] *Ibid*, p 239.

[14] Pride, B., *op cit*, p 21.

[15] Mordan, F. & Co, *Pens, Inks and Inkstands*, W. Kent & Co, London, 1858, p 27.

[16] Warrell, W., *Scribes Ancient and Modern*, Lindsey & Co, London, 1889, p 39, quoting from Salamanca, *The Philosophy of Handwriting*.

[17] *The Saturday Magazine*, 1834 and 1838-39, Article I, *The History of the Quill Pen*.

[18] Pride, B., *op cit*, p 3.

[19] *An Account of the Allowances of Stationary [sic] to the Gentlemen of the Exchequer, April, 1807*, a manuscript account book in the collection of Philip Poole, Esq.

[20] Yciar, Juan de, *Arte Subtilissima*, originally published Saragossa, 1550, in facsimile with a translation by Shuckburgh, Evelyn, Oxford University Press, 1960, p 39.

[21] Knight, J. W., *Doctors Commons in 1870, Fifty Years' Recollections of Doctors Commons and the Probate and Divorce Registries, Somerset House*, manuscript, undated circa 1920. (From a copy in the possession of Mr D. F. Hale, to whom I am indebted).

[22] Wilkes, John, *The Art of Making Pens Scientifically*, London, 1799.

[23] I am indebted to Mr A. E. Hennell for drawing these pens to my attention, and for allowing me to photograph and publish them.

III The Scribe's Knife

[1] Pierce, Rev H. K., *The Instruments of Writing, translated from the writing book of Giovanbattista Palatino, Rome, 1540*, Berry Hill Press, Newport, Rhode Island, 1953, and Yciar, Juan de, *Arte subtilissima*, a facsimile of the 1550 Edition, translated by Shuckburgh, Evelyn, Lion and Unicorn Press, London, 1958.

[2] Pride, B., *The Art of Pen-Cutting*, London, 1812, p 26.

[3] *Ibid*, p 25.

[4] Whalley, Joyce Irene, *Writing Implements and Accessories*, David and Charles, Newton Abbot and London, 1980, p 38, quoting from *The Technical Repository*, 1827.

[5] Billingsley, Martin, *The Pen's Excellencie [or] the Secretaries Delighte*, Sudbury and Humble, London, 1618.

[6] Nicholson, William, (Ed), *The Journal of Natural Philosophy, Chemistry, and the Arts*, Volume VII, 1804, p. 300.

[7] Fairbank, Alfred, *A Book of Scripts*, Faber, London and Boston, 1977, plate 52.

[8] Hayward, J. F., *English Cutlery, Sixteenth to Eighteenth Century*, HMSO, London, 1957, 2nd Impression, 1969.

[9] *Ibid*, p 17, Plate XXIII (a) and (b).

[10] *Ex Inf:* Miss Molly Pearce of Sheffield City Museum.

[11] Hayward, J. F., *op cit*, p 17., Plate XXIII (a).

[12] Wilkes, John, *The Art of Making Pens Scientifically*, Farnham, 1799. (From a copy in the Shorthand Collection of the Social Sciences Library, Manchester Central Library, No 514 A12.)

[13] Smith, Joseph, *Explanation or Key, to the Various Manufactures of Sheffield, with Engravings of each Article*, Sheffield, 1816, reprinted by the Early American Industries Association, 1975.

[14] Pearce, Molly, an article, *Collecting Penknives*, Antique Finder, April, 1976, gives a comprehensive account of the Sheffield-made and the French penknives in the Sheffield City Museum collections, of which the Camille Pagé Collection, purchased in 1922, forms a part.

[15] Pride, B., *op cit*, p 26.

[16] Keefe, H. J., *A Century in print, the story of Hazells, 1839-1939*, Hazell, Watson and Viney, Ltd, London, 1939, p 165.

[17] As note [4] above.

[18] Grosart, Rev A. B., *The Spending of the Money of Robert Nowell of Reade Hall, Lancashire*, Townley Hall Mss Series, Privately Printed, 1877, p 272.

[19] Woodforde, James, *The Diary of a Country Parson, 1758-1802*, Edited by Beresford, John, Oxford University Press, 1978.

[20] Pride, B., *op cit*, p 26.

[21] From a copy in the possession of Philip Poole, Esq.

IV Mechanical Quill-cutting and the Quill Nib

[1] McNeil, Ian, *Joseph Bramah, A Century of Invention, 1749-1851*, David and Charles, London, 1968.

[2] Bramah, Joseph, Patent No 3260 of 1809, Pens for Writing, 21st November, 1809.

[3] De La Chaumette, Isaac, Patent no 434 of 1729, Ordnance, Small Arms, etc, 12th August, 1729.

[4] Sale Catalogue, *The Spitzer Collection of Objéts d'Art*, Paris, 33 Rue de Villejust, 17th April – 16th June, 1893, Lot No 2518.

[5] Wilkes, John, *The Art of Making Pens Scientifically*, Farnham, 1799, p. 9.

[6] McNeil, Ian, *op cit*, plate 17.

[7] The Church of Latter Day Saints, Microfiche Regional Survey, Sussex.

[8] *The Mirror*, No 715, Saturday, 18th April, 1835, p 254.

[9] *Quarterly Bulletin*, The Bank of England, March, 1972: *The use of the quill, patent and steel pens by the Bank of England during the nineteenth century.*

[10] *Ex inf: Lowndes's, Kent's, Robson's, Kelly's* and the *Post Office London Directories*, 1795-1846; copies at Westminster City Library, Victoria.

[11] Wilkes, John, *op cit*, p 58.

[12] *Transactions of the Society for the Encouragement of the Arts, Manufactures and Commerce*, Vol. XXXVI, 1819, pp 74-76, Vol. XXXVIII, 1821, pp 121-123 and Vol. XL, 1823, pp 250-253.

[13] Richmond, Lesley and Stockford, Bridget, *Company Archives*, Gower, Aldershot, 1986.

[14] Lacroux, Jean-Pierre and Van Cleem, Lionel, *La mémoire des Sergent-Major*, Ramsay/Quintette, Paris, 1988, p 28.

V Ink, Parchment and Paper

[1] F. Mordan and Co, *Pens, Inks and Inkstands*, W. Kent & Co, London, 1858.

[2] *The Saturday Magazine*, 3rd November, 1838, p 174.

[3] Lehner, Sigmund and Mitchell, C. Ainsworth, (trans.), *Ink Manufacture*, Scott Greenwood & Son, London, 1926.

[4] Public Record Office, Ref No C47/34/1/3.

[5] Clement, Francis, *The Petie Schole, 1587*, in facsimile, Scolar, Menston, 1967.

[6] Whalley, Joyce Irene, *Writing Implements and Accessories*, David and Charles, London, 1980, p 78.

[7] Lehner and Mitchell, *op cit*, p 29.

[8] Holman, Charles, Patent No 258 of 1688.

[9] British Museum, Heal Collection, Ref: 92.14.

[10] Stilitz, Ivor, *An Early Ink Advertisement*, Journal of the Writing Equipment Society, No 12, 1985.

[11] Cumbria Record Office, Carlisle: *Cumberland Pacquet and Whitehaven Advertiser*, Issue No 66, 18th January, 1776, p 2, col 4.

[12] British Museum, Heal Collection, Ref: 92.34.

[13] *Ibid*, Ref: 92.33.

[14] *Ibid*, Ref: 92.18.

[15] *Ibid*, Ref: 92.29.

[16] Dring, John, Patent No 906 of 1768.

[17] British Museum, Heal Collection, Ref: 92.31.

[18] Grosart, Rev A. B., *The Spending of the Money of Robert Nowell of Reade Hall, Lancashire*, Townley Hall Mss Series, Privately printed, 1877.

[19] Greenland, Maureen, *A Peep into the Past*, Journal of the Writing Equipment Society, No 3, 1982.

[20] *The Post Office London Directory*, 1830.

[21] A printed broadsheet of C. Clark, Bookseller, Lancaster, dated November, 1833, advertising James Perry's Pens and Inks on the reverse, in the author's collection.

[22] Stephens, Henry, and Nash, Ebenezer, Patent No 7342 of 1837.

[23] Diringer, David, *The Hand Produced Book*, Hutchinson, London, 1953, pp 170 *et seq.*

[24] *The Saturday Magazine*, 1838, p 133.

[25] Diringer, David, *op cit*, p 194.

[26] Grant, J. G., Bailey, F. W. and Harrison, H. Ainsworth, *Paper Making*, The Technical Section of the British Paper and Board Makers' Association, Kenley, 1950.

[27] Bower, Peter, *Paper*, a chapter in *The Calligrapher's Handbook*, A & C. Black, London, 1985, p 85.

[28] Grant, J. G., *et al*, *op cit*, p 14.

[29] Dawe, Edward, A, *Paper and Its Uses*, Crosby Lockwood and Son, London, 1919, p 2.

[30] Grant, J. G., *et al*, *op cit*, p 14.

[31] Cumbria Record Office, *The Cumberland Pacquet and Whitehaven Advertiser*, Issue 90, 4th July, 1776.

[32] Grant, J. G., *et al*, *op cit*, p 16.

[33] *List of Paper Mills in England, Scotland & Ireland, Parchment & Vellum Makers in London, etc*, Printed by J. Bradshaw, Sale, Cheshire, undated, circa 1853.

[34] Grant, J. G., *et al*, *op cit*, pp 16 and 17.

VI The Pounce-Pot or Sander

[1] Warrell, W., *Scribes, Ancient and Modern*, Lindsay and Company, London, 1889, p 45.

[2] Bower, Peter, *Hand-made Paper*, a lecture given to the Society of Scribes and Illuminators, October, 1983, reviewed in *The Scribe*, Spring, 1984.

[3] Quoted by Thomas, Charles, and Groves, Sylvia, in an article *Pounce-boxes and their Uses*, in *Country Life*, October 5th, 1951. (It should be noted that the steel 'sand-boxes' described in the same article are in fact tobacco boxes – see my note in the *Journal of the Writing Equipment Society*, No 14, 1985).

[4] Osley, A. S., *Scribes and Sources*, Faber, London and Boston, 1980.

[5] *Ibid*, a chapter contributed by Wolpe, Berthold, *John de Beauchesne and the first English writing-books*, p. 227.

[6] Clayton, Michael, *The Collector's Dictionary of the Silver and Gold of Great Britain and North America*, Country Life, London, 1971.

[7] Covill, William, E., Jr, *Ink bottles and inkwells*, Sullwold, Taunton, Massachusetts, 1971, Figs 1725 to 1727.

[8] *Ibid*, Figs 1731 to 1734.

[9] Thomas, Charles and Groves, Sylvia, *op cit*, as note [3] above.

[10] Osley, A. S., *op cit*, p 223, (translating Plantin, *La première partie des dialogues françois pour les jeunes enfants*, Part II, Dialogue 9).

VII Inkhorns, Inkwells and Standishes

[1] *Naissance de l'écriture, cunéiformes et hiéroglyphes*, Catalogue of the Exhibition at the Galeries Nationales du Grand Palais, 7th May – 9th August, 1982, pp 342-346, and plates.

[2] *The Saturday Magazine*, 22nd December, 1838.

[3] Oxford, Bodleian Library, Ms Bodley 717, illustrated in Parkes, M. B. and Watson, Andrew G., *Medieval Scribes, Manuscripts and Libraries*, Scolar, London, 1978, pl 19.

[4] Riddell, J. R., *A Few Historical Notes on the Worshipful Company of Stationers*, Saint Bride Foundation Printing School, London, 1921, p 8.

[5] Whalley, Joyce Irene, *Writing Implements and Accessories*, David and Charles, Newton Abbot and London, 1975, p 89.

[6] Shakespeare, William, *Henry VI, Part II*, Act IV, Scene II.

[7] *Ex Inf*: V. and A Museum, Accession Register, No W.44-1917.

[8] Curzon, R., *Catalogue of Materials for Writing, etc, . . . in the Library of the Honourable Robert Curzon*, Nicol, London, 1849.

[9] Osley, Dr A. S., *Scribes and Sources*, Faber and Faber, London, 1980, p. 42.

[10] *A Directory of Sheffield*, a reprint of the 1787 edition, Da Capo Press, New York, 1969.

[11] Rice, D. G, *Rockingham Porcelain Inkstands*, The Antique Dealer and Collector's Guide, March, 1976, quoting Cox, A. and A., *The Rockingham Works*, 1974.

[12] British Patent No 5105 of 26th February, 1825.

[13] *The Saturday Magazine*, 1838, part VIII, fig. 5.

[14] Godden, Geoffrey, *Some Trifles from Lowestoft*, The Antique Dealer and Collector's Guide, March, 1970, fig. 1.

[15] For a comprehensive survey of commercial ink-bottles and inkwells, mainly of the nineteenth century, see Covill, William, E., Jr, *Ink bottles and inkwells*, Sullwold, Taunton, Mass, 1971.

VIII The Quill Fountain-Pen

[1] A manuscript copy of the original work is held in the Library of the School of Oriental and African Studies of the University of London, No 188 in the Catalogue by Gacek, Adam, 1981. I am much indebted for his considerable work in transcribing and translating this manuscript on my behalf, to Mr A. D. H. Bivar, Lecturer in Central Asian Art and Archeology, who also kindly provided me with the following item –

[2] Mamoud, Hassan El-Basha, *A Tenth-Century Fountain-Pen*, an article in *The Bulletin*, The Egyptian Education Bureau, London, September, 1951, published here by courtesy of the present Director, Professor Younes A. El-Batrik.

[3] *Journal of the Society of Arts*, No 2763, Vol. LIII, 3rd November, 1905.

[4] A facsimile of the illustration is on display in the Charles Thomas Collection of Writing Equipment, Museum of Science and Industry, Birmingham.

[5] Wagner, Eberhard, *Der Füllfederhalter*, an article in *Historische Bürowelt*, Issue No 4, based on Eule, Wilhelm, *Mit Stift und Feder*, Leipzig, 1955.

[6] Whalley, Joyce Irene, *Writing Implements and Accessories*, David and Charles, Newton Abbot and London, 1975.

[7] A Society of Gentlemen, *A Dictionary of Arts and Sciences*, 2nd Edition, Owen, London, 1764.

[8] Clayton, Michael, *The Collector's Dictionary of the Silver and Gold of Great Britain and North America*, Country Life/Hamlyn, London, 1971, pp 138-9.

[9] As note [5] above.

[10] Fölsch, Frederick Bartholemew, Patent No 3214 of 9th May, 1809, reprinted in *The Repertory of Arts and Manufactures and Agriculture*, Second Series, January, 1810.

[11] Bramah, Joseph, Patent No 3260 of 23rd September, 1809.

[12] Scheffer, John, Patent No 4389 of 8th July, 1819.

[13] *The Engineer's and Mechanic's Encyclopaedia*, 1843, reprinted by Philip Poole and Co, circa 1979, p 282.

[14] Jackson, Donald, *The Story of Writing*, Parker Pen Co, 1981, p 132.

[15] Lewis, James Henry, Patent No 4426 of 20th December, 1819.

[16] Lewis, James Henry, *The Best Method of Pen-Making . . . the Art of Writing . . . etc*, undated, circa 1826.

[17] Johnston, William, Patent No 5392 of 24th July, 1826.

[18] Poulton, George, Patent No 5517 of 4th July, 1827.

[19] Parker, John Jacob, Patent No 6288 of 26th July, 1832.

[20] As note [13] above.

[21] As note [3] above.

IX Metallic Pens

[1] Job, Ch XIX, v 24 and Jeremiah, Ch XVII, v 1.

[2] Bore, Henry, *The Story of the Invention of Steel Pens*, Perry & Co, London, 1892, p 7.

[3] *Ibid*, p 9.

[4] Neudörffer, Johann, *Kurze Anweisung wie man einen Kiel zum Schrieben erwählen, bereiten, schneiden und temperiren, auch die Feder recht führen müsse*, Nürnberg, 1544.

[5] Saint Beure, *History of Port Royal*, Paris, 1867, quoted by Bore, Henry, *op cit*, p 7.

[6] Bore, Henry, *op cit*, p 26.

[7] *Ibid*, pp 14-16.

[8] Yciar, Juan de, *Arte Subtilissima*, Saragossa, 1550, translated by Shuckburgh, Evelyn, Lion and Unicorn Press, London, 1958, p 30.

[9] Noted in display material in the Charles Thomas Collection of Writing Equipment, in the Museum of Science and Industry, Birmingham.

[10] Bore, Henry, *op cit*, p 12.

[11] *Ibid*, p 13, quoting from *Remains*, Vol. I, p 39, referred to in *London Notes and Queries*, 5th Series, Vol. III, p 395.

[12] *Ibid*, pp 17 and 30.

[13] *The Saturday Magazine*, 1838, reprinted by Poole, Philip, 182 Drury Lane, London, undated, circa 1977.

[14] *Holden's London Directory*, 1805 and 1811.

[15] *Pigot's London Directory*, 1822/3 and 1828/9.

[16] *The Engineer's and Mechanic's Encyclopaedia*, 1843, p 277.

[17] Bore, Henry, *op cit*, pp 18-20.

[18] Greenland, Maureen, *Bryan Donkin, Inventor*, an article in *The Journal of the Writing Equipment Society*, No 10, 1984.

[19] *The Engineer's and Mechanic's Encyclopaedia*, 1843, p 277.

[20] Display material, Charles Thomas Collection, as note [9].

[21] Benker, Gertrud, *Alte Bestecke*, Callwey, München, 1978, plate 55, p 57.

[22] Bore, Henry, *op cit*, p 9.

[23] Grimshaw, M. E., *Silver Medals, Badges and Trophies from Schools in the British Isles, 1550-1850*, privately printed.

[24] Bore, Henry, *op cit*, p 13.

[25] Kronberg, B. I., Coatsworth, L. L. and Usselman, M. C., *The Artefact as Historical Document, Part II: The Palladium and Rhodium of W. H. Wollaston*, an article in *Ambix*, Vol. 28, Part I, March, 1981.

[26] *Ibid*, pp 29, 30 and footnote.

[27] From a manuscript account of gold pen-making by Frank Crosbie, of Francis Mordan and Company, circa 1892, in the author's collection.

[28] *Robson's London Commercial Directory*, 1826-27.

[29] *The Saturday Magazine*, 1838.

30 *Ex Inf:* D. F. Wallis, Esq. An example so inscribed was offered for sale in a London street market during 1987.

31 Hawkins, John Isaac, and Mordan, Sampson, Patent No 4742, of 20th December, 1822.

32 Foley, John, *The History of Foley's Diamond Pointed Gold Pens*, New York, undated, circa 1875.

33 *Pigot's Metropolitan New Alphabetical Directory of London*, 1827, illustrated in Whalley, J. I., *Writing Implements and Accessories*, David and Charles, Newton Abbott, 1975, p 19.

34 Institute of Civil Engineering, *Minutes of Proceedings*, Vol. 25, 1865-66, p 512.

35 Foley, John, *op cit*, p 50.

36 *Ibid*, pp 52-74.

37 Francis Mordan and Co, *The Everlasting Gold Pen and How it is Made*, London, 1892.

38 From a manuscript account by Frank Crosbie – see Finlay, Michael, *The Journal of the Writing Equipment Society*, No 16, 1986.

X Pencils and *Porte-crayons*

1 Jackson, Donald, *The Story of Writing*, pp 82-3.

2 Berol Ltd, *Berol: The Pencil, its History and Manufacture,* – Advertising leaflet, undated, circa 1980.

3 Catich, Father Edward, M., *The Origin of the Serif*, Catfish Press, 1968.

4 Collingwood, W. G., *Lake District History*, Titus Wilson, Kendal, p 128.

5 Lefebure, Molly, *Cumberland Heritage*, Victor Gollancz, London, 1970, p 76., referring to B. M. Sloane Ms 2487, (an inventory of the equipment and furniture of the Mines Royal at all their establishments in the Lake country, 1586.)

6 *Ibid*, Chapter Three.

7 Collingwood, W. G., *op cit*, p 131, quoting Postlethwaite, John, *Mines and Mining in the Lake District*, Whitehaven, 1877.

8 Lefebure, Molly, *op cit*, pp 78 and 91.

9 Cumbria Record Office, Carlisle, DB/1/55, a proof of an article for the *Stationery Trades Review*, undated, circa 1941.

10 Webb, K. R., of University College, Southampton, in a letter to *The Sunday Times*, 17th July, 1949, quoting from Parkes, S., *Chemical Essays*, London, 1815, Vol. 2, p 335.

11 *Ibid*, referring to the writer's contribution to *Notes and Queries*, 1943, Vol. 184, pp 236 and 293, and Vol. 185, p 57.

12 Cumbria Record Office, Carlisle, *The Cumberland Pacquet and Whitehaven Advertiser*, Issue No 63, 28th December, 1775, p 3, col 3.

13 Lefebure, Molly, *op cit*, p 93.

14 Cumbria Record Office, Carlisle, P 1830, Will of Jacob Banks, the elder, of Keswick, Parish of Crosthwaite, late Black lead Pencil Maker.

15 Lefebure, Molly, *op cit*, p 83.

16 Nicholson, Joseph, and Burn, Richard, *The History and Antiquities of the Counties of Westmorland and Cumberland*, London, 1777, Vol. II, p 81.

17 *A Book of Values of Merchandize imported, according to which, EXCIZE is to be paid by the First Buyer*, London, Henry Hills and John Field, Printers to His Highness, 1657; author's collection.

18 Lefebure, Molly, *op cit*, p 84, quoting from Robinson's *Natural History of Westmorland and Cumberland*, 1704.

19 *Ibid*, p 87, quoting from *The Cumberland Pacquet*, 1851.

20 *Ibid*, p 89, quoting Hatchett's account of a tour through the North in 1796.

21 Cumbria Record Office, DB/1/56, *The Illustrated Magazine of Art*, 1854, p 252.

22 Mannix and Whellan, *Directory & History of Cumberland*, 1847.

23 Cumbria Record Office, Carlisle, P 1860, Will of Joseph Banks, of Keswick, Pencil Manufacturer.

24 Bulmer, T., *Directory of West Cumberland*, 1883, and *Directory of Cumberland*, 1901.

25 Lefebure, Molly, *op cit*, p 97.

26 *Ibid*, p 98.

27 *The Cumberland and Westmorland Herald*, Keswick Edition, 21st December, 1941.

28 Cumbria Record Office, Carlisle, P 1905, Will of Richard Hogarth, and P 1912, Administration of the Probate of George Hogarth.

29 *Sale Particulars, Coledale House*, including 'Remains of Building lately used as Pencil Mill', 6th May, 1899, kindly shown to me by the former owners of the Coledale Inn (formerly Coledale House), Mr and Mrs L. S. Swift, October, 1981.

30 *The Post Office Commercial Directory of Westmorland and Cumberland*, 1858.

31. Lefebure, Molly, *op cit*, p 97.

32 Lysons, Daniel, *Magna Brittania*, Vol. IV, Cumberland, London, 1816, pp CXXIV-V.

33 Whalley, Joyce Irene, *Writing Implements and Accessories*, David and Charles, Newton Abbot and London, 2nd Impression, 1980, quoting from *The Complete Book of Trades*, 1843.

34 Guildhall Library, London Directories: *New Complete Guide*, 1777; *Bailey's British Directory*, 1784 and 1785.

35 Lambeth Archives Department, London Directories: *Johnstone's London Commercial Guide*, 1817; *Robson's London Directory*, 1826; *Pigot's London & Provincial Commercial Directory*, 1834; *The Post Office Directory*, 1840.

36 *The Carlisle Journal*, 12 March, 1901.

37 Stilitz, Ivor, *The Three Fabers*, Writing Equipment Society Journal No 8, 1983.

38 Cumbria Record Office, DB/1/55, see 9 above.

39 British Patent No 9977, 8th December, 1843, discussed by Cooper, Michael, *William Brockendon, FRS*, Writing Equipment Society Journal, No 17, 1986.

40 Cooper, Michael, *Sir Henry Bessemer, FRS*, Writing Equipment Society Journal, No 10, 1984.

41 Cooper, Michael, *William Brockendon, FRS*, as 39 above.

42 Whalley, Joyce Irene, *op cit*, p. 121 (plate).

43 *The Saturday Magazine*, 1838-39 and 1834, reprinted by Philip Poole, London, circa 1979.

44 Public Record Office, C13/2366, L 1C 1083, Sampson Mordan & Gabriel Riddle vs Joseph Willmore, in Chancery, discussed in detail in Eldred, Edward, *Sampson Mordan & Co*, privately printed, 1986.

45 Cooper, Michael, *Lead Pencils*, Writing Equipment Society Journal, No 18, 1987.

46 Riddle, William, British Patent No 12383, 21st December, 1848.

47 Jonas, (sic) Jonas, Patent No 1409, 17th December, 1783

48 Eldred, Edward, *In Chancery – Mordan and Riddle*, Writing Equipment Society Journal, No 18, 1987.

[49] Jaggard, William, a contribution to *Notes and Queries*, 10th April, 1943, p 237.

[50] *Description of a Machine for Making Slate-pencils, Invented by Mr J. Brockbank, of Whirlpipin near Whitehaven, in Cumberland*, the Society for the Encouragement of Arts, Manufactures and Commerce, *Transactions*, 1811.

XI Seals and Sealing

[1] For a useful general history of the subject, see *The New Encyclopaedia Brittanica*, 15th Edition, 1985, Volume 20, p 673 *et seq*, to which due acknowledgement is made.

[2] Moring, Thomas, *A Catalogue of Seal Engraving*, undated, late nineteenth century.

[3] *The Saturday Magazine*, 1830s, reprinted by Poole, Philip, 182 Drury Lane, London, undated, circa 1977.

[4] Moring, Thomas, *op cit*, p 7.

[5] Jenkinson, Hilary, *A Guide to Seals in the Public Record Office*, HMSO, London, 1954, pp 12-13.

[6] *The Saturday Magazine*, as note [3] above.

[7] Davis, Isaac, Patent No 9153, 11th November, 1841.

[8] Jenkinson, Hilary, *op cit*, gives a detailed account of the different methods of appending seals as well as all other aspects of seals of the medieval period.

[9] *The Saturday Magazine*, as note [3] above.

[10] Cox, Matthew, British Patent No 82, 6th June 1635.

Colour Plates

I
Holbein's portrait of the Hanseatic merchant Georg
Gisze. Painted in 1532, it includes a wealth of detail
depicting contemporary writing implements.
*Courtesy Gemäldegalerie Staatliche Museen Preussischer
Kulturbesitz, Berlin (West)*
Photo: Jörg P Anders, Berlin

I

72

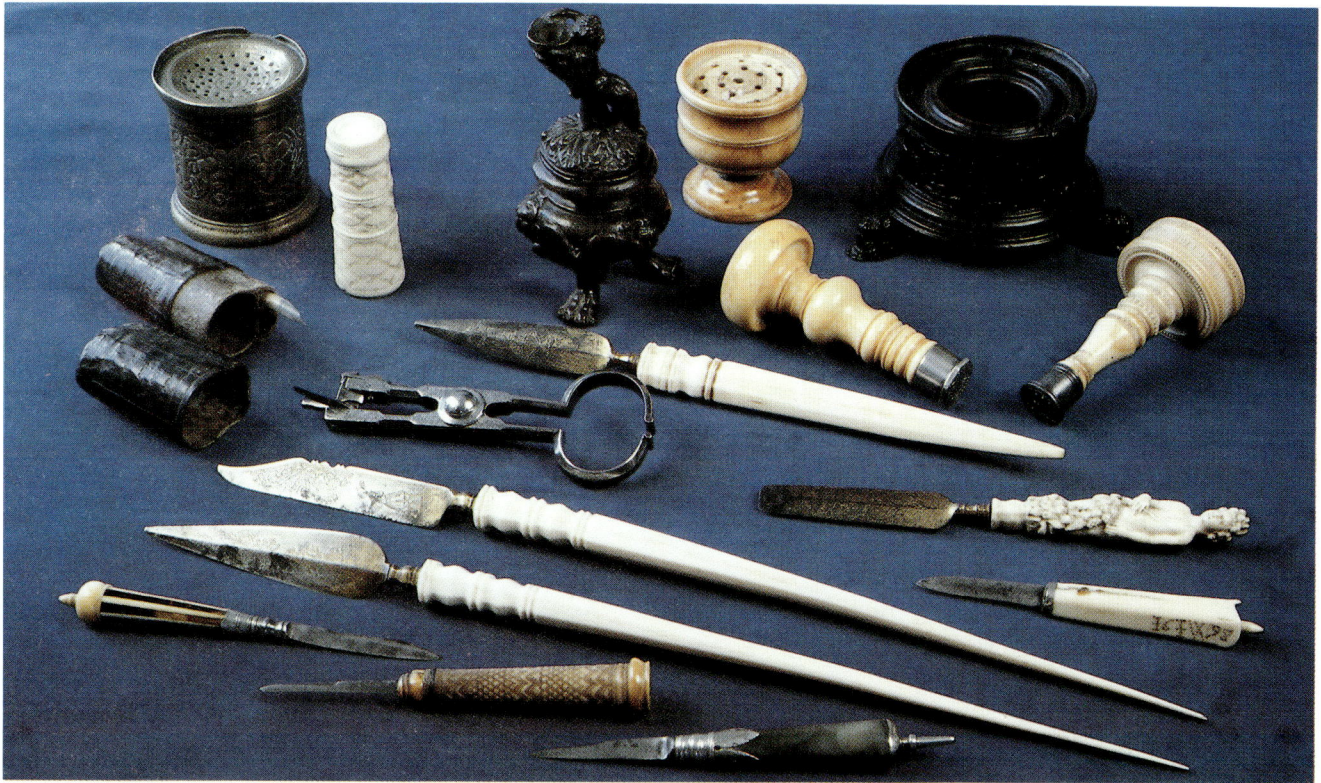

(i)

(ii)

II

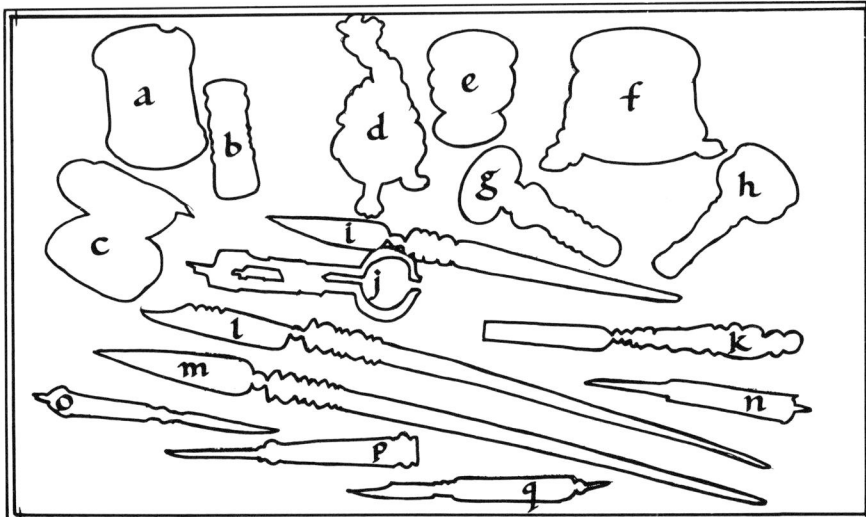

II(i)
Group of seventeenth-century writing implements, details of which, apart from i and q, will be found in the captions to the black and white plates as under:

- a Brass pounce pot, **(161)**
- b Bone penner, **(186)**
- c Case for b above.
- d Bronze inkwell, **(225)**
- e Ivory sander, **(160)**
- f Bronze inkwell, **(226)**
- g Ivory and silver seal, **(322)**
- h Ivory and steel seal, **(321)**
- i Erasing knife with gilt-etched steel blade and ivory handle, South German or Italian, early seventeenth century.
- j Steel quill-cutting device, **(119)**
- k Steel and ivory scribe's knife, **(39)**
- l }Pair of steel and ivory scribe's
- m }knives, **(38)**
- n Steel and ivory pen-knife, **(50)**
- o Steel, tortoiseshell and ivory pen-knife, **(69)**
- p Steel and bone pen-knife, **(49)**
- q Jade-handled steel pen-knife with engraved silver mounts, circa 1695.

II(ii)
Trompe l'oeil painting by Edward Collier, painted in 1703. Collier's closely-observed still-life includes a quill, horn penner and pen-knife with unusual 'peg'.
Courtesy Rafael Valls Fine Paintings

III(i)

a

Pen-knife with ornamented brass scales and ring terminal for suspension, with traces of original gilding. Excavated from the Thames and dating from the twelfth to the fourteenth century, this is the earliest pen-knife so far identified. 126 mm.

b

All steel pen-knife, circa 1530. Excavated from the Thames, this knife is similar in character to that of circa 1530 shown in Plate 46 and another, partly visible, in Holbein's portrait of Georg Gisze, painted in 1532.(Colour plate I). No earlier pen-knife having the chamfered back edge common to many later pen-knives appears to be recorded. 145 mm.

c

Late medieval latten seal with the legend + S'(IGILLUM): D'(E):TORRUS:DE:RIRESCET

d

Medieval bone parchment-pricker, excavated from the mud of the Thames, its iron point corroded away.

III(ii)

Fine George IV pen-knife, the facetted citrine handle having foliate-chased gold mounts, the blade impressed THOMAS, for John Thomas, a working cutler of 425 Oxford Street, London, circa 1825. 117 mm.

III(iii)

Three French penners of the late eighteenth century, all of which contain gold pens.

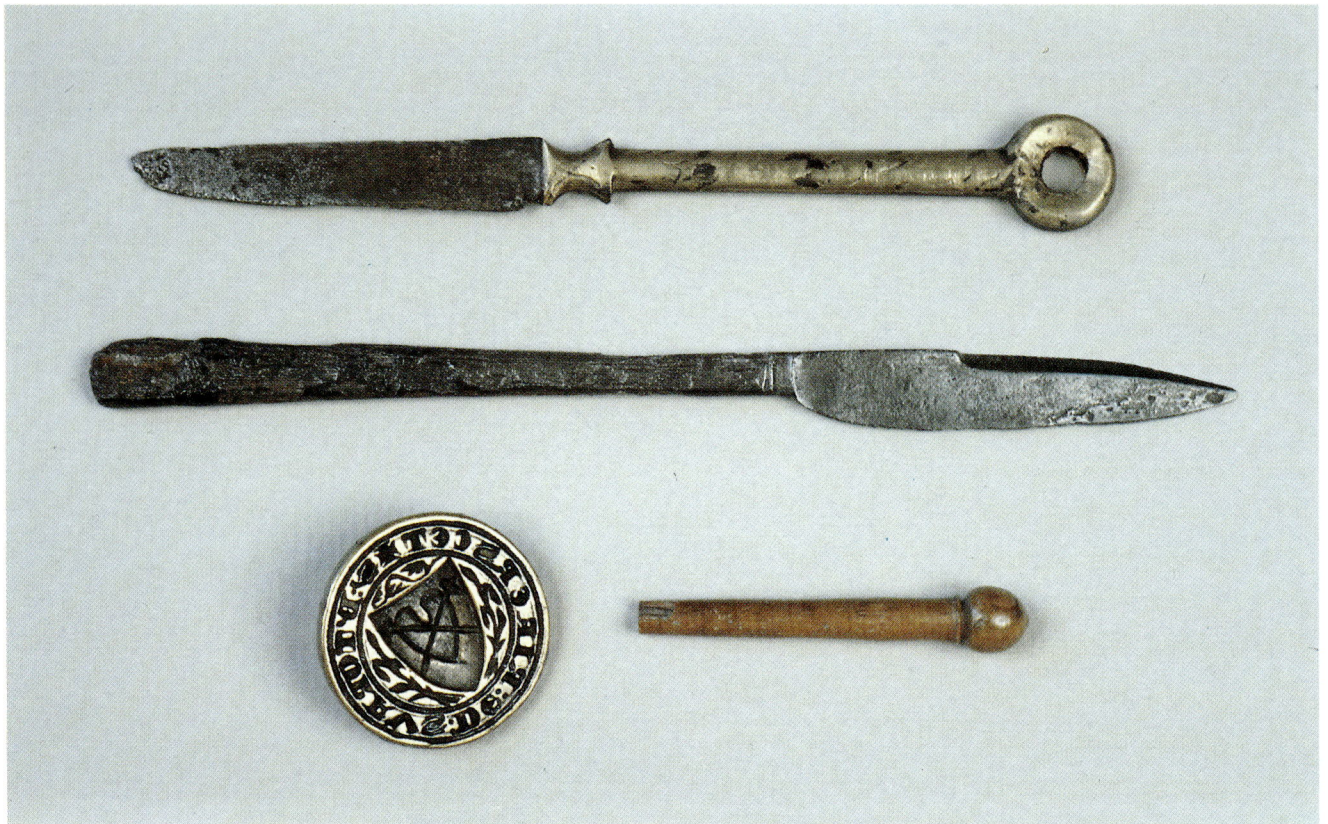

(i)

(ii)

III

(iii)

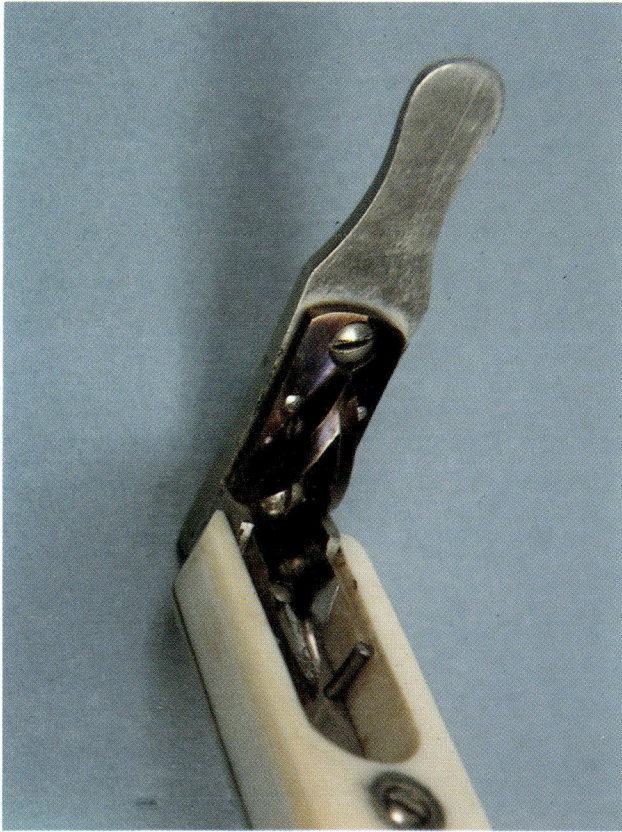

(i)

(ii)

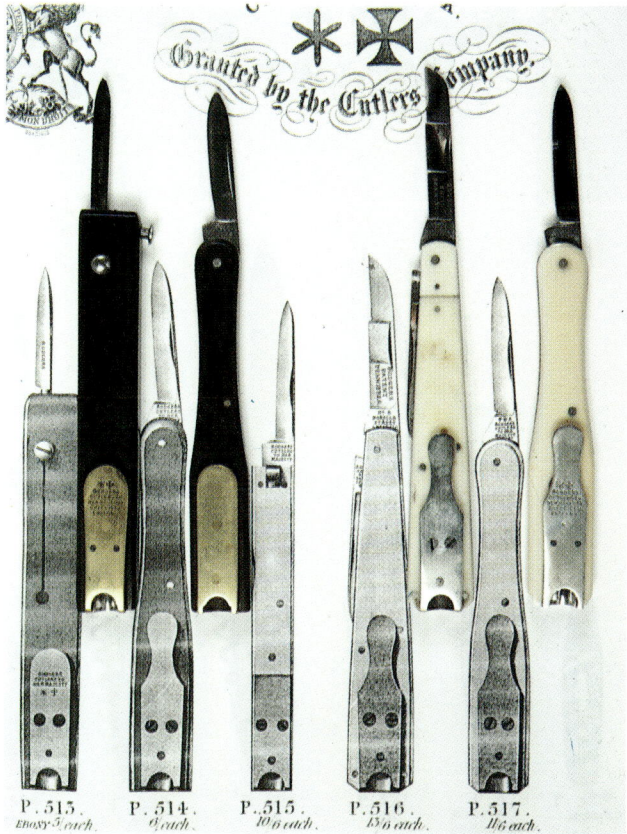

(iii)

IV

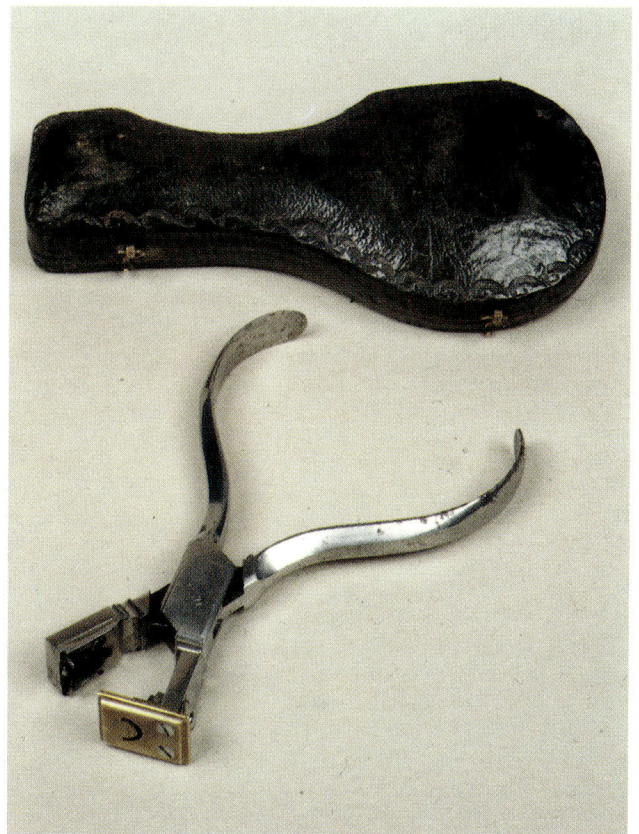

(iv)

IV(i)
The basic mechanism of all mechanical quill-cutters: a
pair of nib-shaped blades working against an anvil of
the same form which cut the profile of the pen while a
central blade forms the slit.

IV(ii)
Made by George Adams, father or son, mathematical
instrument makers to George III and the Prince Regent,
this fine silver quill-cutter with steel key retains its
silver-mounted green shagreen case. English, 1770-95.
62 mm high.

IV(iii)
Group of Joseph Rodgers pocket quill-cutting machines
of a type made from the 1830s into the twentieth
century; these are all impressed 'CUTLERS TO HER
MAJESTY' and have paper slip-cases. The wood-
engraved plate from the firm's cutlery catalogue of circa
1869 shows a typical range of designs with wood or
ivory scales. Tortoiseshell, horn and mother-of-pearl
were also used.

IV(iv)
Pair of steel and gilt-brass quill-cutting 'pliers' with
their original gold-tooled green leather case, French,
first half eighteenth century, 130 mm.

V(i)
John Middleton, pencil-maker, of Vine Street, London,
painted in oils on a cedar panel, circa 1770. 43 x 33 cm.

V(ii)
Thomas Palmer, (1752-1821), founder of one of the most
successful firms of quill pen-makers, at East Grinstead,
from a somewhat faded portrait miniature in the
possession of his descendants.
Courtesy Mrs J. K. Davies

V(iii)
Portrait of a Naval Commander, oil on canvas, English
School, circa 1780. 620 x 510 mm. When, as here, three
fob seals were worn together, they were usually
engraved with the owner's crest, his arms and a cypher
of his initials, respectively.
Courtesy Wilkins & Wilkins

V(iv)
Minute stick of red sealing-wax impressed DAVIS
BROTHERS and PATENT, sufficient for one personal
seal and with one end coated to ignite by friction, circa
1841. 15 mm long.

(i)

(ii)

(iii)

V

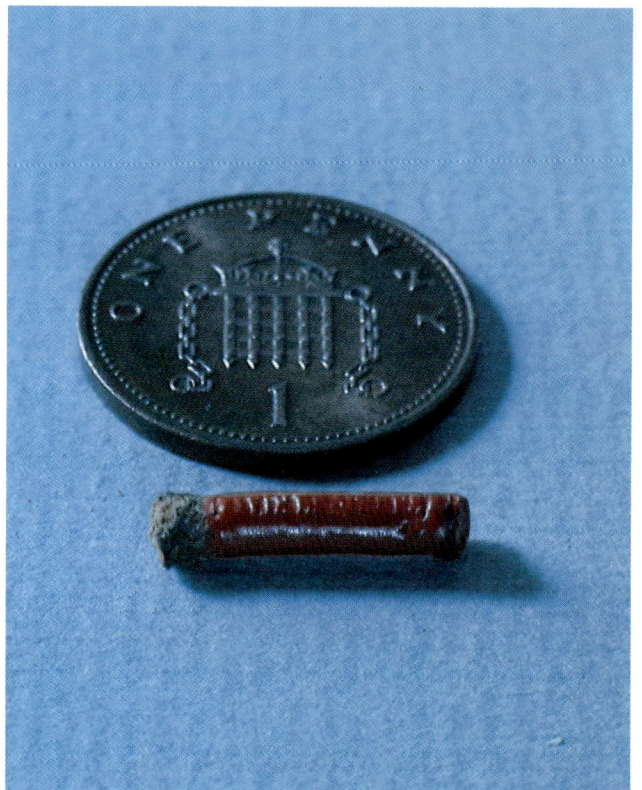

(iv)

(i)

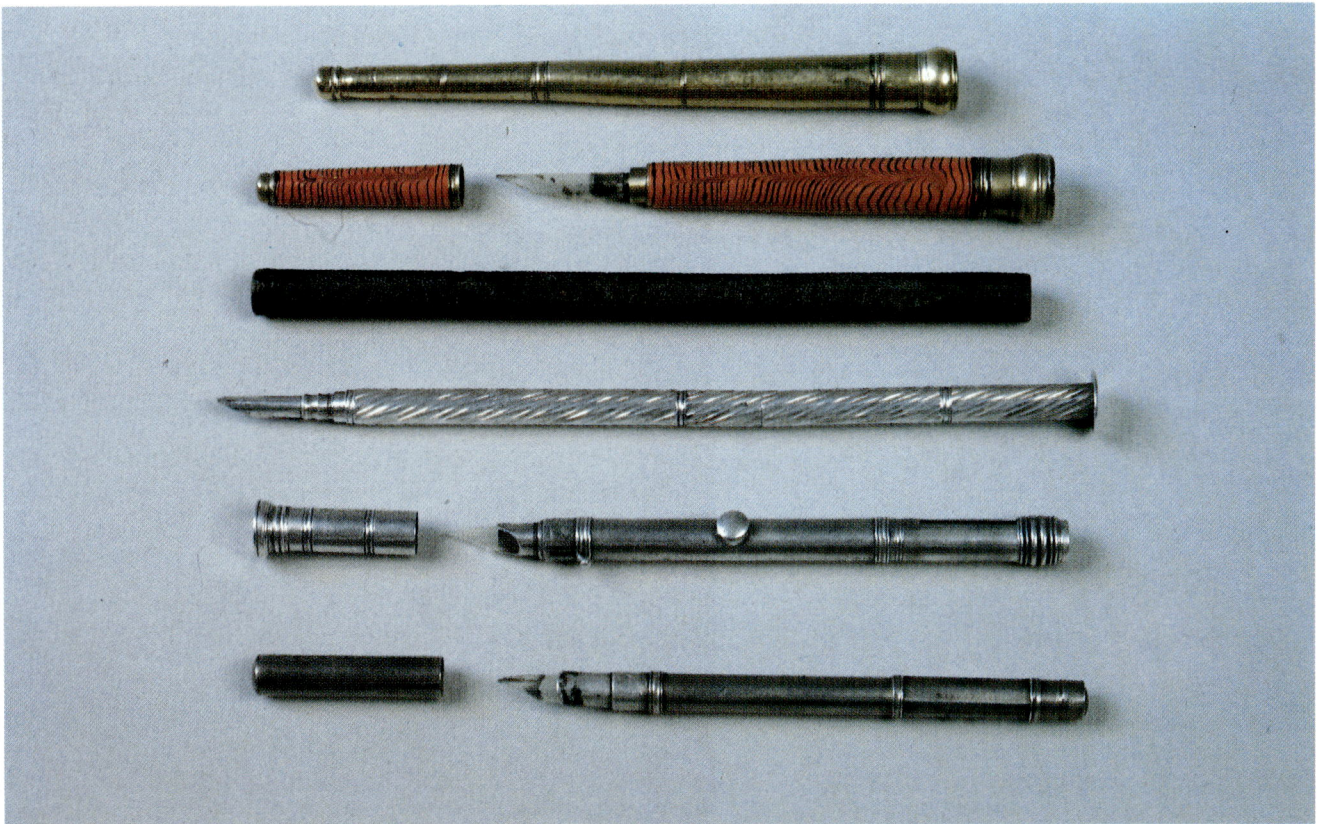

(ii)

VI

VI(i)

The earliest fountain-pen so far discovered. Made of
brass and engraved with the name of its original owner
William Line, it is dated 1702. It uses a quill nib which
is fed with ink from the pen barrel by a simple gravity
feed. The seal terminal is engraved with a lion
rampant, a rebus of the owner's name. 131 mm.
Courtesy Bruce A. Nichol, Esq

VI(ii)

Fountain-pens:

a and b

Two early brass fountain-pens on the Bion principle,
each having a seal terminal, one with red and black
hard wax decoration, retaining its *cuir bouilli* case. (See
plate 260). Mid-eighteenth century. 122 and 129 mm.

c

Extremely rare mid-eighteenth century silver pen,
unmarked, with its original black ray-skin case; in
1757, such fountain pens cost £2.10s. 151 mm.

d

Silver pen conforming to Scheffer's Penographic patent,
hallmarked London, 1823 and made by W. Robson,
who must have acquired the patent rights between 1819
and this time. It is impressed 'W. ROBSON & CO,
PATENTEES, LONDON, 2945'. 123 mm long.

e

The first self-filling pen, patented by John Jacob Parker
in 1832. (British Patent No 6288). Impressed 'PARKER'S
PATENT, LONDON. No 6047' and hallmarked London,
1833, maker M.J. 116 mm.

VII(i)
Fine gold-mounted ivory-handled desk seal carved with hands representing 'Age and Youth', the jasper matrix engraved with an armorial. Circa 1840. 112 mm high. (See also Plate 327).

VII(ii)
Silver desk seal cast as a gamecock trimmed for the fight, the matrix engraved with a crest. Hallmarked London, 1828. 53 mm high.

VII(iii)
Superb quality gold-mounted purpurine-handled desk seal, the chalcedony matrix engraved with the armorial of Lord Brownlow of Belton House, Leicestershire, circa 1825. 71 mm high.

VII(iv)
Agate-handled gold-mounted desk seal with bloodstone matrix engraved in blackletter 'Belton House', circa 1825. 60 mm high. (Belton House, formerly the home of Lord Brownlow, is now the property of the National Trust).

(i)

(ii)

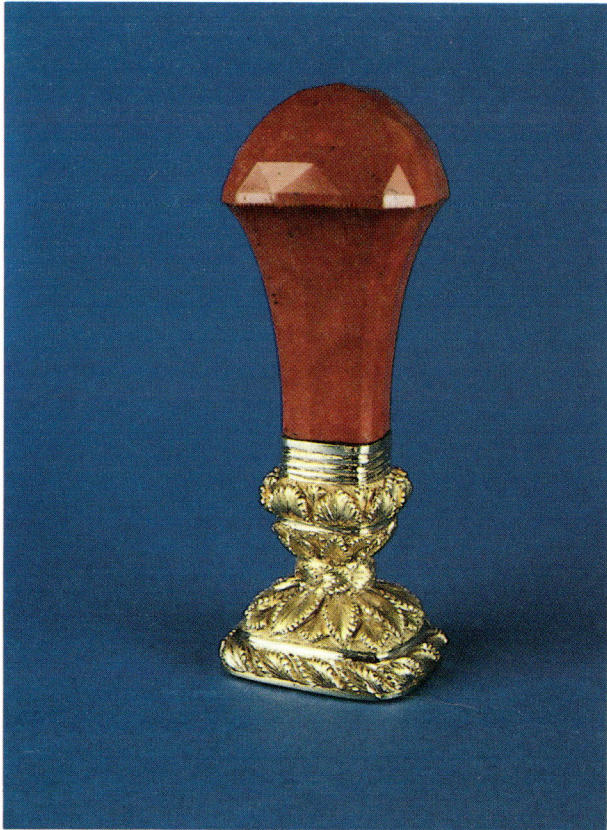

(iii)

VII

(iv)

LAMBERT & RAWLINGS
GOLDSMITHS & JEWELLERS
TO THEIR MAJESTIES
Coventry Street London

VIII

VIII
Medallion wafers, made from opaque white and
transparent coloured glue from engraved intaglios and
sold by Lambert and Rawlings, Goldsmiths and
Jewellers to the Royal Family. They were moistened
and used to seal folded letters. Circa 1832.

Monochrome Plates

1
Mosaic of St Matthew at work on his
gospel, a quill pen among his tools, part
of the mural decoration of the Church of
San Vitale in Ravenna; dating from circa
546-8, this may be the earliest depiction of
a quill pen extant.
Courtesy Archivi Alinari, Florence

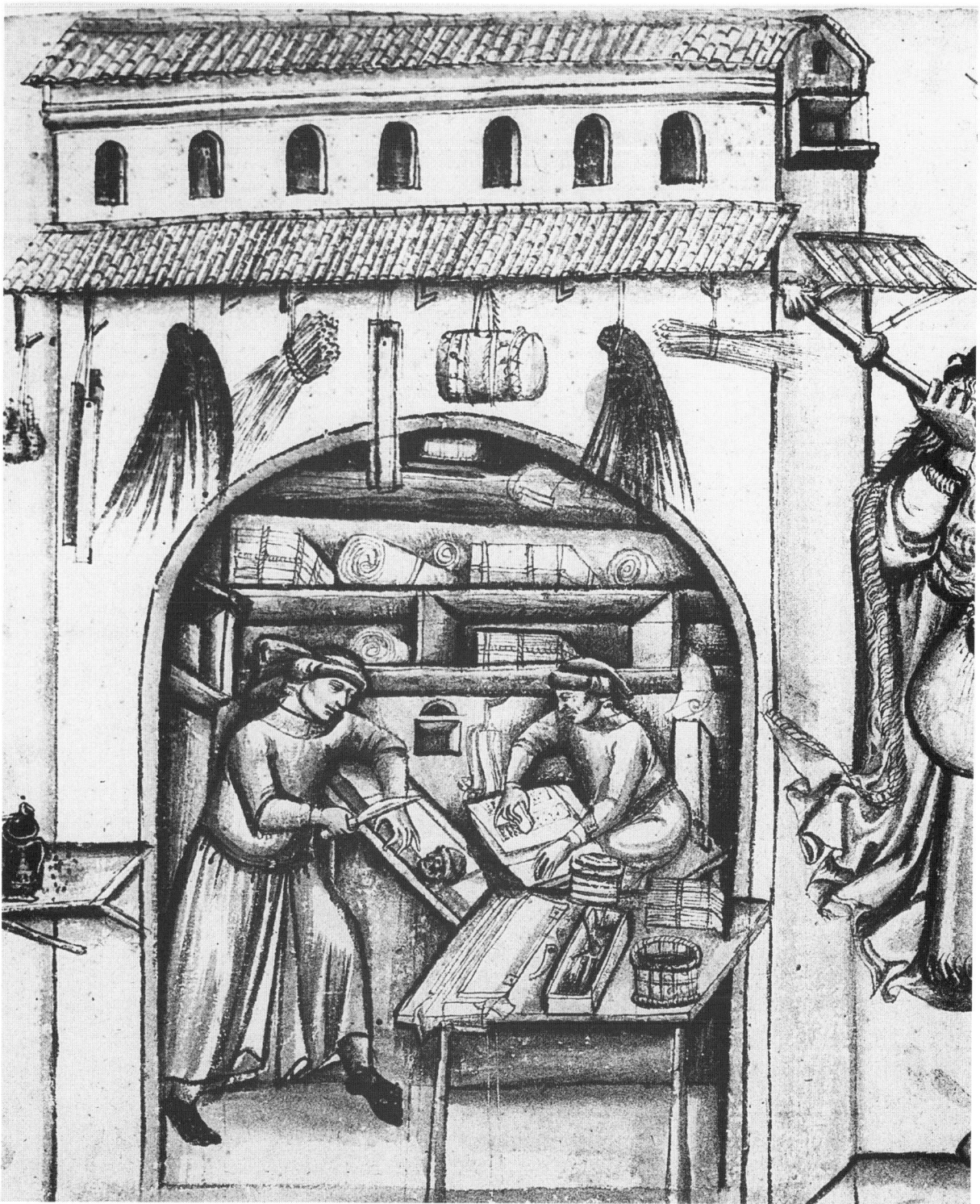

2
Stationer's shop, Bologna, fifteenth century. Bundles of
quills and wings hang from the eaves. Inside, one man
is erasing writing from a sheet of parchment with a
pumice stone, for re-use; another is trimming a bundle
of sheets to size.
Courtesy Biblioteca Universitaria, Bologna
BUB Ms, 1456, c 4ʳ

89

3

Stationer's advertisement for the sale of quill pens, from the *Edinburgh Evening Courant*, Thursday, 6th November, 1787. *Courtesy Philip Poole, Esq*

3

4

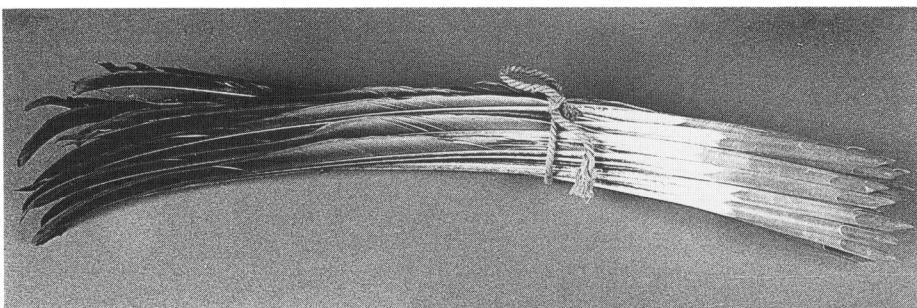

4
Original bundle of Hudson's Bay quill pens, bound with puce wool twine, nineteenth century.
350 mm.

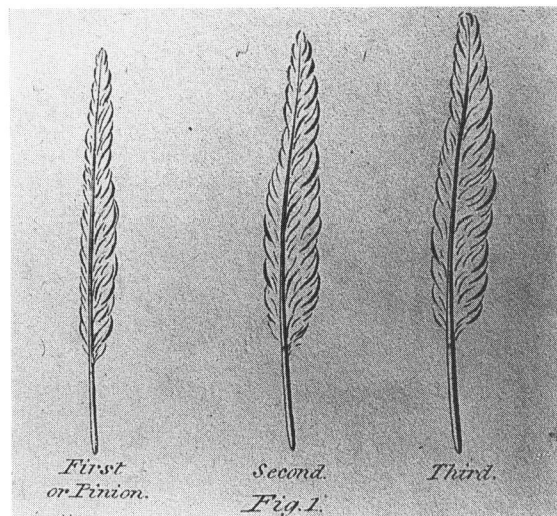

5

5
The main flight feathers used for making quill pens; engraving from B. Pride's *The Art of Pen-Cutting*, 1812.

6
Pinion, Second and Third from the left wing of a goose.

6

Sir Joseph Causton & Sons, London. 79

QUILL PENS.

GOOSE QUILL.

Warranted to be cut by hand.

Yellow	String	..	..	..	per 100 4/0
Pink	,,	..	..	..	,, 6/0
Orange	,,	..	..	..	,, 8/0
Pink and Blue	,,	..	..	..	,, 10/0
Orange and Blue	,,	..	..	..	,, 12/0
Full Pink	,,	..	..	..	,, 15/0

PINION QUILL .. .. per 100 1/3, 1/6, 2/0 & 2/6

Fig. 1166.

OFFICE or BANK QUILL.

These Pens are of superior quality, but having been *once used*, are sold at a great reduction.

Orange String	..	..	..	..	..	..	per 100	1/6
Red	,,	..	..	..	..	..	,,	2/3
Blue	,,	..	..	..	..	..	,,	3/0
Pink	,,	..	..	..	..	..	,,	3/9

TURKEY QUILL.

These Pens are used chiefly for Engrossing and Law Writing, and are well adapted for Red Ink.

Green String	..	..	..	..	..	..	per 100	4/6
Red	,,	..	..	..	..	..	,,	5/6
Pink	,,	..	..	..	..	..	,,	7/0

CROW QUILL.

For Architectural Drawing, &c.	..	..	..	per 100	5/0
Superior quality do.	..	..	..	,,	9/0

HUDSON'S BAY QUILL.

Much used in the Houses of Parliament and the Law Courts, and remarkable for their hardness and durability.

Pink String	..	..	..	..	..	..	per 100	22/6
Pink and Green String	..	..	..	..	..	..	,,	30/0
,, Yellow ,,	..	..	..	..	..	..	,,	37/6
,, Purple ,,	..	..	..	..	..	..	,,	45/0
,, ,, and Yellow String	..	..	..	..	..	..	,,	63/0

Cheaper qualities, in boxes of 25, 1/6 and 3/0 per box.

SWAN QUILL.

The very finest Pens obtainable.

Pink String	..	..	..	..	..	..	per 100	30/0
,, and Yellow String	..	..	..	..	..	..	,,	37/6
,, and Purple ,,	..	..	..	..	..	..	,,	45/0
,, and Blue ,,	..	..	..	..	..	..	,,	52/6
,, Green and Orange, *very large, selected*	..	..	..	..	..	,,	63/0

** Any of the above may be had *uncut* if desired.

QUILL PEN NIBS.

Fig. 1167.

Warranted cut with a Knife.	1st Quality.		2nd Quality.	
	s.	d.	s.	d.
25 Superior Nibs, in Box ..	1	0	0	6
50 ,, ,, ,, ..	2	0	1	0
100 ,, ,, ,, ..	3	3	2	0

89, 91, 93 & 114, Southwark Street, and Zoar Street, S.E.

G

7
Page from a wholesale stationer's catalogue of 1890, showing the wide range of quills and quill pens available.

8
Victorian bundle of 21 of an original package of 25 high quality goose quill pens, tied with cerise woollen twine, the nibs protected by a tied carton priced '2/6' in ink, anonymous. 330 mm.

7

9

10

11

9
Victorian box of Canada Goose quill pens by Watkins and McCombie, circa 1880, 216 mm. Established before 1840 by Thomas Watkins, this firm was taken over before 1910 by Cooper, Dennison and Walkden.

10
Victorian box of quill pens, anonymous, late nineteenth century. 208 mm.

11
Victorian box of London-made quill pens, anonymous, late nineteenth century. 205 mm. The original price of '1d each' is written in pencil on the underside of the box.

12
Victorian box of Hudson's Bay quill pens, containing 18 of its original 25 Canada Goose quill pens wrapped in tissue, anonymous. 229 mm.

13
Late Victorian box of goose quill pens by J. J. Field, London.
Courtesy Museum of Science and Industry, Birmingham, Charles Thomas Collection

14
Late Victorian box of goose quill pens, anonymous, containing 10 of its original 25 pens. 232 mm.

93

15
Screw-topped cedar box of quill
nibs, Palmer's Royal Portable
Pens, circa 1805. 74 mm diameter.

16
Sycamore box with sliding lid,
Palmer & Sons, East Grinstead,
labelled underneath
'GENTLEMENS PENS' with the
handwritten figure '50' in ink,
early nineteenth century. 125 mm
long.

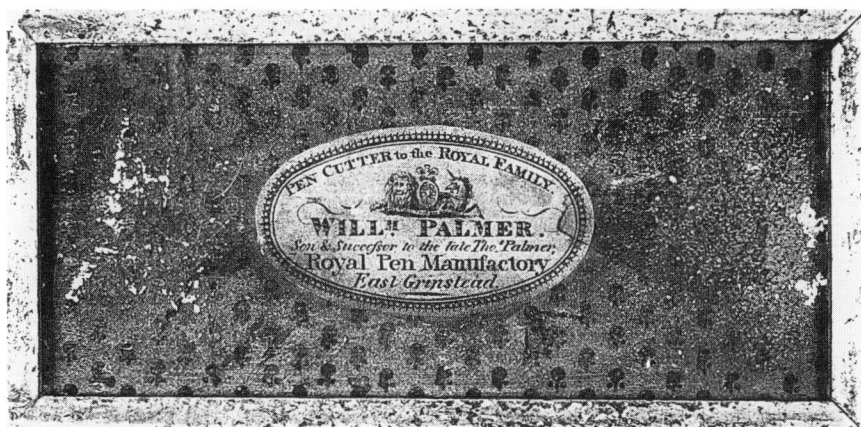

17
Similar box of William Palmer's
'LADIES PENS', early nineteenth
century. 125 mm long.

18
Trade Card, printed in blue, of Palmer & Sons, East
Grinstead, early nineteenth century. 76 mm long.

94

19, 20
Advertising broadsheets of Palmers, East Grinstead, 1808-9.
Courtesy of the Trustees of the British Museum, Banks Collection, 92.11

21
Price list of Thomas J. Palmer, East Grinstead, circa 1860s. Thomas J. Palmer succeeded William Palmer, (1784-1861), son of the founder of the firm, Thomas Palmer, (1752-1821).

22

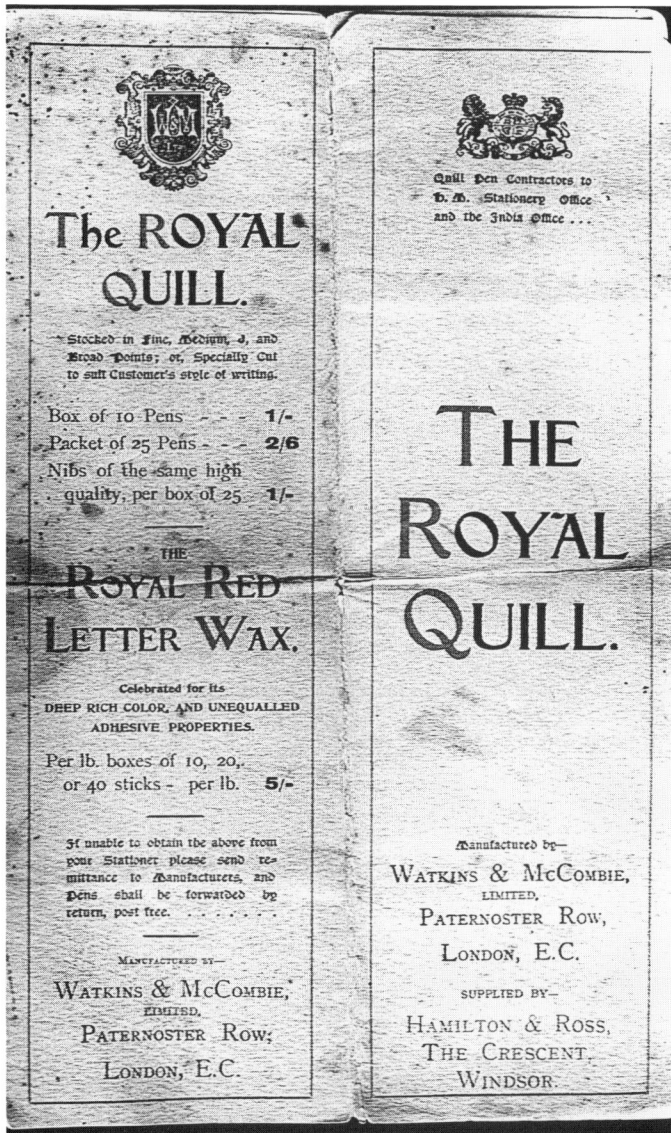

23

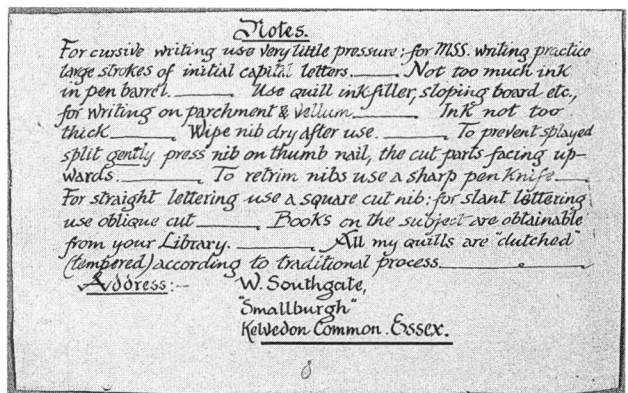

24

22
Box of Hill's Metallised Quills, also known as 'The Metkalamos' Quills, containing 5 of its original 25 goose quill pens with gold-plated nibs, circa 1908. 348 mm.

23
Advertising leaflet from a box of 'The Royal Quill' pens by Watkins and McCombie, late nineteenth century.

24
Hand-written leaflet enclosed with quill pens supplied by William Southgate, early twentieth century. 170 mm long.

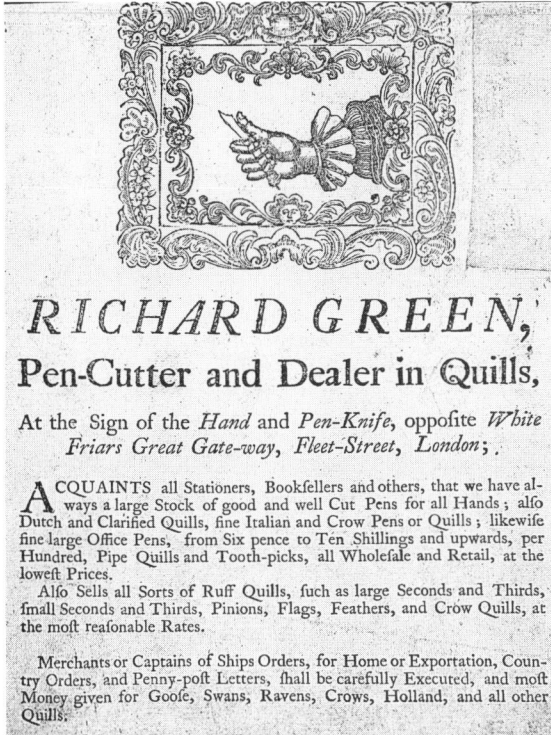

RICHARD GREEN,
Pen-Cutter and Dealer in Quills,

At the Sign of the *Hand* and *Pen-Knife*, oppofite *White Friars Great Gate-way, Fleet-Street, London;*.

ACQUAINTS all Stationers, Bookfellers and others, that we have always a large Stock of good and well Cut Pens for all Hands ; alfo Dutch and Clarified Quills, fine Italian and Crow Pens or Quills ; likewife fine large Office Pens, from Six pence to Ten Shillings and upwards, per Hundred, Pipe Quills and Tooth-picks, all Wholefale and Retail, at the lowest Prices.

Alfo Sells all Sorts of Ruff Quills, such as large Seconds and Thirds, fmall Seconds and Thirds, Pinions, Flags, Feathers, and Crow Quills, at the moft reafonable Rates.

Merchants or Captains of Ships Orders, for Home or Exportation, Country Orders, and Penny-poft Letters, fhall be carefully Executed, and moft Money given for Goofe, Swans, Ravens, Crows, Holland, and all other Quills.

25

26

25
Mid-eighteenth century pen-cutter's trade card. Compare the knife with that in Plate 64.
Courtesy of the Trustees of the British Museum, Heal Collection, 92.12

26
Fine example of rococo style engraving – a pen-cutter's trade card of circa 1760.
Courtesy of the Trustees of the British Museum, Heal Collection, 92.8

27
Trade card of a London quill-dresser in the early nineteenth century.

28
Part of an original bundle of quill pens which have been clarified with their ends intact, causing 'snapping'; modern practice is to cut off the tips before 'dutching' to allow the expanding air to escape freely.

27

28

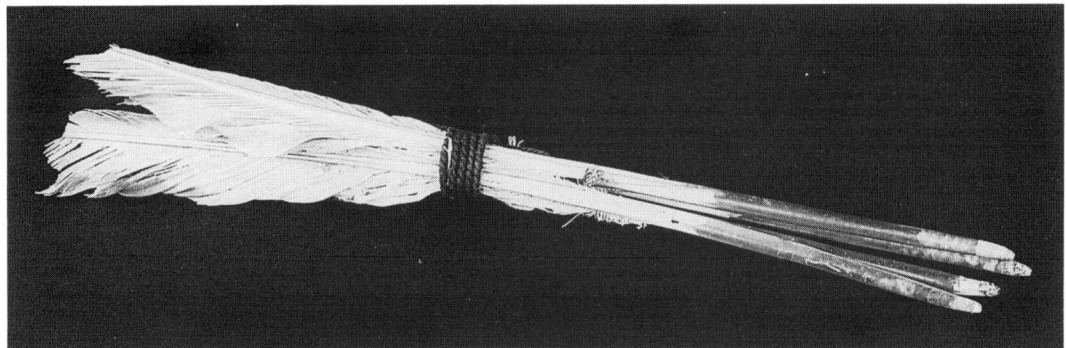

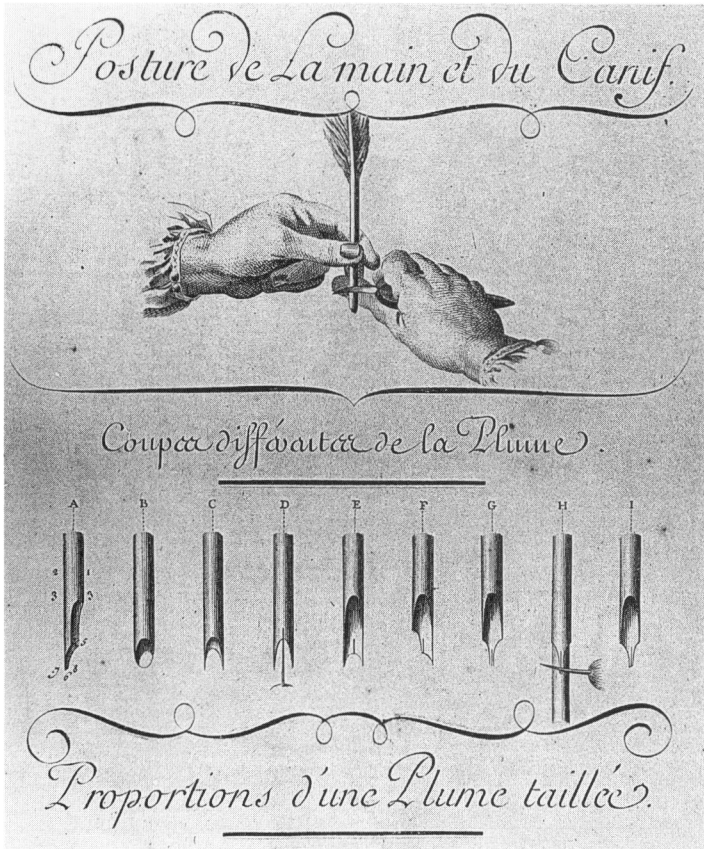

29

Posture de la main et du Canif.

Coupes différentes de la Plume.

Proportions d'une Plume taillée.

29
The stages in cutting a quill pen. From Paillason's 'L'Arte d'Écrire, late eighteenth century.

30
The variety of pen-angles cut for different hands. From George Shelley's *The Second Part of Natural Writing*, 1714.

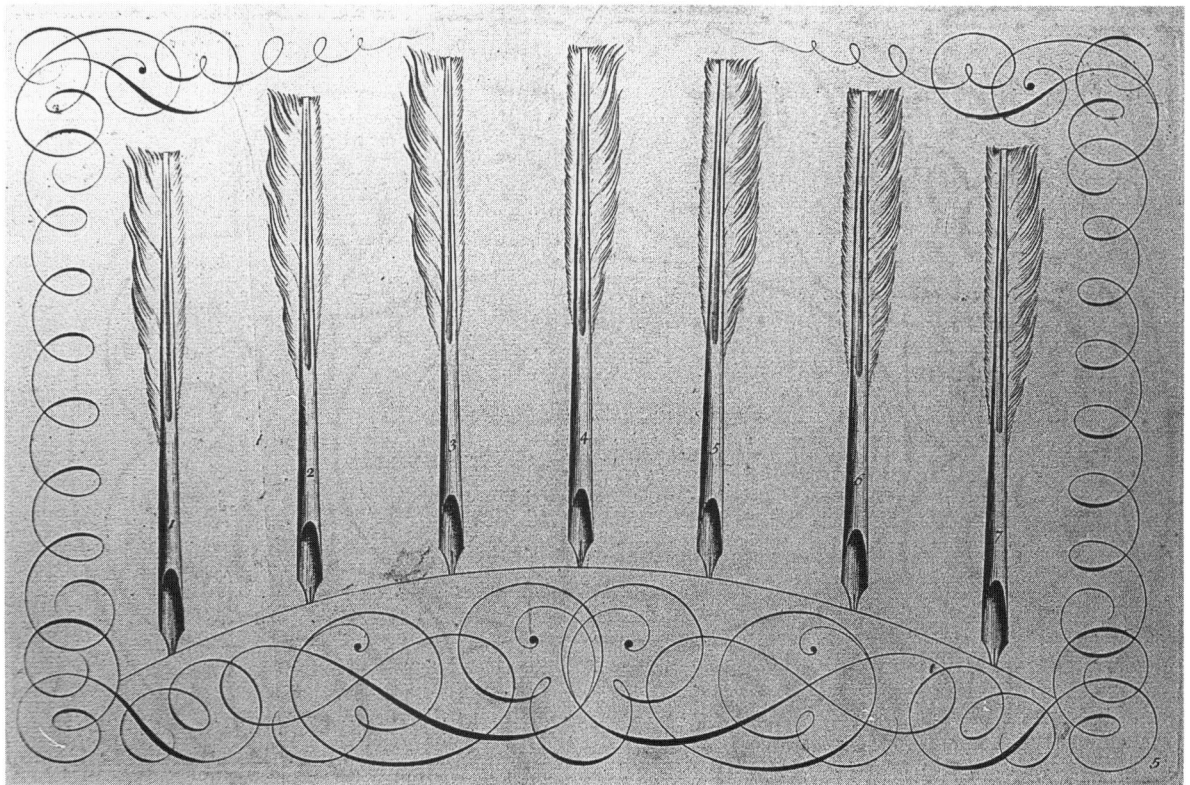

30

31
Copperplate engraved copy book for the Round
Hand, one of a series of such books for different
hands, published by R. Langford in 1821.

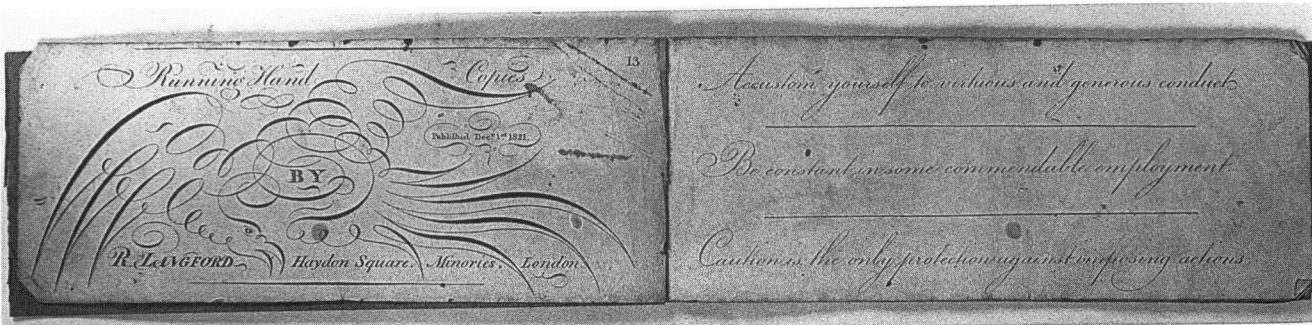

32
Copy book for the Running Hand, a more cursive
version of the Round Hand, also from the Langford
series. Both hands would now be regarded as
'copperplate'.

33
Title page and a page of copies from a late
eighteenth century book of German Text copies.
Written by Samuel Brown, Writing Master, this is
one of an apparently unrecorded series of copy
books published in 1798 under the general title of
The New Modern British Penman.

99

34
The German Text Hand as exemplified by George
Shelley in his *Second Part of Natural Writing*, 1714. The
elaborate flourishing of the initial D is typical of the
way in which writing masters vied with each other to
advertise their skills as penmen.

35
The ancient Court Hand, one of Shelley's copies, which
was easily legible only to the trained eyes of the legal
profession and still used well into the nineteenth
century.

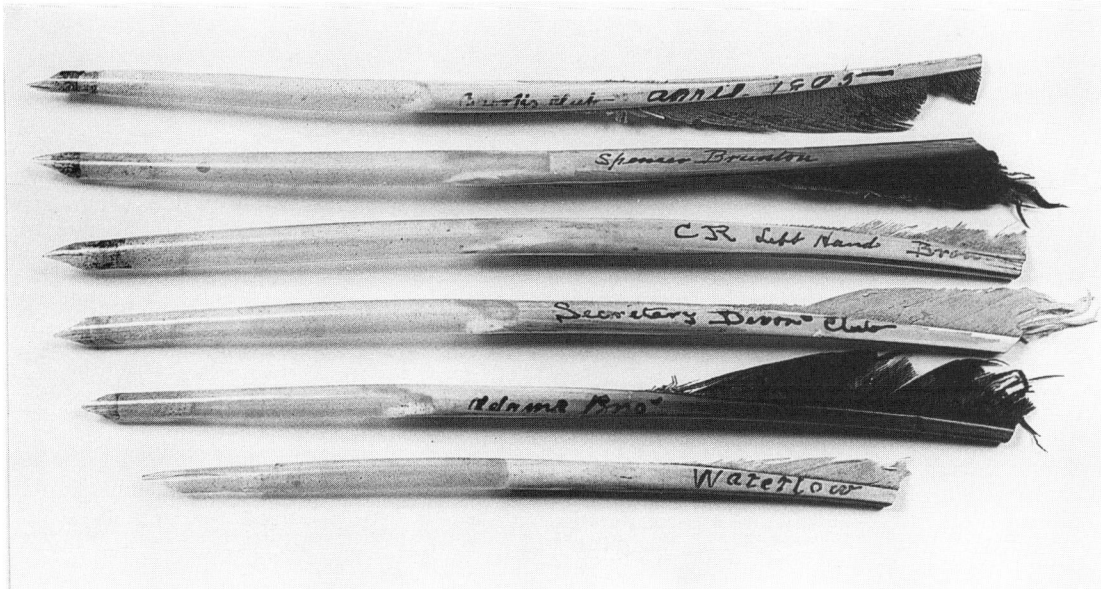

36
Group of 'pattern' quills from a pen-cutting establishment in East London in the early nineteenth century; these are inscribed with the names of the customers to ensure the exact repetition of pens which had given satisfaction
Private Collection

37
Springy undulations in the vellum, making pen control difficult, were held down by the point of the scribe's knife as in this depiction of Saint Jerome from the *Diepenveen Bible* of 1450-3.
Courtesy of the Trustees of the Victoria and Albert Museum, AL 1663-1902; Reid Ms 23. Photograph by courtesy of the Conway Library, Courtauld Institute of Art

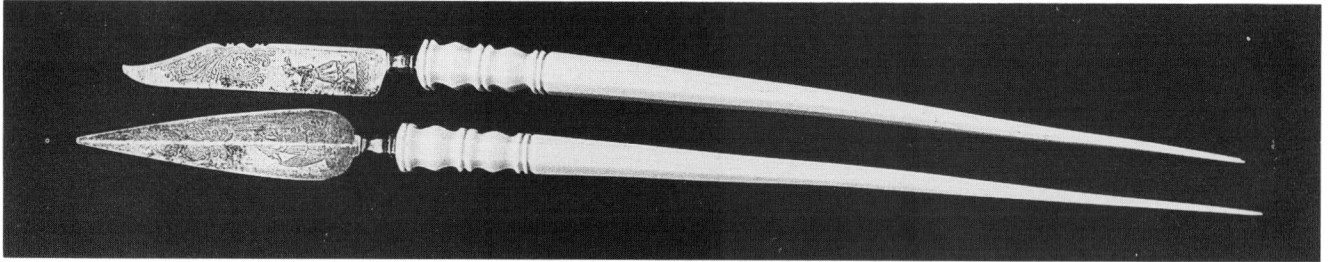

38
Rare South German or Italian ivory-handled scribe's knife and eraser, the art quality gilded steel blades finely etched with classical figures and scrollwork, early seventeenth century. 392 and 385 mm.

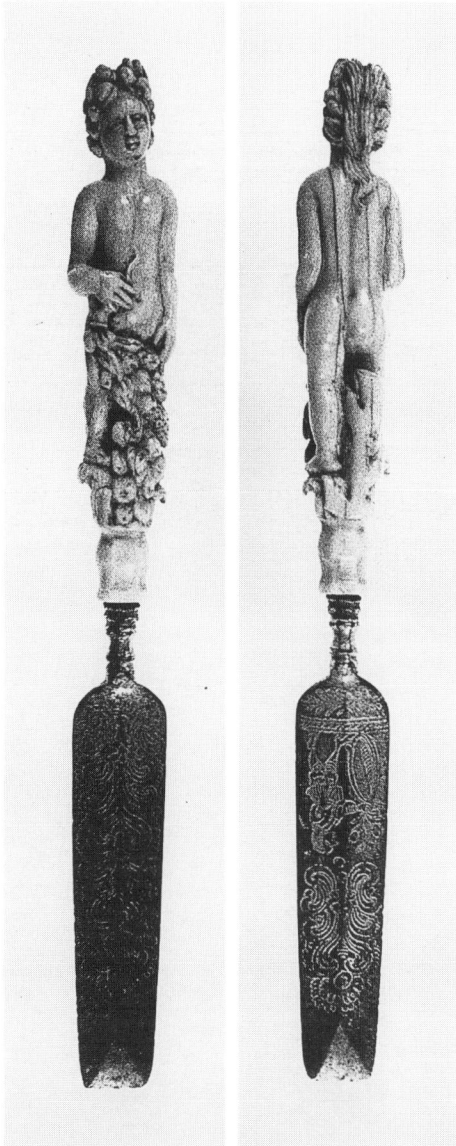

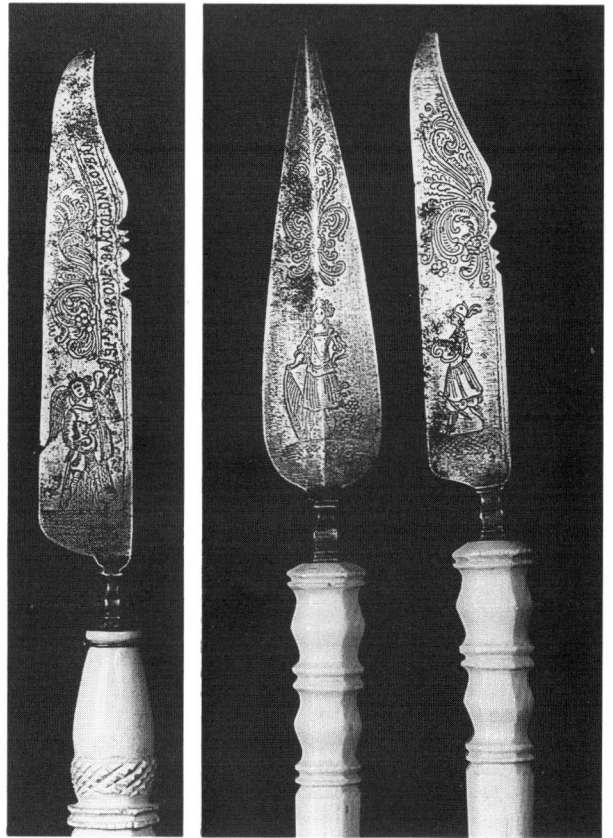

40   38 a

39

39
South German or Italian desk knife with etched and gilt chisel-shaped blade, the ivory handle carved with a female figure holding a cornucopia of fruit symbolic of 'Plenty', early seventeenth century. 184 mm.
Photo: the author, courtesy R. Beresford-Jones, Esq

40
South German or Italian scribe's knife which has a typically long ivory handle, the blade engraved with the name of its original owner *Signore Barone Bartolomeo Braschini*, early seventeenth century. 394 mm.

102

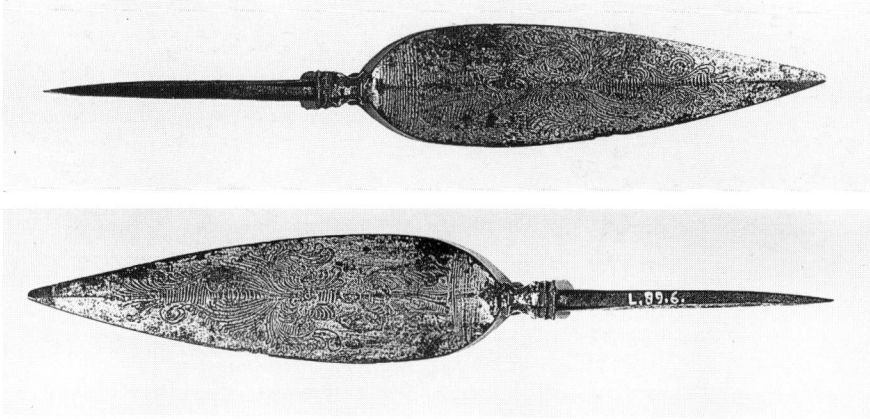

41
Erasing blade, Italian or South German, early
seventeenth century.
Courtesy City of Sheffield Museum

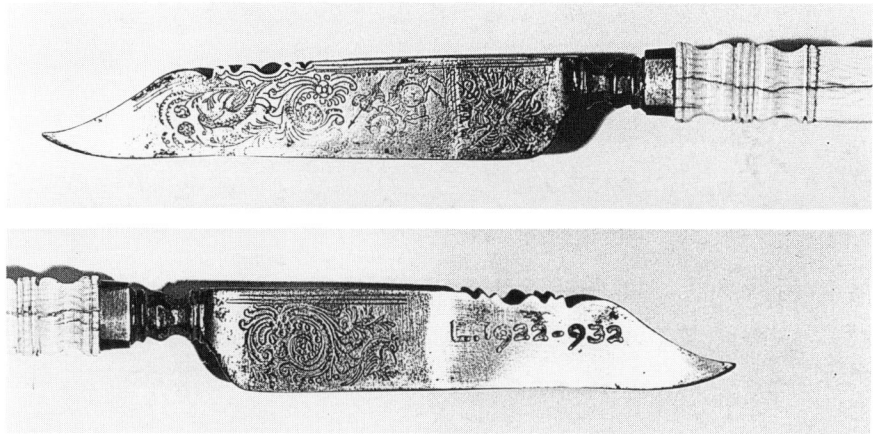

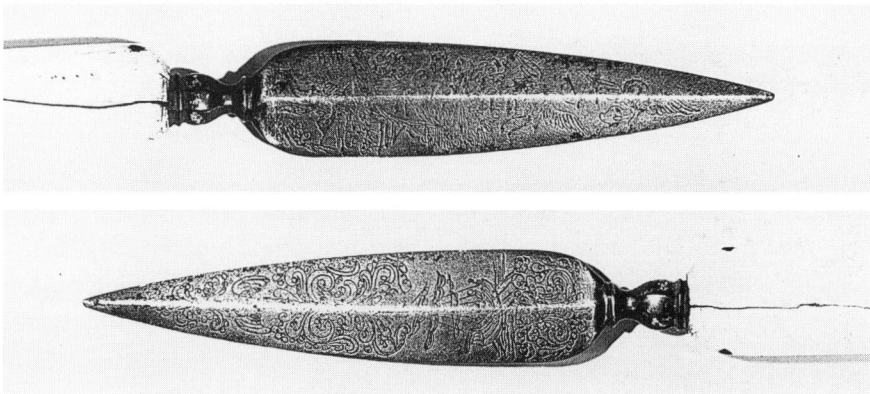

42
Scribe's knife with cutting blade, Italian or South
German, early seventeenth century.
Courtesy City of Sheffield Museum

43
Scribe's knife with erasing blade, Italian or South
German, early seventeenth century.
Courtesy City of Sheffield Museum

44
Two French quill pen-knives, one with a peg, the other
with pointed handle for the same purpose, and an
erasing knife, from *L'Arte d'Écrire*, circa 1780.

46 – opposite page
Portrait of Margaret Tudor, (1489-1541).
Her writing equipment includes a pen-
knife similar to that of Colour plate III(i)b.
*Private Collection. Courtesy of the Trustees
of the Scottish National Portrait Gallery
Photo: Tom Scott*

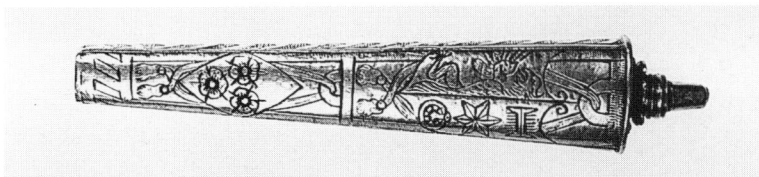

45. Engraved silver handle of a Friesian
pen-knife, with peg, engraved with the
owner's name and dated 1576. 86 mm.

46

46a

47

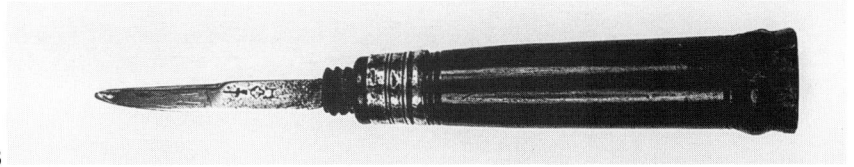

48

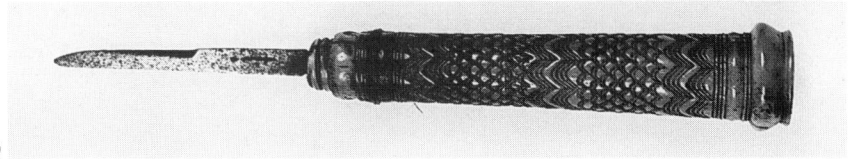

49

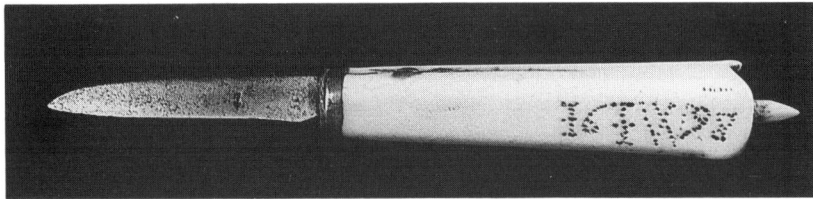

50

47
Excavated pen-knife with peg, the ivory handle stained a deep brown from long burial in the mud of the Thames; cutler's mark of Joseph Surbert, circa 1630. 140 mm.

48
Pen-knife with doubly-chamfered blade (reversible for the pocket) which has a peg attached to the blade, the handle of silver-mounted black horn; cutler's mark a quatrefoil above H, and dagger. Circa 1660. 130 mm overall.

49
Rose engine-turned bone-handled pen-knife of similar form; cutler's mark a 'flaming' sword, a mark used by Nicholas Croucher, a sword cutler working in London at the end of the seventeenth century. 136 mm overall.

50
Pen-knife dated 1698. Ivory handle of lozenge section with peg; straight-edged blade without bolster. Cutler's mark a broad arrow. 125 mm. Compare with that in Plate 51.

opposite page
51
Trompe l'oeil still life by Edward Collier, oils on canvas, circa 1700. Note the lozenge section of the pen-knife, top right.
Courtesy of the Trustees of the Hunterian Art Gallery, (Smiley Collection), University of Glasgow

52
Still life by Edward Collier, circa 1700. The pen-knife, top left, has a most unusual curved peg, simple bolster and straight-edged blade.
Courtesy Christies

51

52

George Shelley S.M.
LONDON

G. Bickham ad vivum delin et sculp.

53
Portrait of George Shelley, from his *Second Part of Natural Writing*, 1714. The knife depicted has a translucent handle, most probably of agate, with peg and straight-edged blade without bolster.

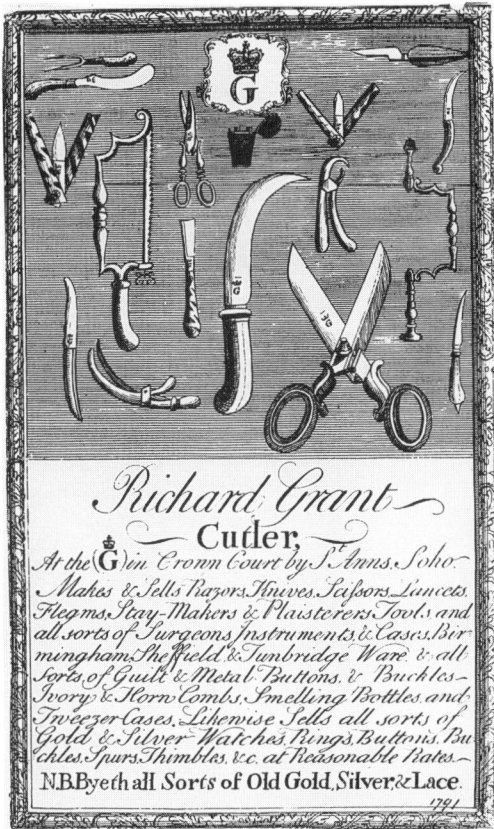

54

55

56

54
Trade Card of Richard Grant, Cutler, London, early eighteenth century.
Courtesy of the Trustees of the British Museum, Heal Collection, 52.51

55
Trade Card of Moses Roberts, Cutler, London, circa 1720.
Courtesy of the Trustees of the British Museum, Heal Collection, 52.88

56
Trade Card of Jacob Gorden, Cutler, London, circa 1740.
Courtesy of the Trustees of the British Museum, Heal Collection, 52.50

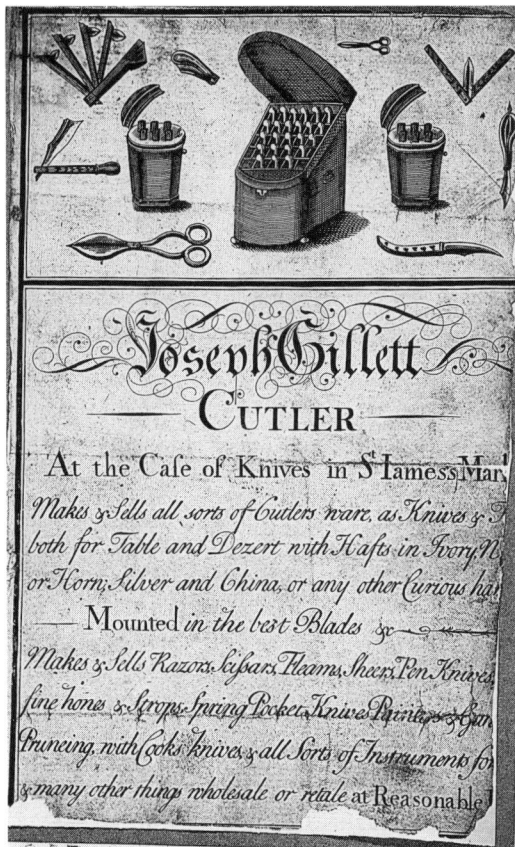

57

58

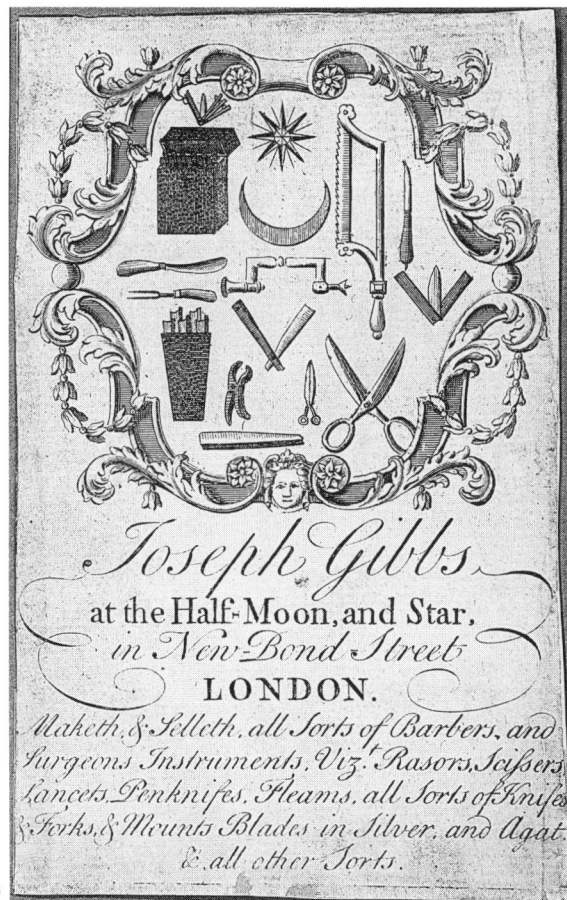

59

57

Trade Card of Joseph Gillett, Cutler, London, circa 1750.
Courtesy of the Trustees of the British Museum, Heal Collection, 52.49

58

Trade Card of Paul Savigny, Cutler, London, first half eighteenth century.
Courtesy of the Trustees of the British Museum, Heal Collection, 52.91

59

Trade Card of Joseph Gibbs, Cutler, London, circa 1759.
Courtesy of the Trustees of the British Museum, Heal Collection, 52.44

60
Trade Card of Henry Patten, Cutler, London, circa 1756.
Courtesy of the Trustees of the British Museum, Heal Collection, 52.77

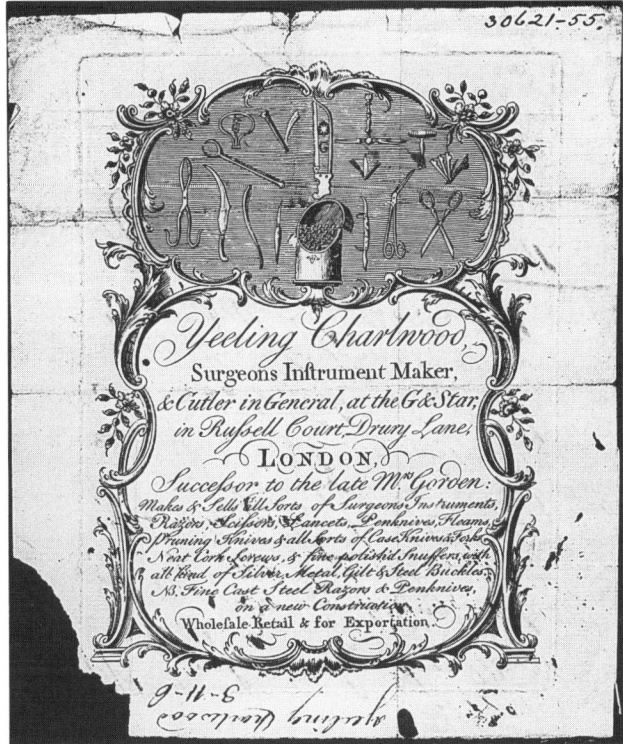

61
Trade Card of Yeeling Charlwood, Cutler, London, circa 1775.
Courtesy of the Trustees of the British Museum, Heal Collection, 52.27

62
Pen-knife, the round handle of agate with silver ferrule and peg; bolstered blade, English, second quarter eighteenth century. 142 mm.

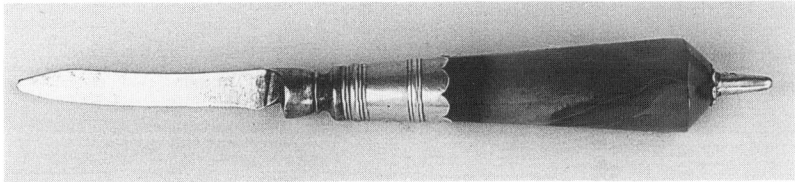

63
Pen-knife with multi-faceted jasper handle, silver-gilt ferrule and peg; bolstered blade with indistinct cutler's mark; of small size, probably for a lady or child. English, second quarter eighteenth century. 130 mm.

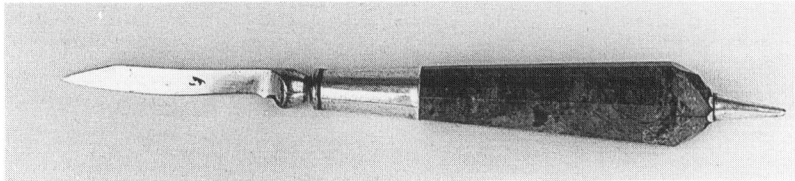

64
Pen-knife, the round handle of moss-agate with silver-gilt ferrule, domed cap and peg, the blade stamped GRAY. Mid-eighteenth century. 146 mm. Compare with Plate 25.

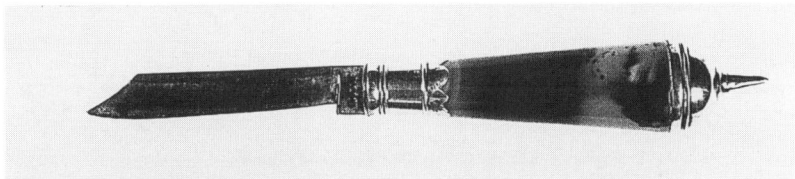

65
Pen-knife with octagonal agate handle, silver ferrule and peg; cutler's mark EVANS under crown. Second half eighteenth century, the handle possibly earlier. 148 mm.

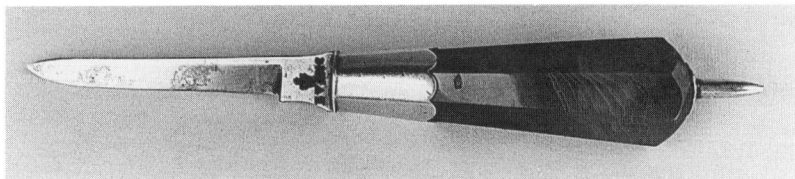

111

66
Pen-knife with faceted ivory handle and peg, the silver ferrule scratch-engraved with leaves. Cutler's mark PARIS, Sheffield, early eighteenth century. 170 mm. (The mark PARIS was entered by John Brough in 1700, reserved to John Justice in 1705-6 and was used by several other cutlers. Paris Justice is listed in the Sheffield Directory of 1787).

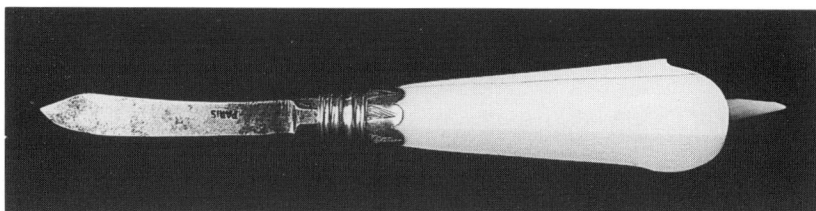

67
Rebladed pen-knife with fluted ivory handle of a type used on eating knives in the early eighteenth century. (See Hayward, J. F., *English Cutlery*, V & A M, 1957, Plate XVII [c]).
The replacement blade is marked RAVEN, the mark of a Sheffield cutler, Joshua Morton, entered in 1760. The mark is not listed in the 1774 Sheffield Directory. 160 mm.

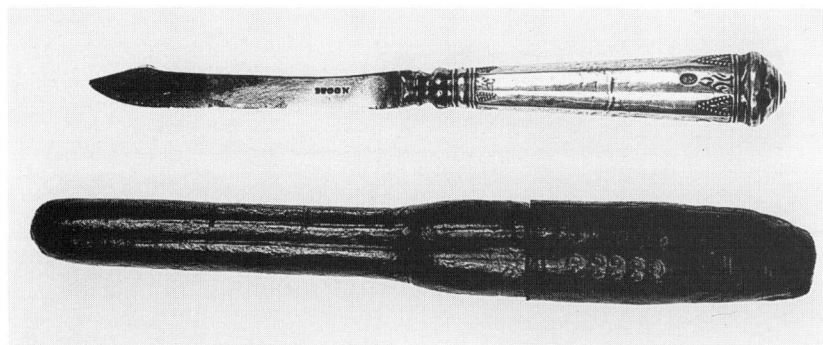

68
Pen-knife, the composition-filled octagonal-faceted silver handle marked I.S in an oval, the blade with the cutler's mark SPOON of John Spooner, Sheffield, circa 1730. 163 mm; in paper and boiled leather case. 180 mm.

69
Pen-knife, the faceted handle of foiled tortoiseshell and ivory with screw-on ivory terminal and peg, the unmarked blade with simple bolster, Sheffield, circa 1700. 140 mm (For an eating knife with similar handle, see Hayward, J. F., *English Cutlery*, V & A M, 1957, Plate XVI [c]).

70. Group of Sheffield-made die-stamped silver-handled pen-knives, second quarter eighteenth century:
a
Small knife with steel peg, possibly for a child. 119 mm.
b
Handle marked I.S in an oval, the scimitar-shaped blade with cutler's mark of John Spooner. 132 mm.
c
Unmarked handle, the blade with cutler's mark Z under a heart, probably of Cotton Watkin. 144 mm.
d
The handle marked I.S above a six-pointed star in a heart, the blade marked SPOON for John Spooner. 140 mm.

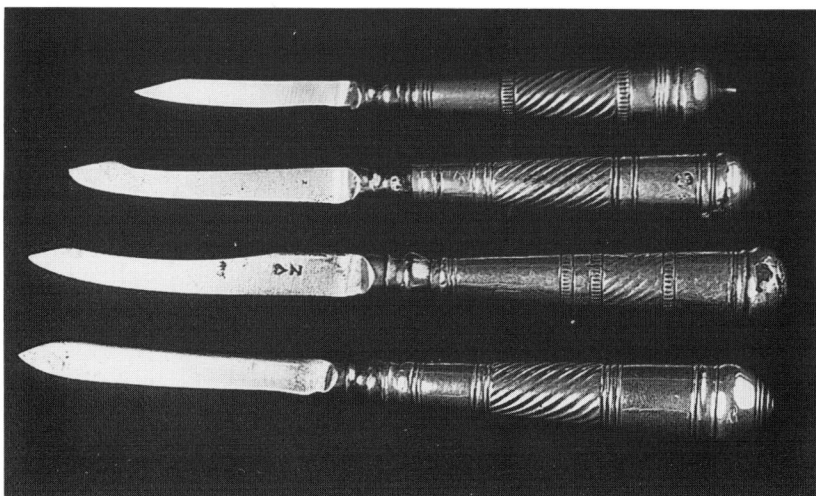

112

71
Sheffield-made pen-knife, the handle of
foiled tortoiseshell inlaid with silver
piqué fronds, with silver ferrule and cap,
second quarter eighteenth century.
115 mm.

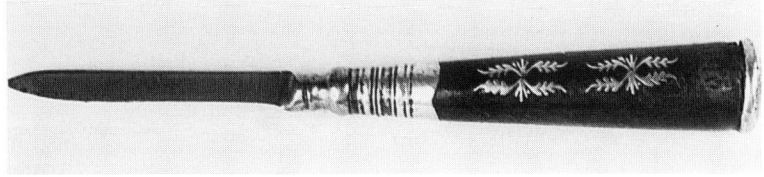

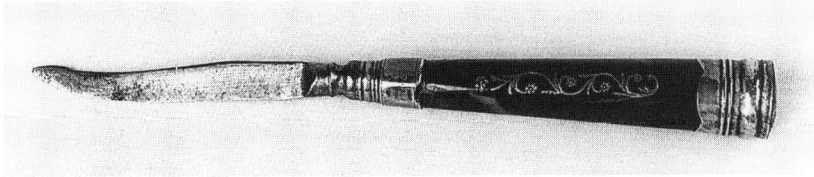

72
Similar knife with leaf scroll piqué
decoration and similarly bolstered blade
of scimitar form. 135 mm.

73
Brass-handled pen-knife with 'wriggled'
decoration, early eighteenth century.
148 mm.

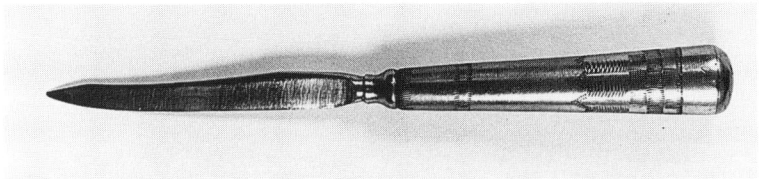

74
Pen-knife with composition-filled die-
stamped Sheffield Plate handle in the neo-
classical style, by English, Royal
Colonade, Brighton, late eighteenth
century. 127 mm.

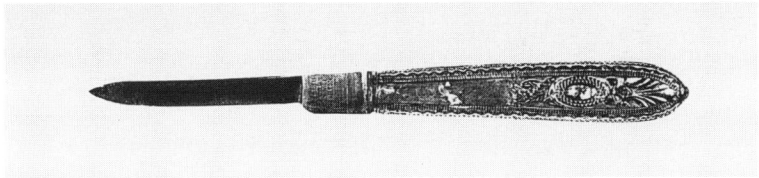

75
French scrivener's knife in black horn with
ivory collars, having four interchangeable
blades, the handle containing a steel
parchment-pricker/bodkin. 157 mm,
overall.

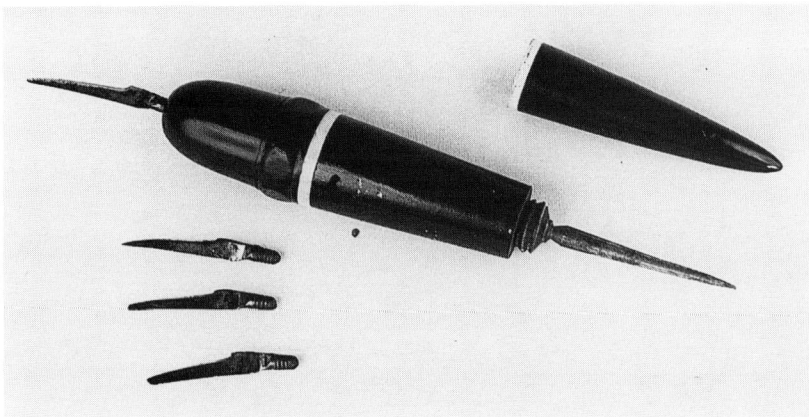

75a

113

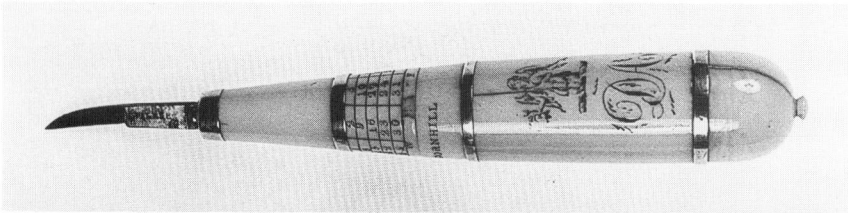

76
Ivory-handled pen-knife with
nickel mounts, by John Wilkes, 57
Cornhill, London, circa 1800. The
handle, which incorporates a
perpetual calendar, unscrews to
reveal spare blades, a small file
and tweezers with ear-pick (used
to provide the wherewithal to
wax thread); there is also a wafer
compartment with chequered
wafer-seal and a round peg which
serves also as a burnisher.
120 mm, overall.

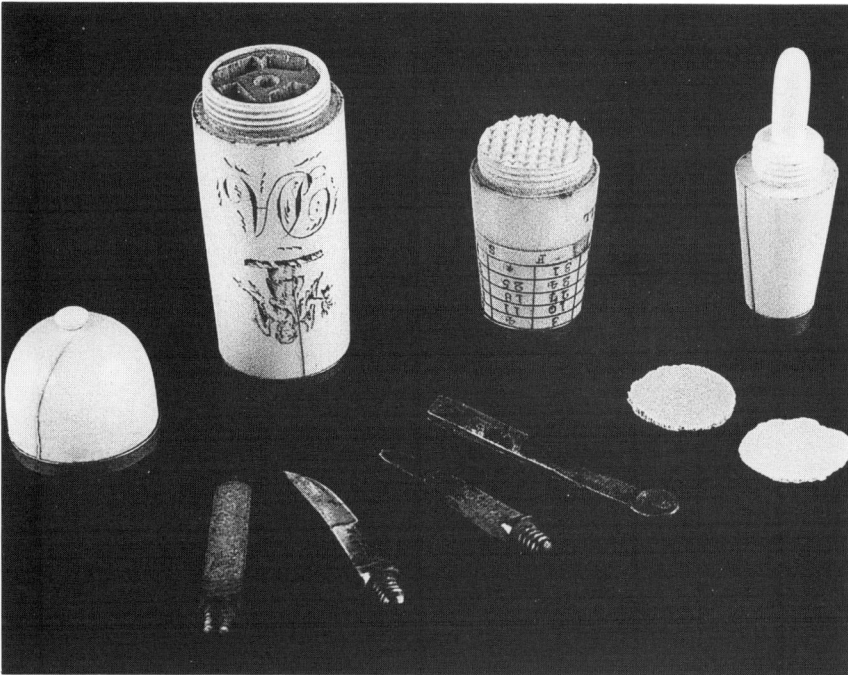

76a

77
Pen-knife by John Wilkes, with
interchangeable pen-nibber, circa 1800.
*Photo: the author, courtesy of the Museum of
Science and Industry, Birmingham, Charles
Thomas Collection*

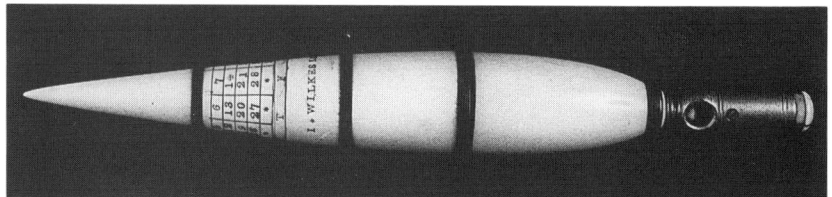

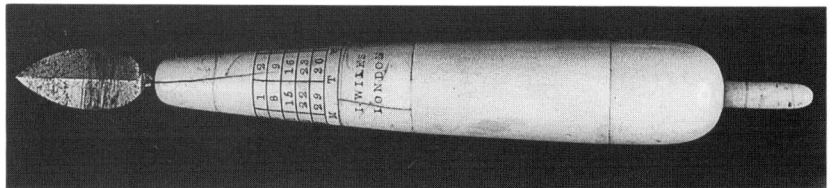

78
Erasing knife by John Wilkes, circa 1800.
*Photo: the author, courtesy of the Museum of
Science and Industry, Birmingham, Charles
Thomas Collection*

79
Folding pen-knife with roebuck
antler scales, having five
interchangeable blades; cutler's
mark REES, early nineteenth
century. 139 mm, open.

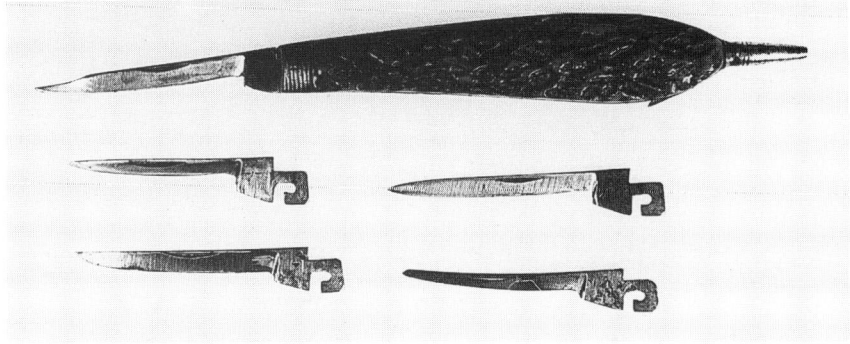

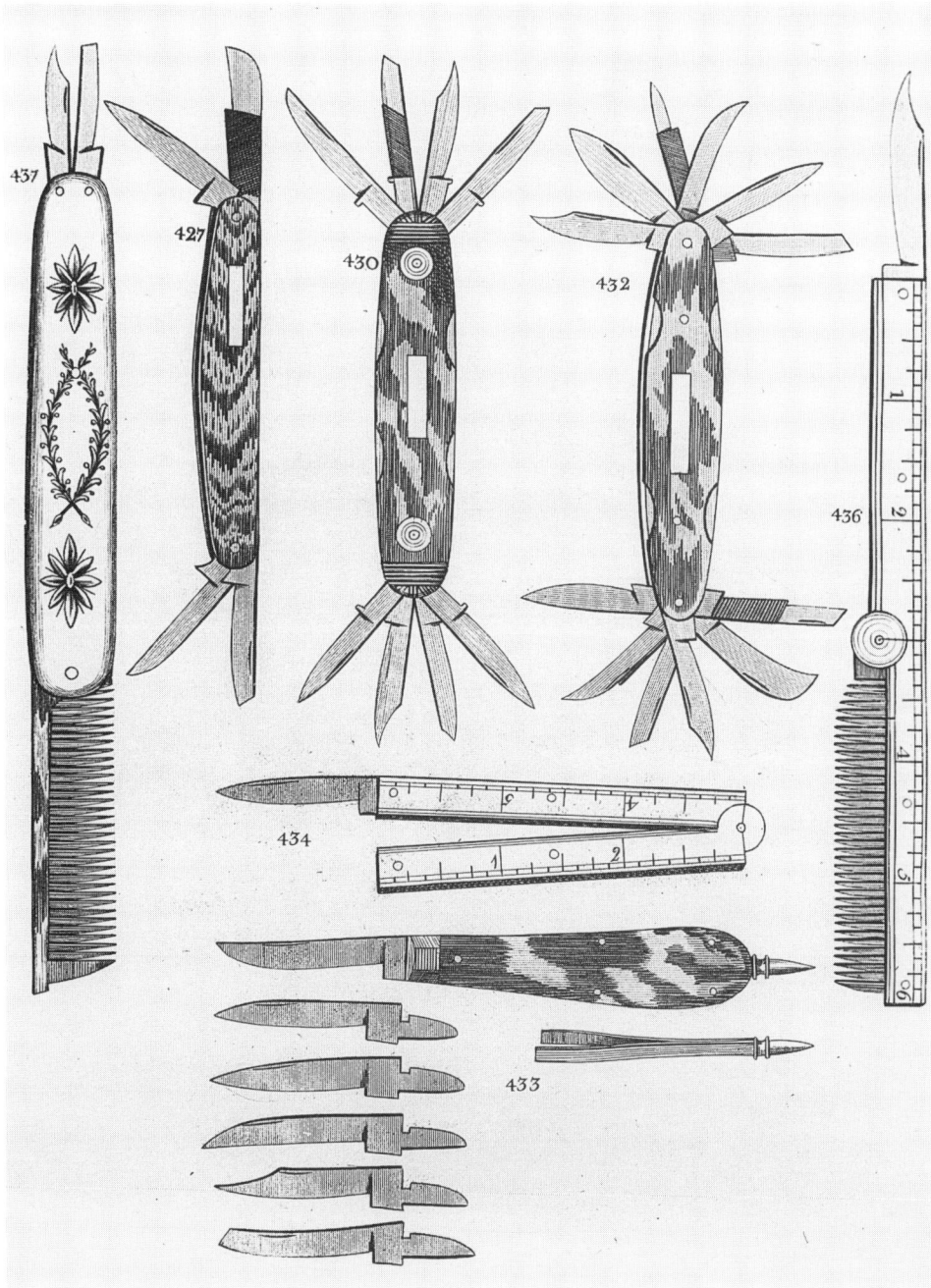

80
Engraved plate from Joseph
Smith's *Key to Sheffield
Manufactures*, circa 1816. Compare
No 433 with previous plate.
Courtesy Sheffield City Libraries

115

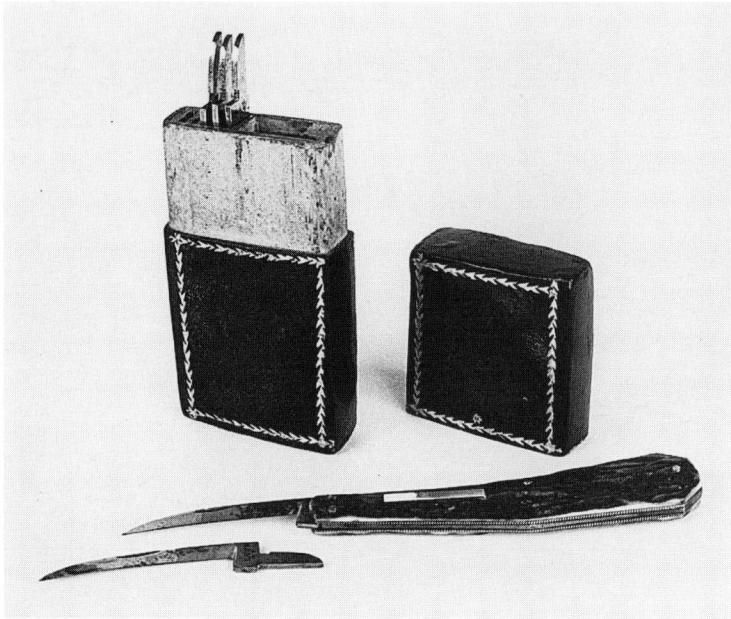

81
Pen-knife with roebuck antler handle scales, having five interchangeable blades marked LUND for Thomas Lund, 57 Cornhill, London, successor to John Wilkes; in gold-tooled leather-covered wooden case, early nineteenth century. 86 mm.

82
Another solution to the need for multi-bladed pen-knives, by Joseph Rodgers, Sheffield, circa 1825. Each blade is marked with the crowned cypher GR, the handle a complete roebuck antler. 210 mm, overall.

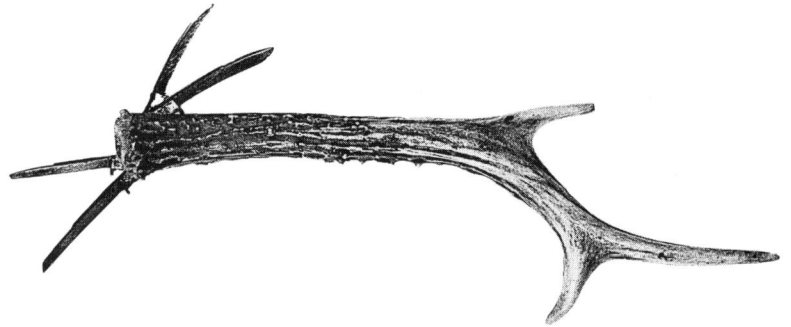

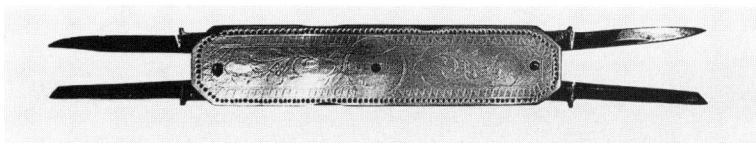

83
Late Georgian four-bladed folding pen-knife with engraved mother-of-pearl scales, the blades marked LONDON, circa 1825. 142 mm, overall.

84
French ebony-handled pen-knife with two sliding blades, mid-nineteenth century. 143 mm, open.

85
French folding pen-knife with ivory scales and steel peg, the blade having a cutler's mark in the form of an earlier pen-knife, early nineteenth century. 145 mm, open.

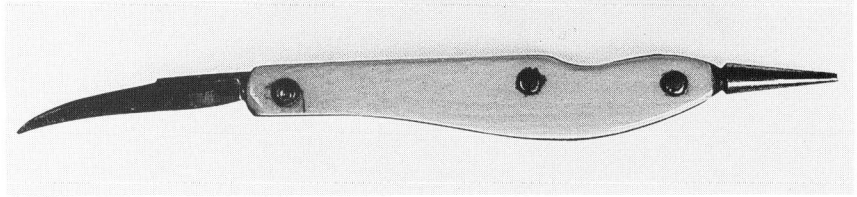

86
Folding pen-knife with tortoiseshell scales and peg, the pen blade with mark of Rodgers, Sheffield, a second blade spring-loaded for nibbing the pen, which is inserted through a hole in the handle scale, early nineteenth century. 147 mm, open.

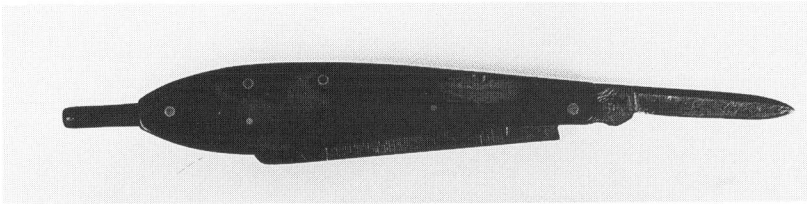

87
Selection of folding pen-knives illustrated in Smith's *Key to Sheffield Manufactures*, circa 1816. *Courtesy Sheffield City Libraries*

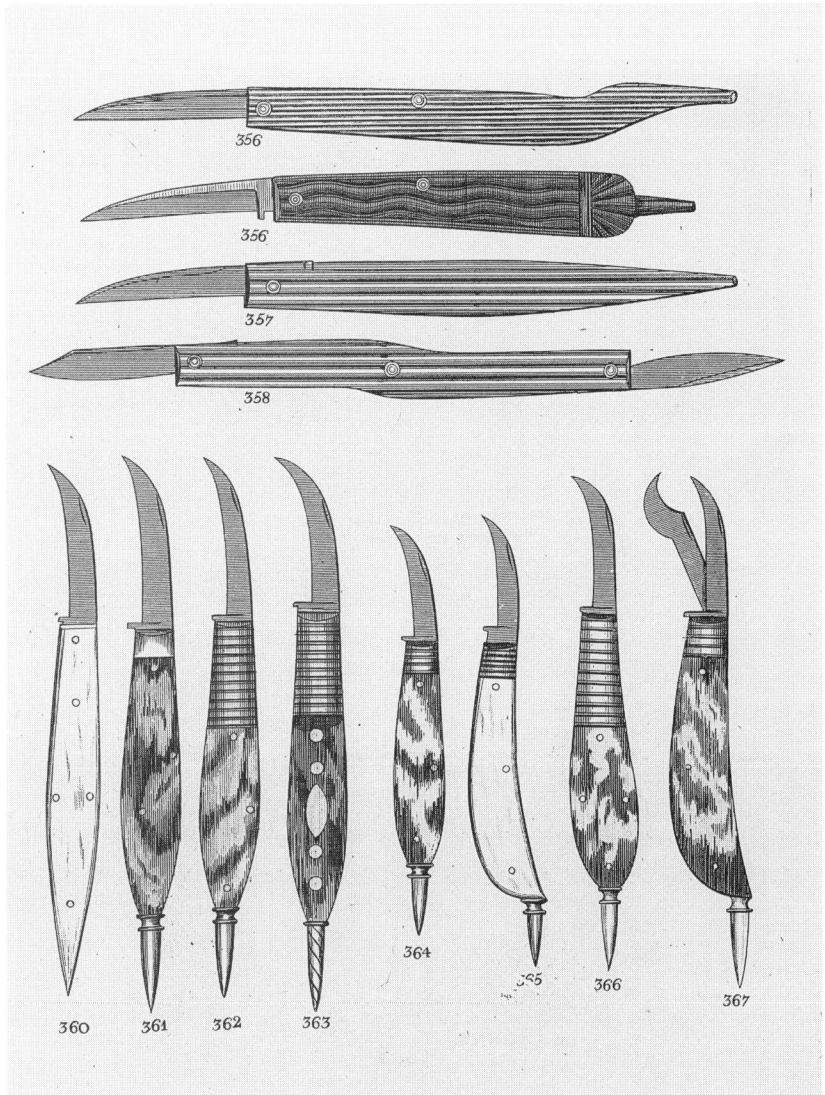

117

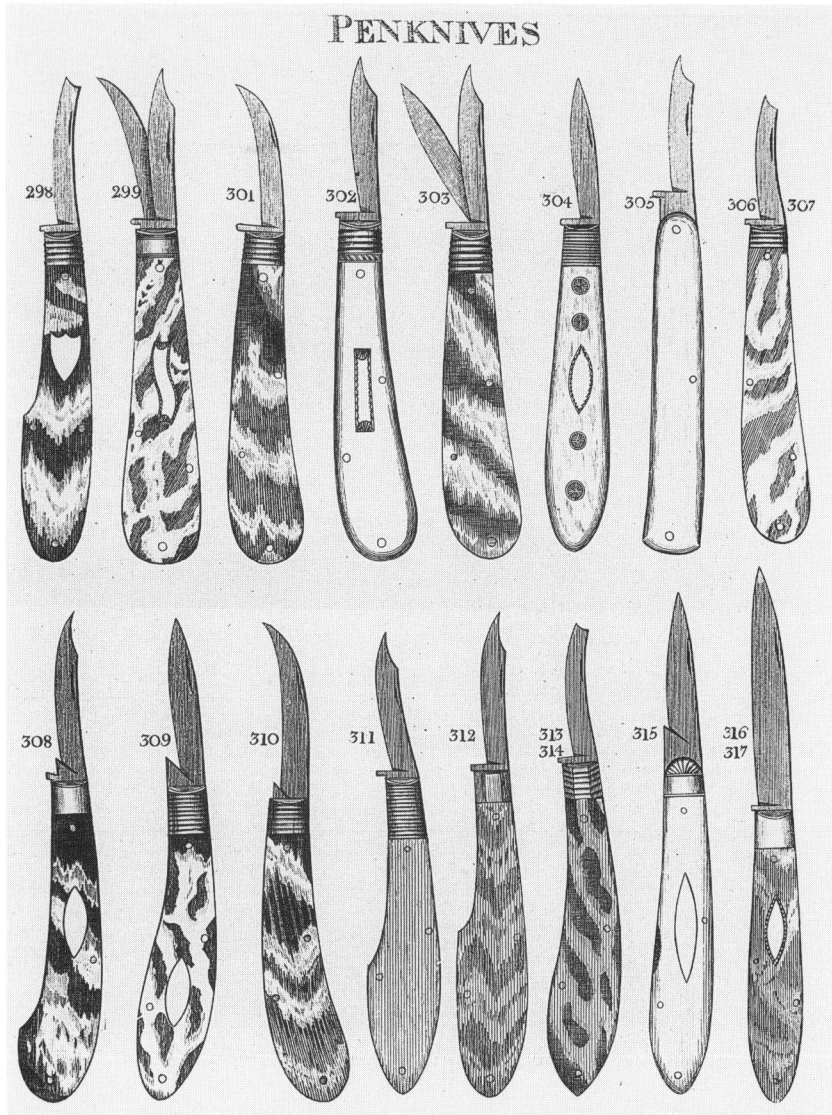

PENKNIVES

89
Folding pen-knife with hollow-pointed
scimitar blade and tortoiseshell scales,
circa 1815. 109 mm, open. Compare with
previous plate, number 308.

88
Further folding pen-knives
illustrated in Smith's *Key to
Sheffield Manufactures*, circa 1816.
Courtesy Sheffield City Libraries

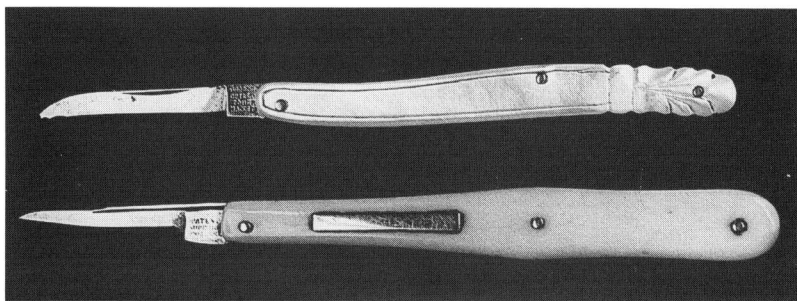

90
Folding pen-knives:
a
Early Victorian knife with carved mother-
of-pearl scales, by Joseph Rodgers, Cutlers
to Her Majesty. 110 mm, open.
b
Late Georgian example with ivory scales
and nickel escutcheon, circa 1825. 117 mm,
open.

91. George IV silver and mother-
of-pearl pen-knife with sliding
pencil holder, the blade marked
with crowned cypher GR and
maker's mark CARRS, circa 1825.
125 mm, overall.
Courtesy Philip Poole, Esq

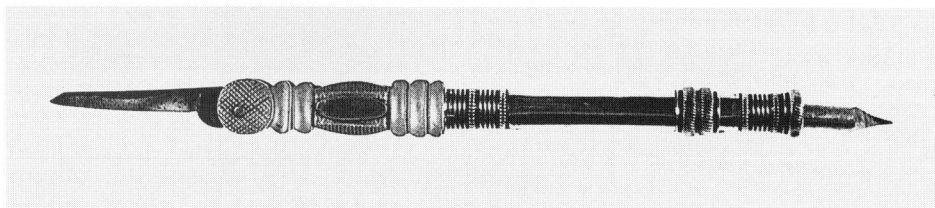

92
Amusing ivory-handled two-bladed folding pen-knife in the form of a human leg, its toe in the grip of the beak of a goose apparently bent on retribution for the plucking of its quills; cutler's mark of I. Stringer, Sheffield, late eighteenth century. 128 mm, open.

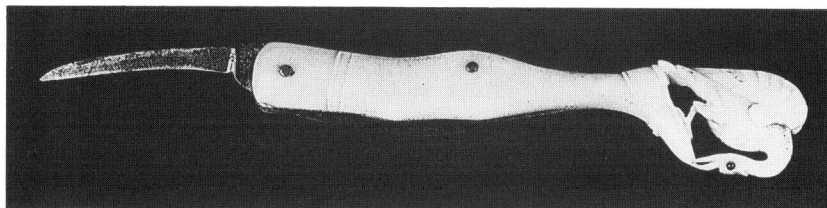

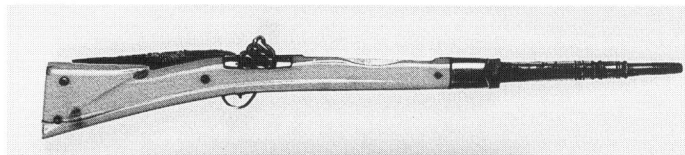

93
Ivory novelty pen-knife in the form of a percussion musket, its 'bayonet' a propelling pencil, with single folding blade. 90 mm, closed. Such knife/pencils are found dated as early as 1842 and were still popular nearly thirty years later when Joseph Rodgers advertised them, in both ivory and ebony, in his general cutlery catalogue.

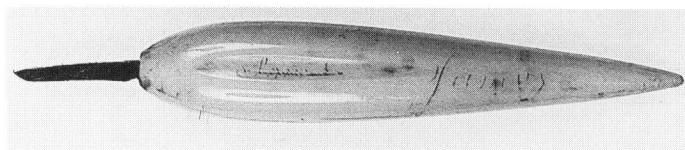

94
Ivory-handled pen-knife, the pointed handle serving as a peg, scratch-engraved with the name of its owner, 'James', late eighteenth century. 133 mm. Compare with that in Plate 44, right.

95
Late eighteenth century pen-knife with fluted ivory handle; blade unmarked, probably Sheffield. 142 mm.

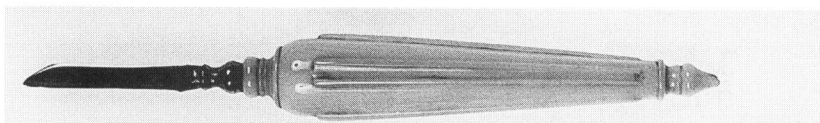

96
Spirally-fluted slab-sided knife with bone handle, the blade marked with an indistinct cypher above a heart. Late eighteenth century. 150 mm.

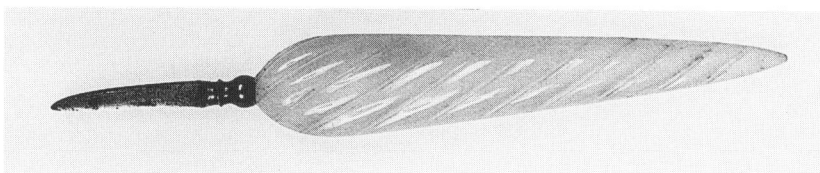

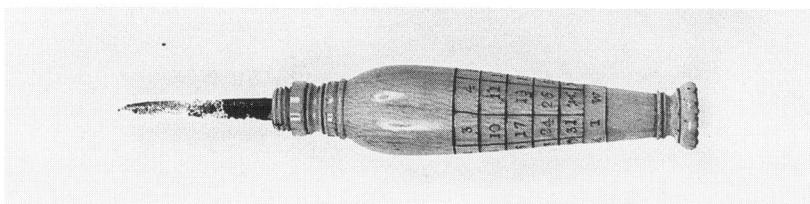

97
Pen-knife with turned ivory handle, perpetual calendar and chequered wafer seal, the blade reversible into the handle for the pocket, circa 1800. 105 mm.

98
Pen-knife with roebuck antler handle, silver mounts and a peg, circa 1800. 129 mm.

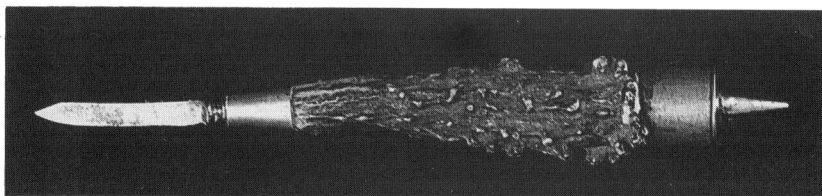

99
Black pressed-horn pen-knife with fluted and shell decoration, having an ivory peg, unmarked, early nineteenth century. 141 mm.

119

100
Pen-knife, the handle a silver-mounted tiger's tooth which would also serve as a burnisher, the blade etched MOSELEY & SIMPSON, COVENT G(ARDEN) ROW, LONDON, circa 1875. 165 mm.

101
All-steel pen-knife, the handle finely etched with birds in foliate scrollwork, the blade marked EVANS, OLD CHANGE, LONDON, circa 1830s. 135 mm. This style of knife was popular in France and is often found in cased desk sets with pen, seal and paperknife.

102
English-made pen-knife in the French style, with carved mother-of-pearl handle, mid-nineteenth century. 163 mm.

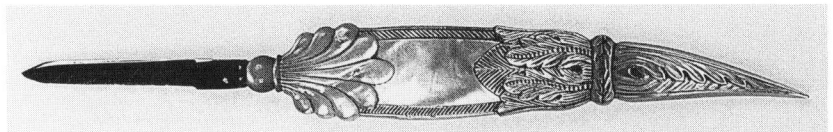

103
Pen-knife with slab-sided ivory handle and peg, the blade marked UNDERWOOD, 56 HAYMARKET, mid-nineteenth century. 145 mm.

104
Pen-knife made from a bone of a racehorse, silver-mounted, hallmarked Birmingham, 1894, maker S. W. Smith, and engraved 'Rosebery, 1872-1894'. 198 mm.

105
Four pen-knives of the type mainly used by professional clerks and other serious writers:
a   With turned and fluted ivory handle engraved with a monogram under a coronet, the blade marked WALKER & HALL, SHEFFIELD, circa 1880. 168 mm.
b   With pointed bone handle, the shoulders carved with palmettes, early nineteenth century. 151 mm.
c   Of slightly rounded slab-sided form in ivory, the blade marked JOSEPH MAPPIN BROTHERS, SHEFFIELD, second half nineteenth century. 165 mm.
d   Of plain slab-sided form in ivory, with peg, as issued to government departments, the rounded blade marked SO under a crown for the Stationery Office, with maker's mark of HUNTER & SON, SHEFFIELD, second half nineteenth century. 168 mm.

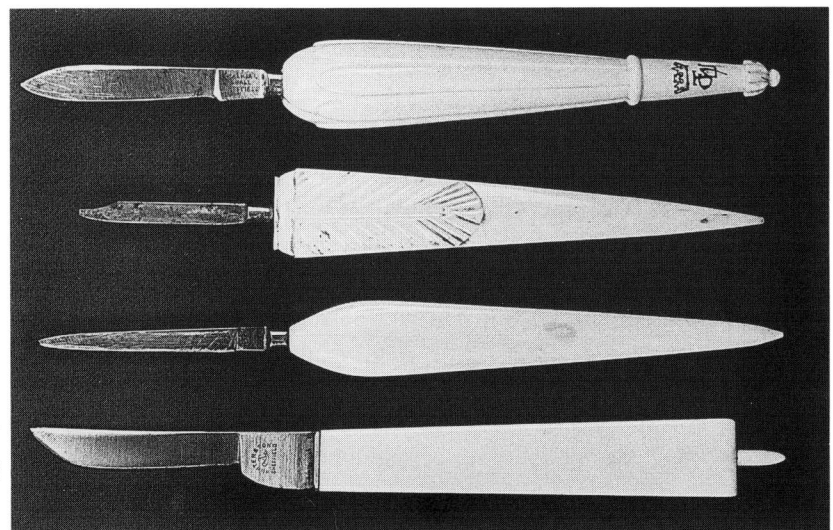

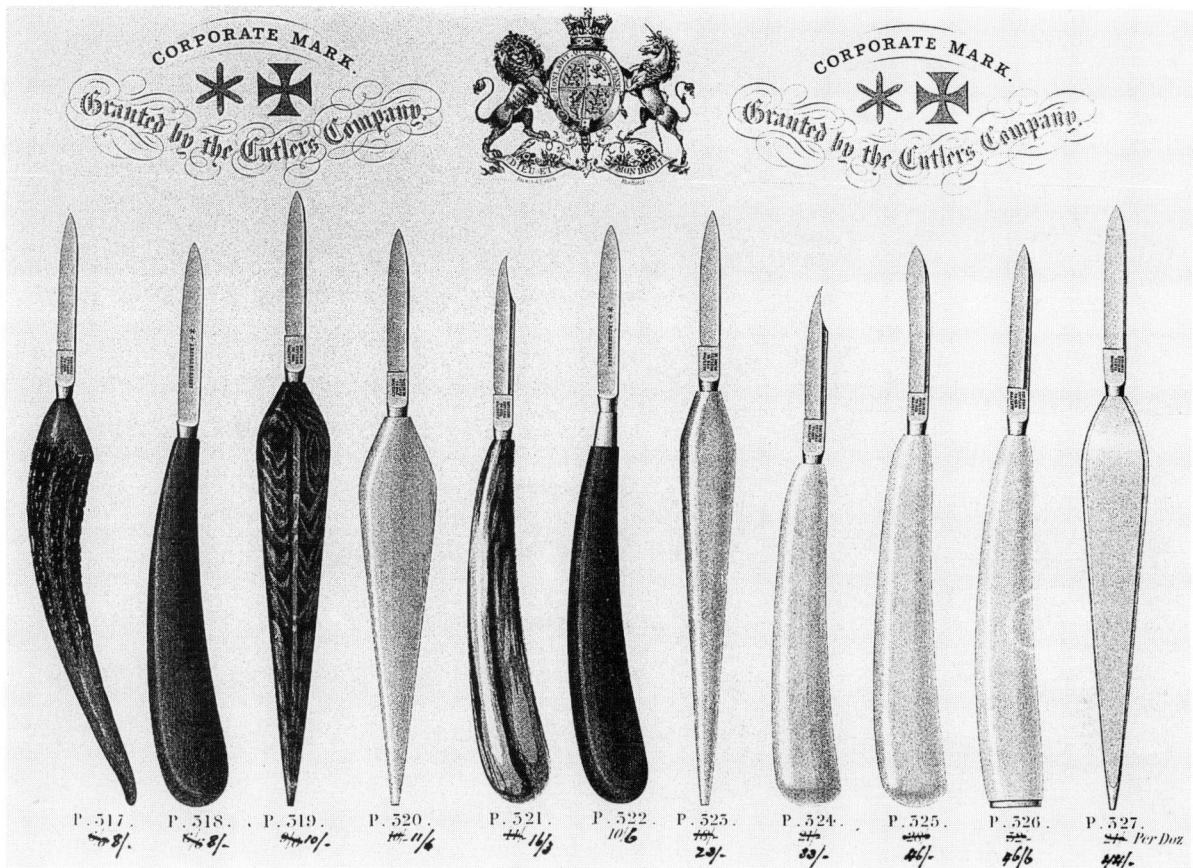

106
Page from Joseph Rodger's cutlery catalogue of the 1860s, with revised prices 1870, showing typical working scribes' pen-knives. Ebony, ivory and cocoa-wood were the most common handle materials; horn and staghorn were also used.
Photo: the author, courtesy Ralph Parr, Esq

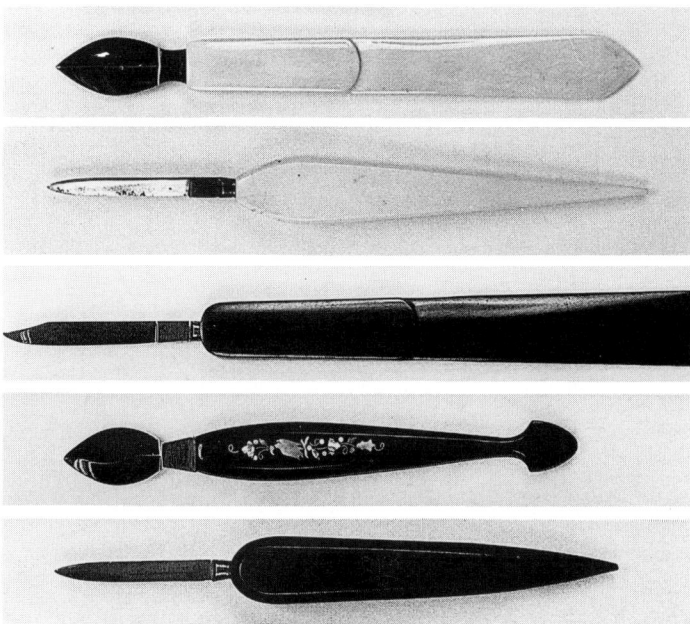

Group of pen-knives and erasers by one of the most prolific makers, Joseph Rodgers of Sheffield:

107 Erasing knife with ivory handle in the form of a folder, the blade marked RODGERS, CUTLERS TO HIS MAJESTY, SHEFFIELD, ENGLAND, with trade marks, circa 1905. 162 mm. Complete with slip-on case impressed JOSEPH RODGERS & SONS SHEFFIELD.

108 Pen-knife with ivory slab-sided pointed handle, the blade marked with Rodgers's trade marks and CUTLERS TO HER MAJESTY, mid-nineteenth century. 162 mm. In paper case impressed JOSEPH RODGERS & SONS.

109 Pen-knife with rosewood handle of folder design, the blade marked J. RODGERS & SONS, 6 NORFOLK ST., SHEFFIELD, mid-nineteenth century. 206 mm.

110 Erasing knife of black thermoplastic with abalone shell and silver piqué work, the end shaped for burnishing, the blade marked RODGERS CUTLERS TO HER MAJESTY, mid-nineteenth century. 143 mm.

111 Pen-knife with slab-sided cocoa-wood handle impressed with crowned cypher VR under crown, the blade marked J. RODGERS & SONS, mid-nineteenth century. 155 mm. In similarly marked paper case.

121

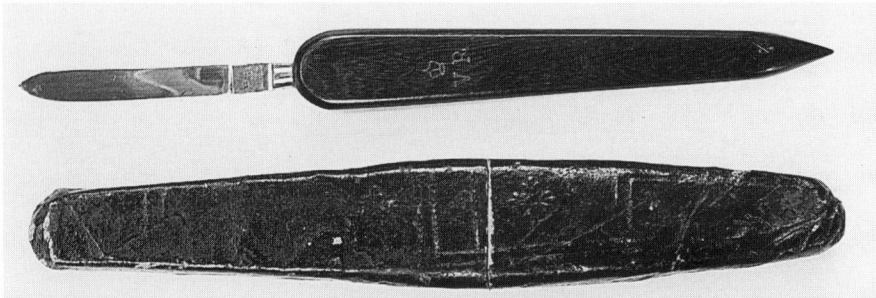

112
Pen-knife with cocoa-wood
handle, the blade marked XL
ALL, PARKIN & MARSHALL,
SHEFFIELD, second half
nineteenth century. 185 mm. With
paper case.

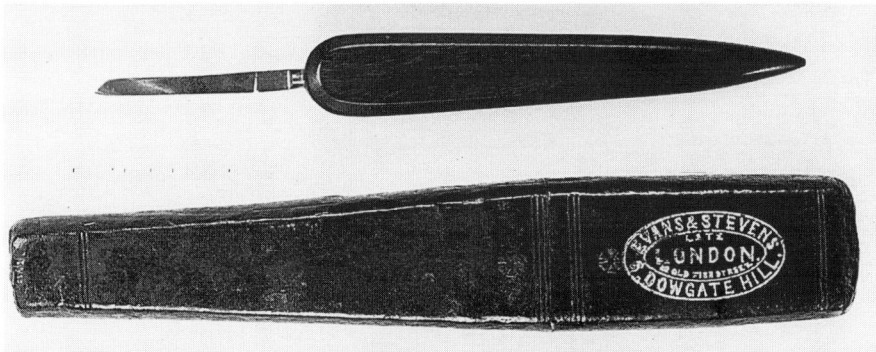

113
Pen-knife with cocoa-wood
handle of pointed slab-sided
form, the blade marked EVANS
AND CO, EXCHANGE,
LONDON. 160 mm. In paper case
gold-tooled EVANS & STEVENS,
6 DOWGATE HILL, LATE 12
OLD FISH STREET, LONDON,
mid-nineteenth century.

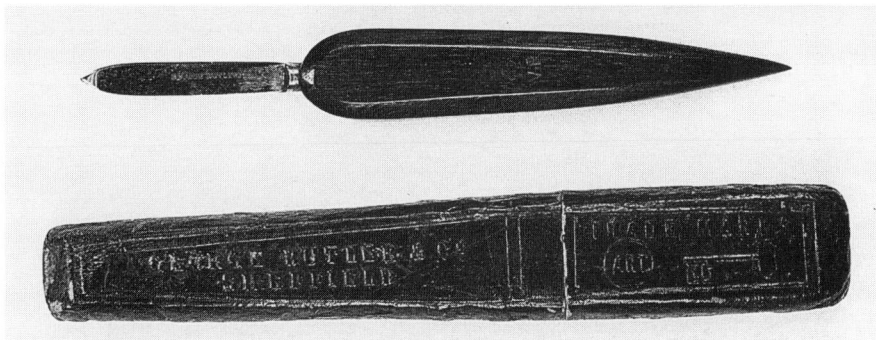

114
Pen-knife, the cocoa-wood handle
of slab-sided form impressed with
crowned cypher VR, the blade
marked GEORGE BUTLER, mid-
nineteenth century. 160 mm. In
paper case impressed GEORGE
BUTLER & CO, SHEFFIELD, with
trade marks.

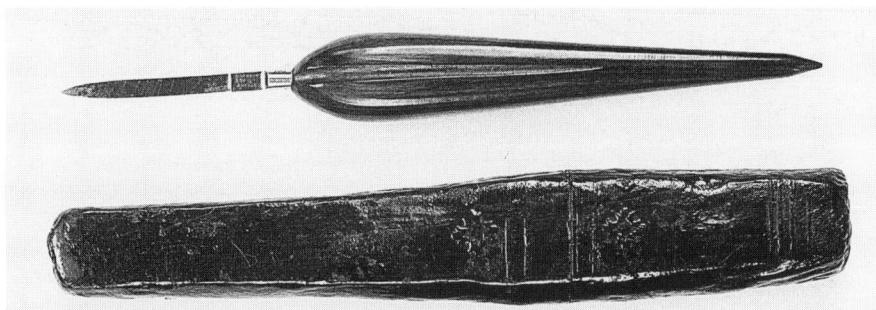

115
Pen-knife with rosewood handle,
the blade marked HARRISON
BROTHERS AND HOWSON,
CUTLERS TO HER MAJESTY,
mid-nineteenth century. 170 mm.
In paper case.

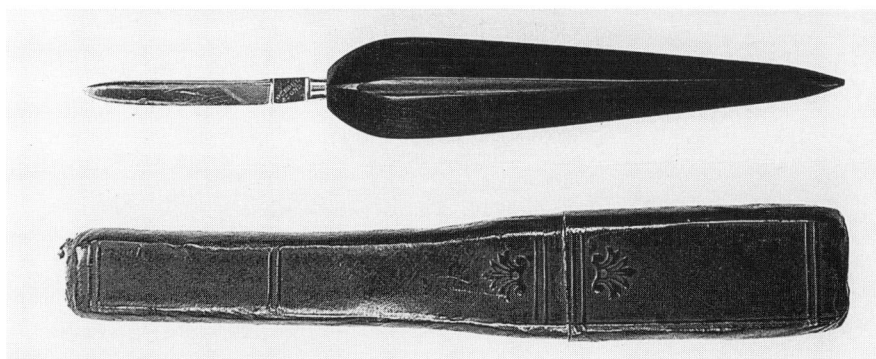

116
Pen-knife with ebony handle of
unusual lozenge section, the
blade marked OSBORNE &
SONS, mid-nineteenth century.
170 mm. In paper case.

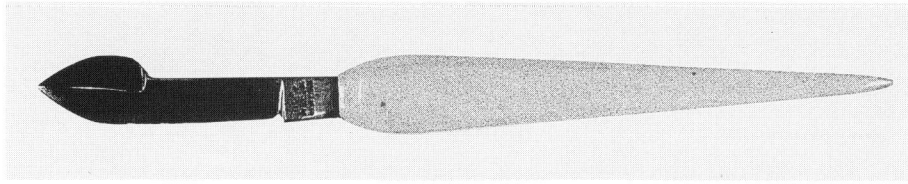

117
Bone-handled desk-knife with blade designed for quill-cutting and erasing, marked MORDAN & CO SHEFFIELD, late nineteenth century. 165 mm.

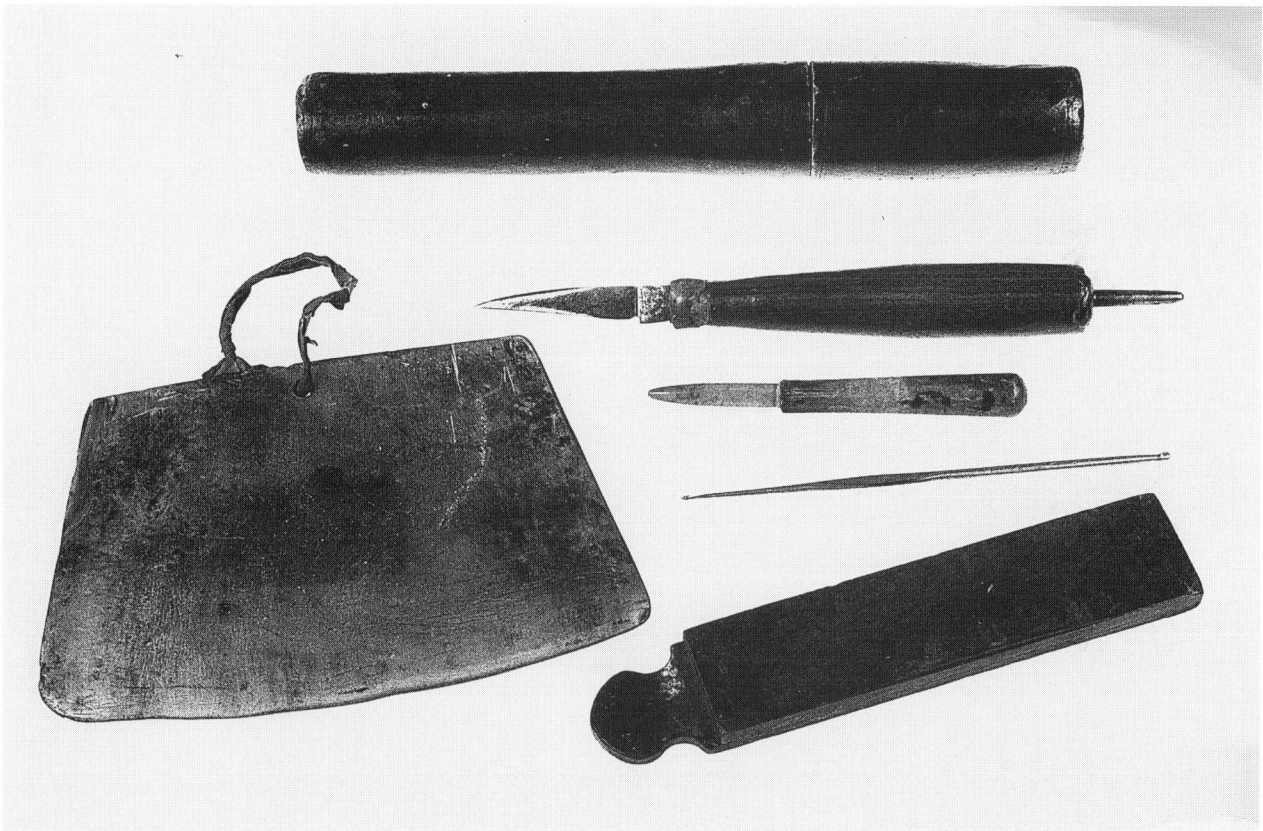

118
Quill pen-knife and other tools belonging to William Southgate, a professional pen-cutter who worked in the late nineteenth and early twentieth centuries. The knife has a wooden handle with brass ferrule, the blade marked JOHN SELLERS AND SONS, SHEFFIELD. 184 mm. With cylindrical paper case. The other items are an Arkansas whetstone, a wooden-handled bone peg which was inserted into the cut pen for the final nibbing of the points and a horn stomach shield on which the nibs of the finished pens were gently tapped to align them for tying into bundles. The crochet hook would be used to remove the internal membrane from the quill barrel.

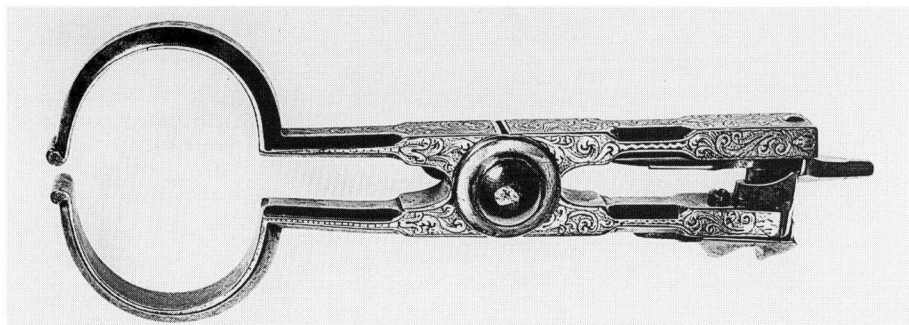

119
Two views of a very rare pair of
steel quill-cutters, finely engraved
with strapwork, birds and foliage.
One arm of the jaws incorporates
a folding blade, the other a 'peg'.
French, first half seventeenth
century. 142 mm.

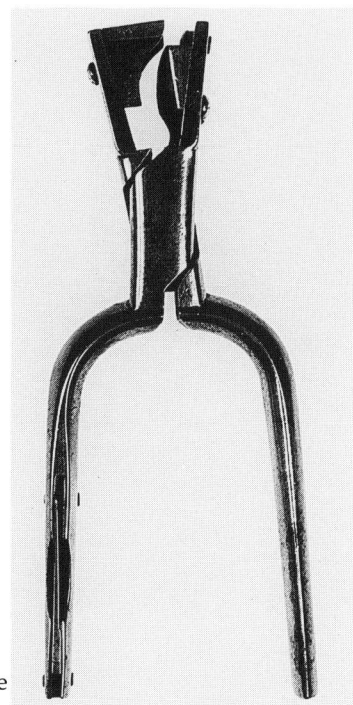

120
Late Georgian pair of English
quill-cutting 'pliers'; in this case
the folding pen-blade is in one
of the handles. Circa 1800.
123 mm.

121
Great rarity dating from the end
of the seventeenth century; the
blades of this brass quill-cutter
are screwed down on to the quill
scoop, first cut using the folding
pen blade. Continental, probably
German. 75 mm.
*Courtesy of the Trustees of the
British Museum, 1910, 5.11-3*

122
Gilt-brass quill-cutter with
folding pen-blade; the screw key
is stamped twice with the maker's
mark. Continental, early
eighteenth century.
*Courtesy of the Trustees of the
Victoria and Albert Museum, M.418,
1936*

123
Ivory and gilt-brass quill-cutter
with folding pen-blade,
Continental, early eighteenth
century. 81 mm high.

124

124
Quill-holders of the early
nineteenth century; the
'compound pens' of Bramah's
Patent of 1809 would have used
similar holders:
a Turned horn double pen-holder
for two quill barrel pens, with
contemporary turmeric-stained
quills.
b Carved bone penstick of French
prisoner-of-war work, the
terminal formed as a clenched fist.

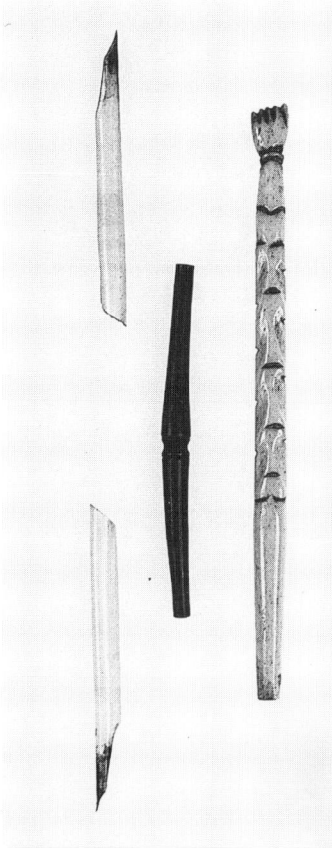

125
Bramah's Patent pen and quill
nibs:
a The 'fragment forms' of his 1809
Patent. These quill nibs were sold
in boxes of twenty-five at three
shillings. By 1822, the price had
come down to three shillings a
hundred.
b The holder, in silver and turned
ivory, is stamped 'J. BRAMAH,
PATENT', circa 1810-20. 140 mm.

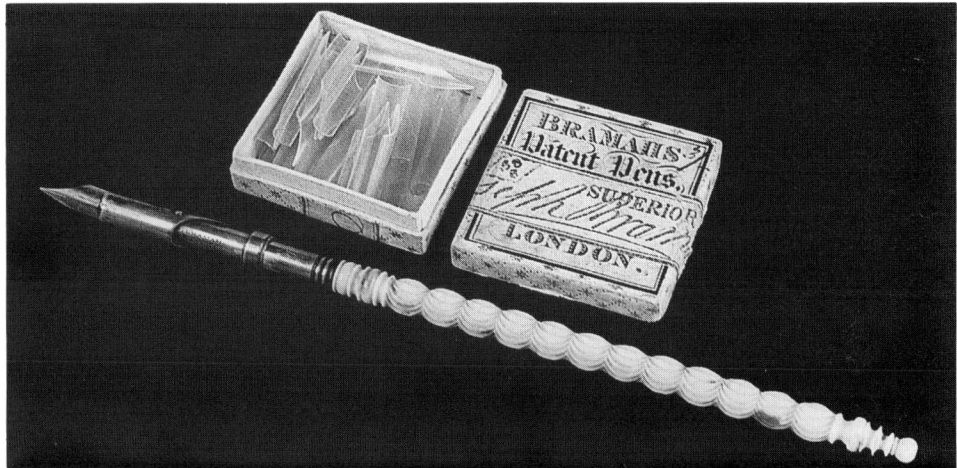

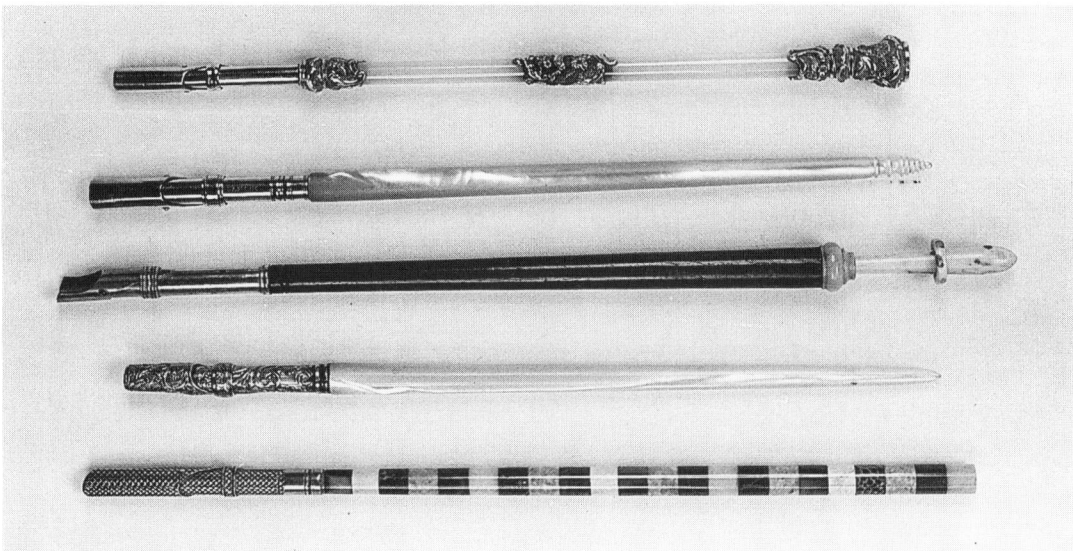

126
Group of pen-holders using the principle of Bramah's
Patent, (top to bottom):
a Cast and chiselled gold-mounted chalcedony pen
with seal terminal, circa 1825. 160 mm.
b Gold-mounted mother-of-pearl pen, stamped 'S.
MORDAN & CO', second quarter nineteenth century.
171 mm.
c Unusual nickel-mounted wooden holder
incorporating an ivory letter scale, circa 1840. 196 mm.
The introduction of postage stamps by Rowland Hill

resulted in the appearance of many novel letter
balances at this time.
d Engraved silver-gilt and mother-of-pearl example
from a fitted morocco writing box by J. Bramah,
Piccadilly, circa 1825. 167 mm.
e Early Victorian engine-turned silver-mounted holder,
the handle formed of sections of various agates and
other hardstones. 184 mm.

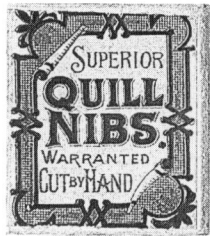

128
The Saturday Magazine of 1838 mentions a 'House in Shoe Lane' which cut about six million pens annually. This may have been Coopers, the makers of these 'Superior Quill Nibs', at 5 Shoe Lane; datable before 1840, when the firm expanded to occupy numbers 6 and 7, these pens cost 6d for twenty-five. 34 mm.

127
Late Victorian quill nibs, all cut by hand with a knife. The brightly coloured but anonymous labels no doubt helped to protect retailing stationers from losing their customers to the makers.

129
Two rare quill-holders:
a
Tortoiseshell and partridge-wood holder for a quill nib with gold ferrule; the nib slides into a U-shaped slot in the solid tortoiseshell. Early nineteenth century. 158 mm.
b
Unusual silver-gilt and mother-of-pearl holder with spring-loaded grip held closed by a sliding ring. Impressed 'WEST LATE PALMER'. Circa 1840. 158 mm.

130
Trade card of George Palmer, Cutler and Dressing Case Maker to the Royal Family; formerly of 20 St James's Street, he moved to No 1 after 1815. He was the son of Thomas Palmer, Quill Pen Manufacturer, of East Grinstead, for whose pens he provided a West End outlet, 1815-20.
Courtesy of the Trustees of the British Museum, Banks Collection, 52.94

126

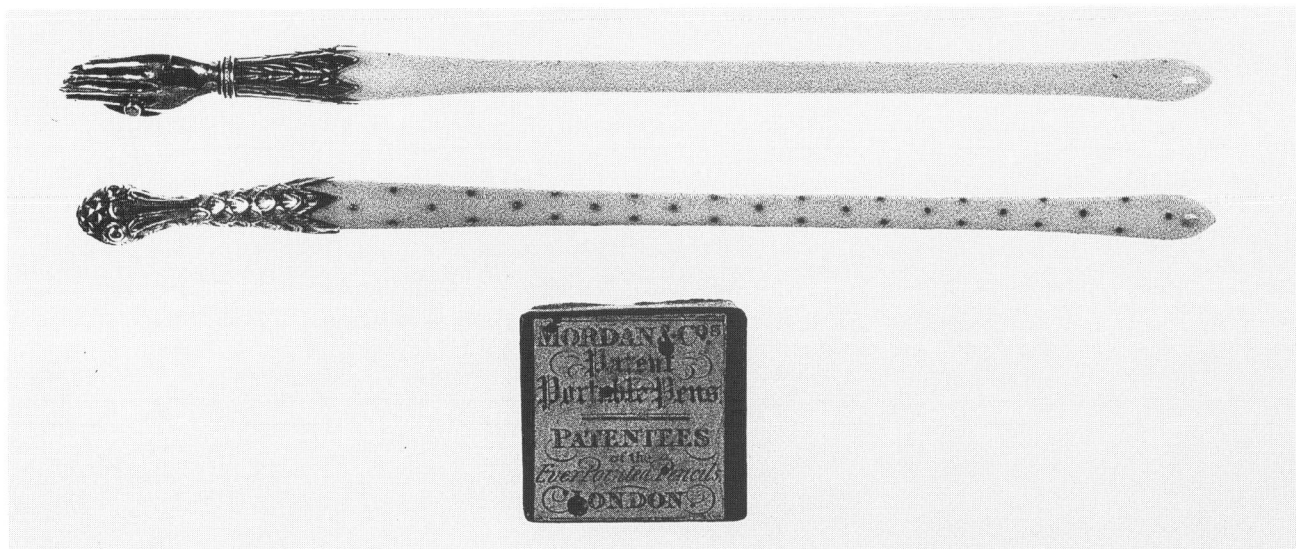

131
Mordan quill nibs and datable holders typical of the quality products for which Mordans were highly regarded:
a
Silver holder in the form of a hand with a gem-set ring, the ivory shank impressed 'S. MORDAN/AUG^T 3 1842/ No 1390', the latter figure the design registration number. 158 mm.

b
Silver and ivory holder, impressed 'MORDAN', the serpent's head grip marked with the Design Registration lozenge mark for 13th March, 1845. 156 mm.
c
Sampson Mordan and Company produced their quill nibs by machine, a box of fifty such as this costing 1s 6d in the 1830s

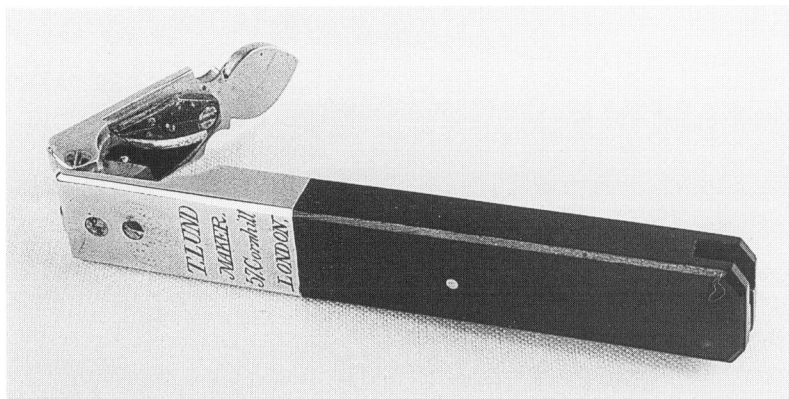

132
Early example of the standard form of pocket quill-cutting machine, in ebony and nickel, with blued steel cutters, by Thomas Lund of 57 Cornhill, London, made before 1817 when he took over adjoining premises at No 56. 83 mm.

133
Thomas Lund's Cornhill shop, circa 1820. Lund took over John Wilkes's Quill and Pen Warehouse at this address in 1803, and by the time of this trade card was clearly selling a wide range of goods. *Courtesy of the Trustees of the British Museum, Heal Collection, 52.66*

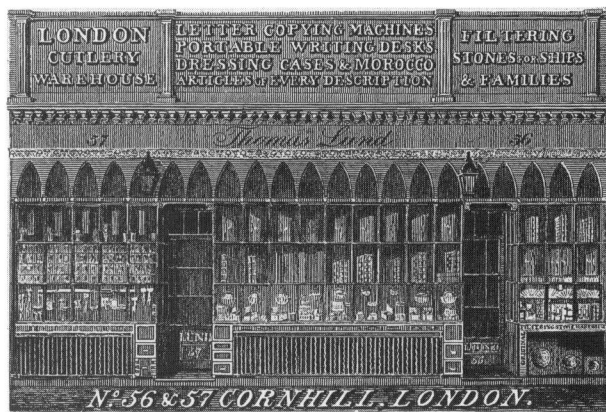

127

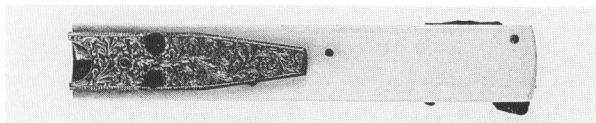

134
Superlative quality quill-cutting machine in ivory and engraved gilt-brass, by 'Thornhill, CUTLER, 144 New Bond Str^t.'. 85 mm.

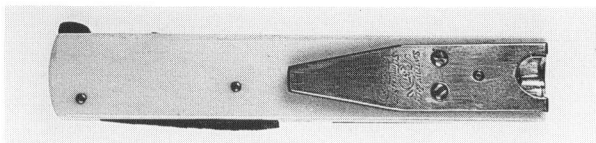

135
Quill-cutter in ivory and gilt-brass, by 'Savigny and Co, 67 St James's Str.', a well-known firm of cutlers and surgical instrument makers. 92 mm.

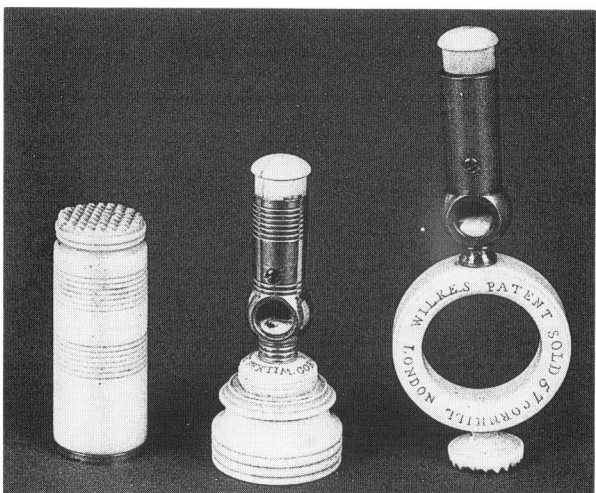

136
Two versions of John Wilkes's 'PATENT PEN NIBBER' in ivory and gilt-brass, (never actually patented), each of which incorporates a tiny guillotine to trim the extreme points of a newly cut pen and could also be used to effect an immediate repair of a worn pen; each also has a chequered wafer seal. Circa 1800. 68 and 50 mm.

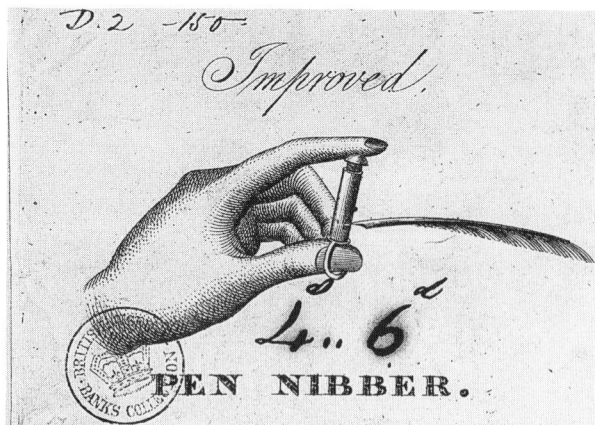

137
Steel pen nibber impressed indistinctly 'W. . . .', probably by John Wilkes, on its original steel watch chain. Circa 1800. 62 mm, (338 mm overall).

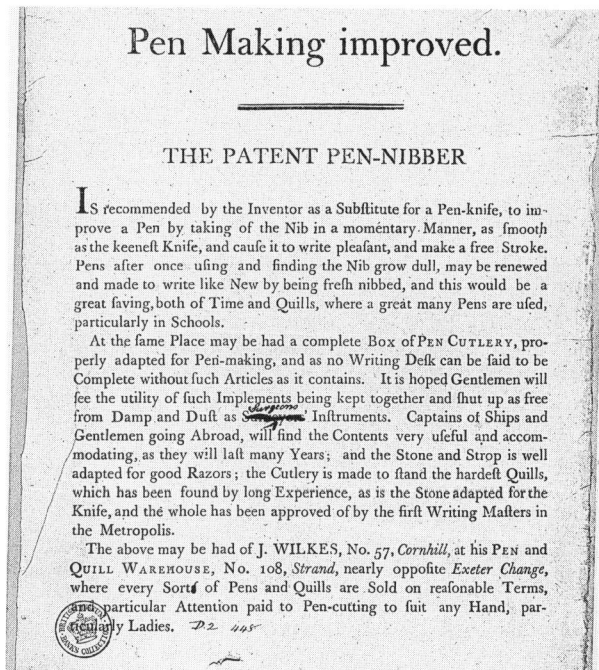

138
Early nineteenth century advertisement for 'The Improved Pen Nibber', at 4s/6d.
Courtesy of the Trustees of the British Museum, Banks Collection, 92.21

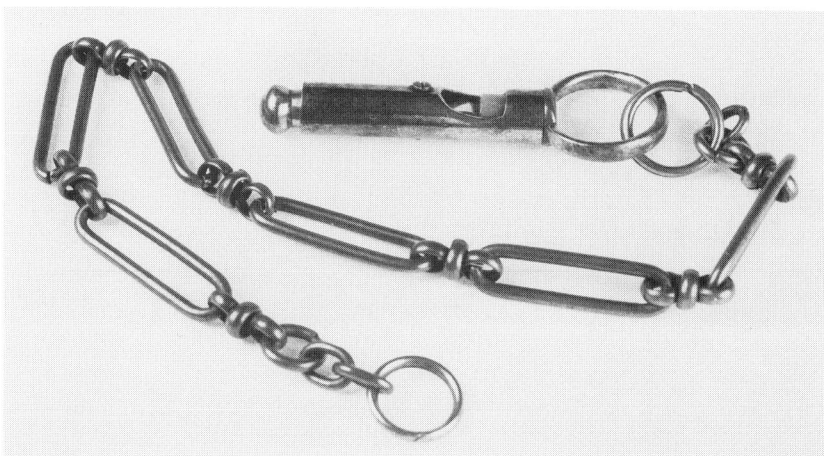

Pen Making improved.

THE PATENT PEN-NIBBER

Is recommended by the Inventor as a Subſtitute for a Pen-knife, to improve a Pen by taking of the Nib in a momentary Manner, as ſmooth as the keeneſt Knife, and cauſe it to write pleaſant, and make a free Stroke. Pens after once uſing and finding the Nib grow dull, may be renewed and made to write like New by being freſh nibbed, and this would be a great ſaving, both of Time and Quills, where a great many Pens are uſed, particularly in Schools.

At the ſame Place may be had a complete Box of Pen Cutlery, properly adapted for Pen-making, and as no Writing Deſk can be ſaid to be Complete without ſuch Articles as it contains. It is hoped Gentlemen will ſee the utility of ſuch Implements being kept together and ſhut up as free from Damp and Duſt as Surgions' Inſtruments. Captains of Ships and Gentlemen going Abroad, will find the Contents very uſeful and accommodating, as they will laſt many Years; and the Stone and Strop is well adapted for good Razors; the Cutlery is made to ſtand the hardeſt Quills, which has been found by long Experience, as is the Stone adapted for the Knife, and the whole has been approved of by the firſt Writing Maſters in the Metropolis.

The above may be had of J. WILKES, No. 57, *Cornhill*, at his Pen and Quill Warehouse, No. 108, *Strand*, nearly oppoſite *Exeter Change*, where every Sort of Pens and Quills are Sold on reaſonable Terms, and particular Attention paid to Pen-cutting to ſuit any Hand, particularly Ladies.

139
John Wilkes's advertisement for his 'Patent Pen-Nibber'. Circa 1800.
Courtesy of the Trustees of the British Museum, Banks Collection, 92.20

140
Silver-mounted folding pen-knife of high quality, incorporating a quill-cutting machine with mother-of-pearl scales, by Doughty, 19 West Strand, complete with its red morocco case, circa 1835. 83 mm.

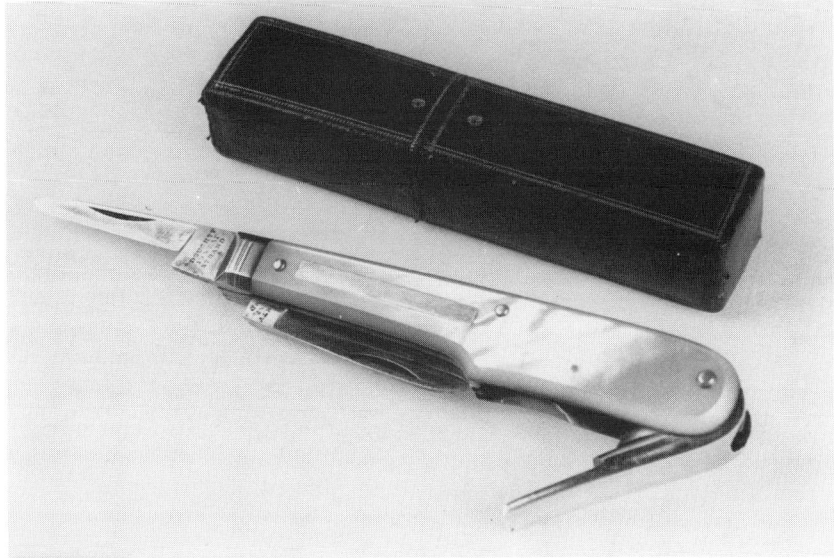

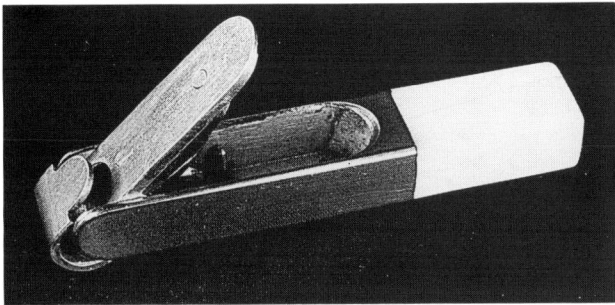

141
Unusual ivory and nickel quill-cutting machine with folding dustproof cover to the quill hole, early nineteenth century. 60 mm.

142
Unusually small Victorian nickel quill-cutting machine by Joseph Rodgers of Sheffield, circa 1840; it retains its original red morocco case. 60 mm long.

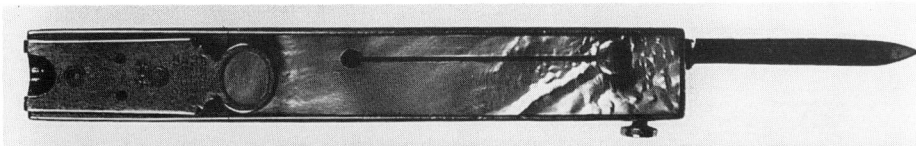

143
Rare Rodgers quill-cutting machine of superlative quality, in nickel-mounted mother-of-pearl. 101 mm.

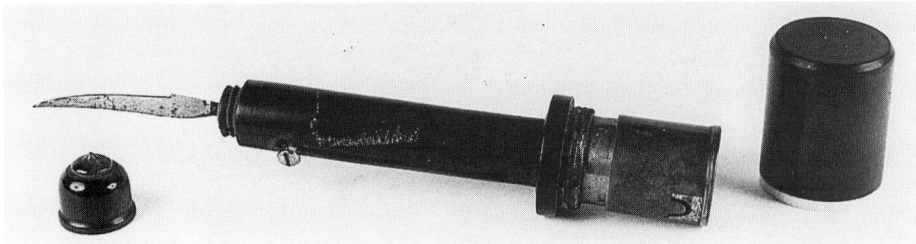

144
French combined quill-knife and pen-cutting machine, impressed 'Lassèrre Brevette'. Circa 1822. The spring-loaded end contains the nib-cutters.
Courtesy the Museum of Science and Industry, Birmingham, the Charles Thomas Collection

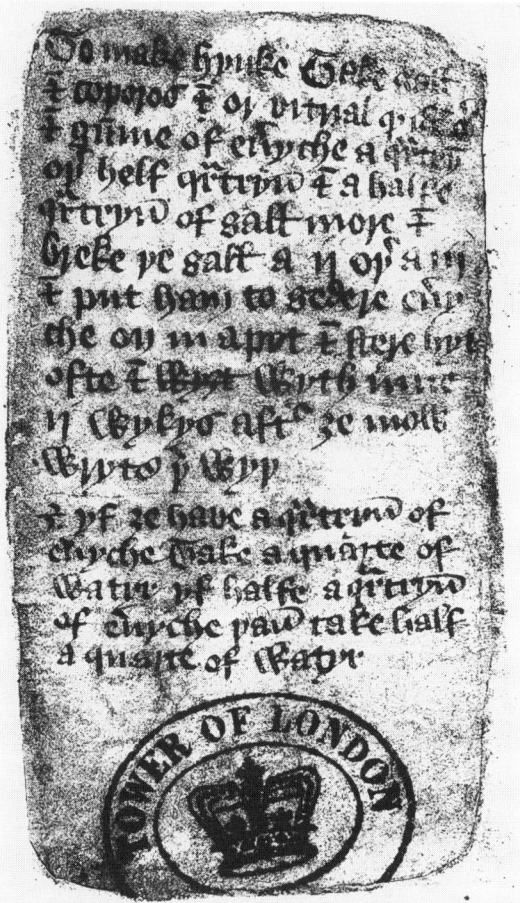

145

146

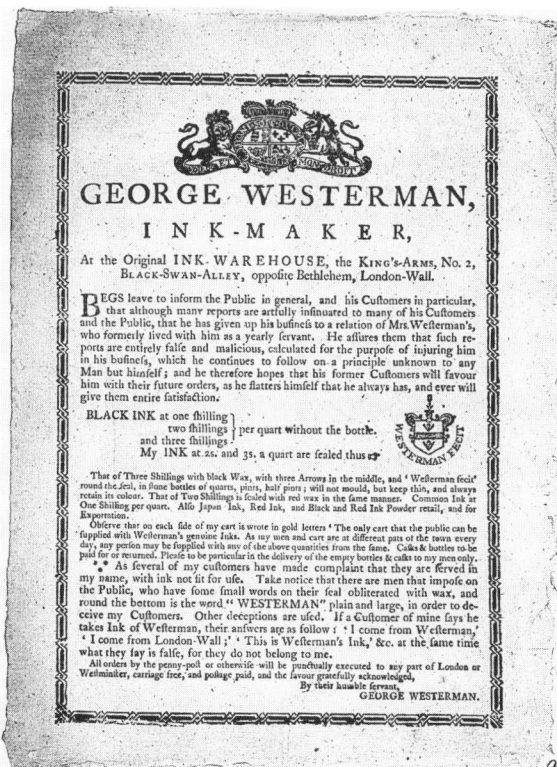

147

145
Recipe for iron-gall ink, containing galls, copperas or vitriol and gum, English, mid- to late fifteenth century.
Courtesy of the Public Record Office, Ref No C/47/34/1/3

146
Trade label for Charles Holman's ink powder which could be added to water, beer, ale or wine to make black writing ink, circa 1690. The patent referred to was granted in 1688.
Courtesy of the Trustees of the British Museum, Heal Collection, 92.14

147
Advertisement of George Westerman, Inkmaker, before 1760. He was succeeded at the same address by Joshua May and Samuel Amess. (See Plate 149).
Courtesy of the Trustees of the British Museum, Heal Collection, 92.34

Fine Writeing Inke
A ma bonne Ancre
Juchiostro fino da scriuere

Mauron pinx:

P Tempest exc:
CumPrivilegie

148   None too prosperous street seller of 'Fine Writeing Inke', with his ink barrel, funnel, measure and a bundle of quill pens, one of a set of *Cries of London* after M. Laroon, circa 1700.
Courtesy of the Trustees of the British Museum, Ref No 170 a.10. p.12, no 40*

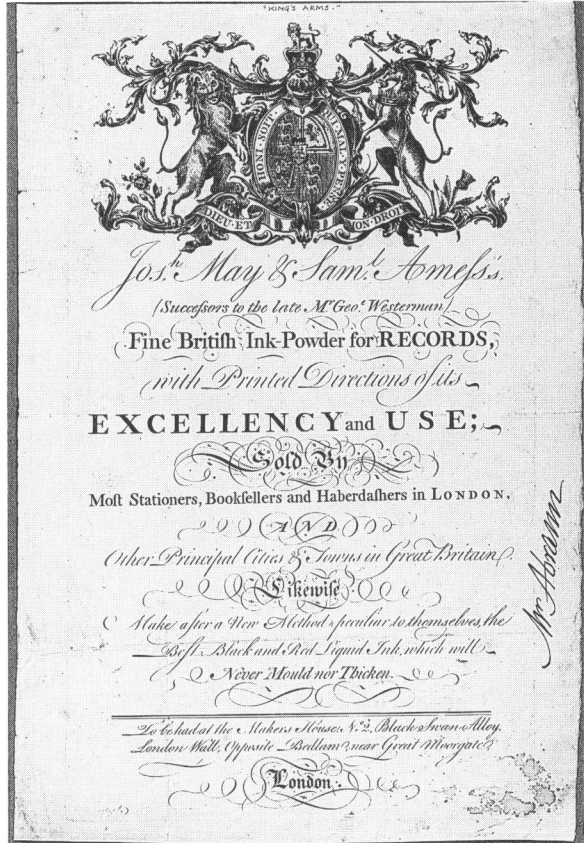

149
Trade card of Joshua May and Samuel Amess. As successors to George Westerman, (Plate 147), they continued to use the same shop sign, The King's Arms, second half eighteenth century.
Courtesy of the Trustees of the British Museum, Heal Collection, 92.18

SCRAPING.

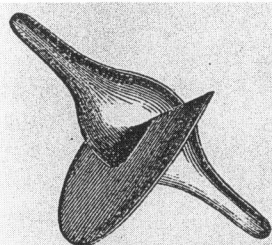

HALF-MOON KNIFE.

GRINDING AND DRAINING.

150   Stages in the making of parchment, and the half-moon knife used for the purpose, from *The Useful Arts and Manufactures of Great Britain*, SPCK, London, undated, circa 1860.

131

151

152

151
Steel-engraved views were popular decoration for writing paper, which was usually in folds of two leaves, during the mid nineteenth century. Printed in black, this is a view of Holme Eden near Carlisle, by Harwood, London, 1846.

152
Lancaster Castle, by one of the great engravers, Lizars of Edinburgh, who also engraved banknotes. Printed in puce on paper watermarked 'TOWGOOD, 1855'.

153
Embossed decorative writing paper with neo-classical frieze and scroll border, the edge stained yellow. Watermarked 'BUTT^W 1801', for Butterworth.

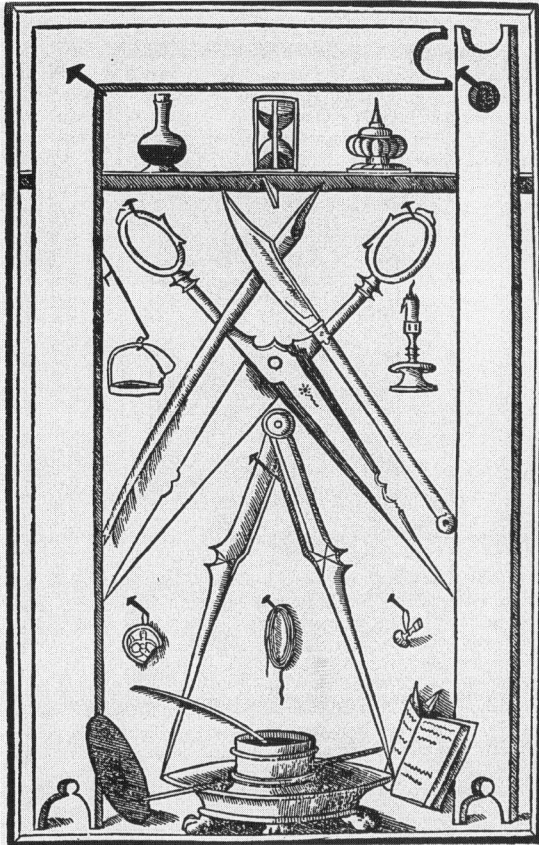

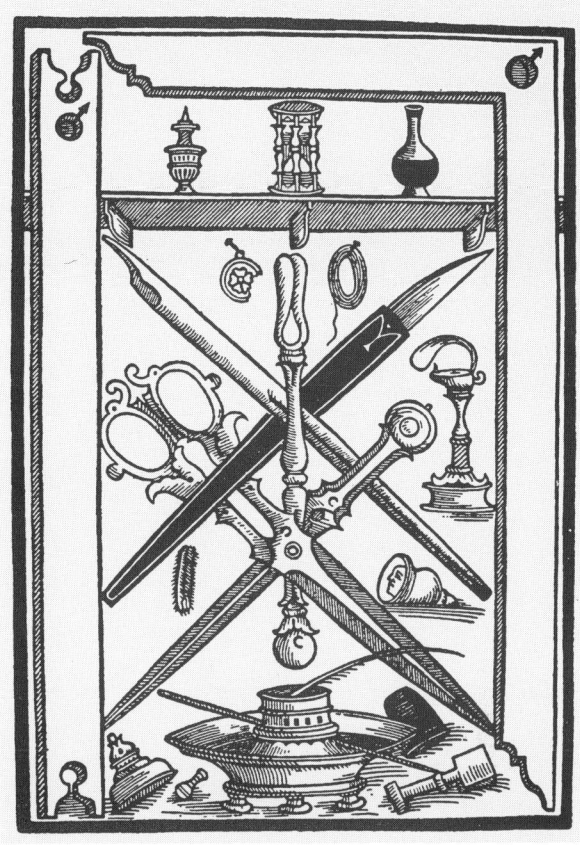

154
The Instruments of Writing from
Tagliente's *Lo presente Libro*, Venice, 1524.
Pounce was contained in the fluted caster,
top right.

155
From Palatino's *Libro nuovo d'imparare a
scrivere*, Rome, 1540; his pounce-pot, top
left, is also of caster form.

156
Portrait of the philosopher Aegidius by
Quentin Matsys, (1466-1530). His bone or
ivory pounce-pot is of a form popular for
the next four centuries.
*Private Collection. Photo: Courtesy of the
Courtauld Institute of Art*

133

157
Turned fruitwood pounce-pot,
English, late seventeenth century.
73 mm high.

158
Sander of turned oak, English,
seventeenth or eighteenth
century. 80 mm high.

159
Turned cedar pounce-pot with
detachable push-on lid, English,
eighteenth century. 74 mm high.

160
Turned ivory sander on foot,
seventeenth century. 65 mm high.

161
Italian brass pounce-pot chased
with a human mask and a
crowing cockerel in leaf
scrollwork, first half seventeenth
century. 73 mm high.

162
South Staffordshire enamelled
sander with polychrome floral
decoration and gilt-metal mounts,
circa 1770. 42 mm high.

163
Derby porcelain sander painted with insects and a
landscape, the latter thought to be the only example of
such decoration by the 'moth painter', circa 1756-58.
52 mm high.

164
German porcelain sander with a
moulded flower finial, painted
with sprays of polychrome
flowers, mid-eighteenth century.
46 mm high.

165
Documentary Liverpool porcelain
sander, Pennington's factory,
1791. 75 mm high.
Courtesy Phillips

167
Chinese export porcelain sander
with underglaze blue landscape
decoration, Nankin, late
eighteenth century. 56 mm high.

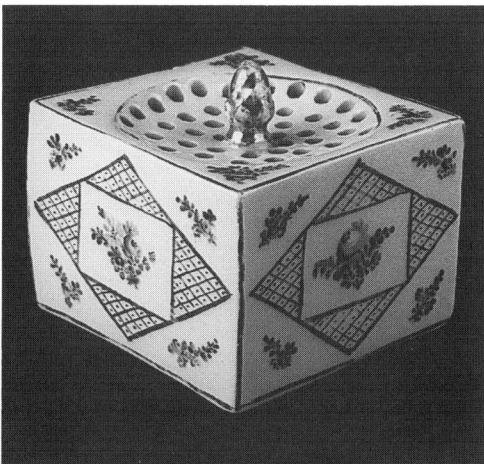

166
Meissen porcelain sander with
gilt diapered and enamelled floral
sprig decoration, circa 1800.
(Crossed swords mark in
underglaze blue). 51 mm high.

168
Chinese export porcelain sander
enamelled with *famille rose*
peonies, *Quianlong*, circa 1750.
49 mm high.

170
Initial 'S' from Gregory the
Great's commentary on Ezekiel,
the scribe holding his inkhorn.
*Courtesy of the Staatsbibliothek,
Munich, Clm. 9511, fol 12ᵛ*

169
The artist-scribe Hildebert, his
desk having two of the simplest
inkwells, literally inkhorns,
second quarter twelfth century.
*Courtesy of the Chapter Library,
Prague, Ms Kap. A21.1*

172
Early sixteenth century horn-lined
inkwell in *cuir bouilli* stamped
with figures of saints, excavated
in Worship Street, London. 47 mm
high.
*Courtesy of the Trustees of the
Museum of London, A28570*

171
Two late medieval horn inkwells
with incised roundel decoration.
47 and 48.5 mm high.
*Courtesy of the Trustees of the
Museum of London, A292 and
A13339*

136

ANNO·DÑI·1541·   ·ETATIS·SVÆ·28·

174
An Unknown Man at his Desk, painted in
1541 by Hans Holbein, showing a *cuir
bouilli* pen-case attached to a covered
metal inkwell.
*Courtesy of the Kunsthistorisches Museum,
Vienna, GG 905*

173
Penner in *cuir bouilli*, gilt-stamped with
the Tudor rose, said to have belonged to
Henry VI, but more probably associated
with Henry, Prince of Wales, son of James
I; formerly in the Victoria and Albert
Museum.
*Reproduced by the author from an old V and
A Museum photograph in the Charles
Thomas Collection, Museum of Science and
Industry, Birmingham*

175
Lead inkwell with a holder for quills, from Finsbury, sixteenth century. About 65 mm high.
Courtesy of the Trustees of the Museum of London

176
Simple lead inkwell of 'beehive' form, date unknown, possibly late medieval. 29 mm high.

177
Serpentine-shaped lead inkwell with quill holes in the corners, mid-eighteenth century, 46 mm high.

178
English professional scribes at the Court of the King's Bench, using penners attached to inkwells by drawstrings, early sixteenth century. From *Archaeologia*, XXXIX, 1863, p. 357.
By permission of the British Library

179
Woodcut from *Stans Puer ad Mensam* by Johannis Sulpitius, printed by Wynken de Worde in 1518. The scribe, even in his *scriptorium*, used a portable pen-case and inkwell.
By permission of the British Library

178

179

138

180 Charles I dictating despatches to his Secretary of War, Sir Edward Walker, who is using a portable silver penner. Artist unknown. *Courtesy of the National Portrait Gallery, No 1961*

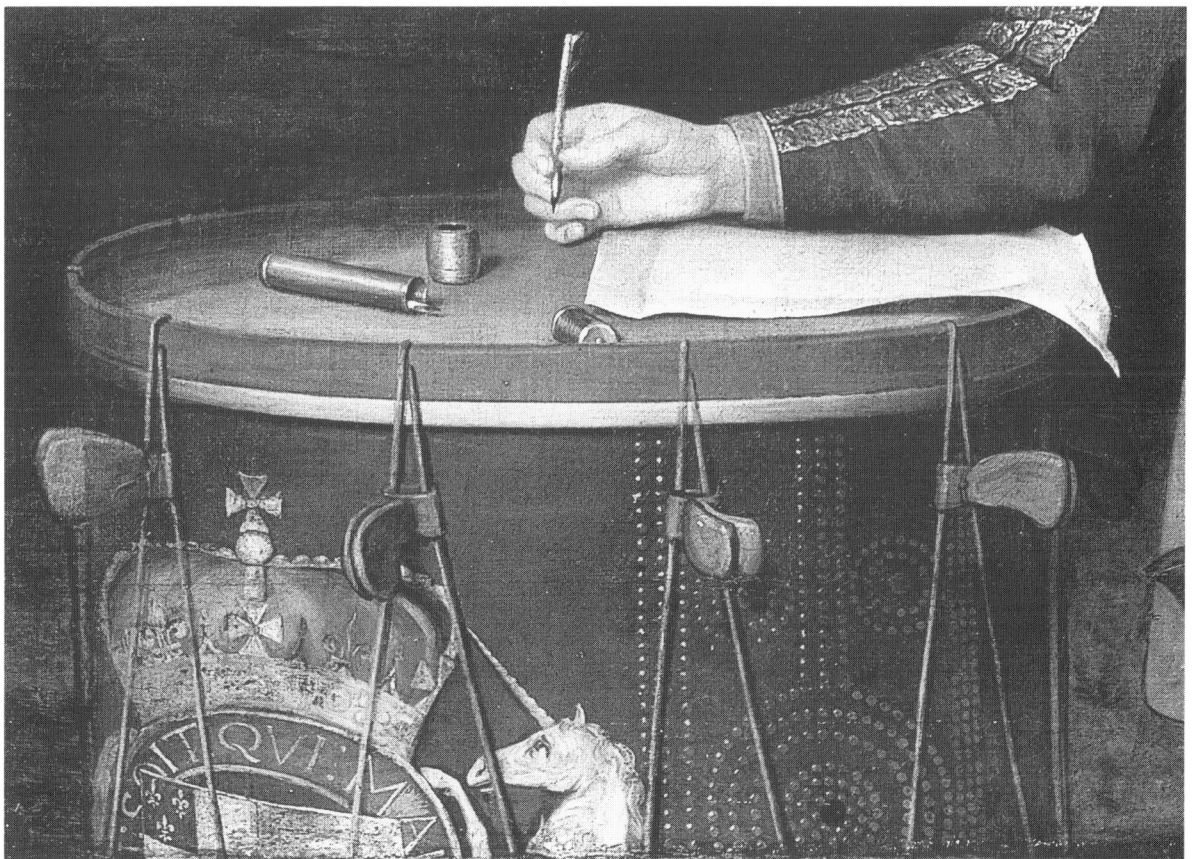

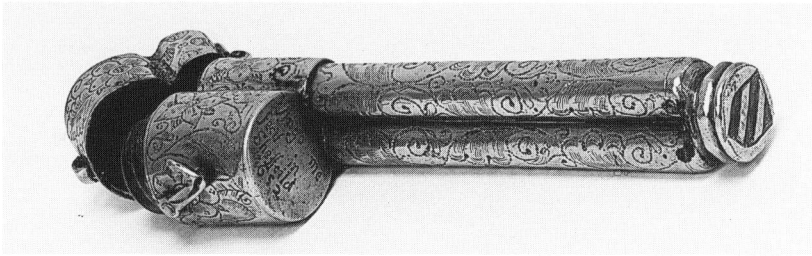

181
Rare brass penner or inkhorn inscribed
'Virgo me fecit in Sheffeild (sic) 1652'.
111 mm long.
*Courtesy of the Trustees of the Victoria and
Albert Museum, M. 201-1914*

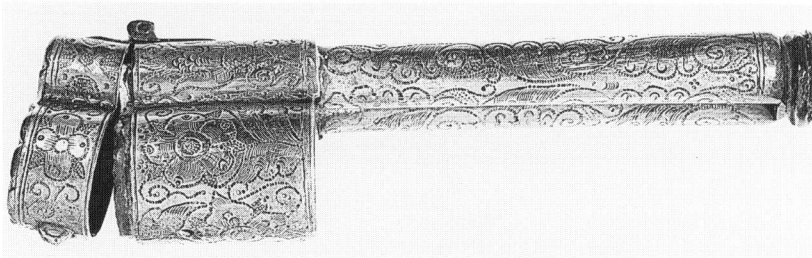

182
Similar brass penner by Virgo, also dated
1652. 111 mm.
*Courtesy of the Trustees of the Museum of
London*

183
Brass pen-case inscribed enigmatically 'I
was in Sheffeild (sic) made & many can
Witness I was not made by any man' and
dated 1655. The answer to the riddle lies
in the name of the maker, who sometimes
signed himself Virgo and is thought to
have been one of a family of metalworkers
called Madin, who worked in Sheffield.
126 mm long.

184
Unique brass pen-case and
inkwell by Virgo of Sheffield,
made for Ann Day in 1657, the
Latin inscription perhaps a
commentary on the religious
bigotry of the Commonwealth. It
may be translated 'There is no
Love in the land and Truth
produces hatred'; the other side
reads 'In writing one learns to
write'. The seal terminal is
engraved with the Day family
arms. 133 mm.
*Courtesy Michael and Jane Dunn,
New York*

140

185

Ivory penner of fine art quality having
engraved floral scrollwork decoration on a
brown-stained ground. The compartments
house a reversible pen-knife blade,
inkwell and pounce box; complete with
boiled leather and paper case. Mid-
seventeenth century. 130 mm long,
excluding knife blade.
Courtesy Edric Van Vredenburgh, Esq

185a

186

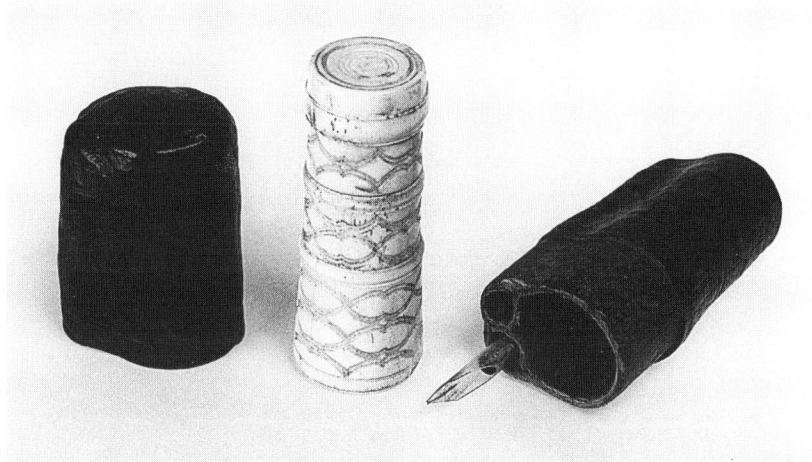

Turned bone penner of three sections, the
first and second for ink (with glass liner)
and pounce (with pierced iron inset), the
third possibly for wafers. The quills are
housed in two separate compartments in
the boiled leather case. Mid-seventeenth
century. 78 mm long.

186a

141

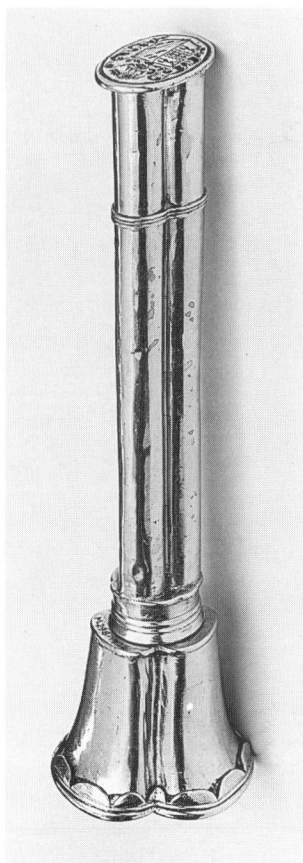

187
Fine silver penner of trefoil section, providing space for three quills above the screw-on inkwell, the seal terminal engraved with the arms of Luttrell impaling Baker, circa 1681. Maker's mark only, WB, three pellets below, struck twice; that this is a London maker is evidenced by a pair of silver candle-snuffers and tray hallmarked London, 1682, by the same maker, sold in London at Sothebys on 19th June, 1986. 110 mm long.
Courtesy of the Trustees of the Victoria and Albert Museum, Ref M. 298-1975

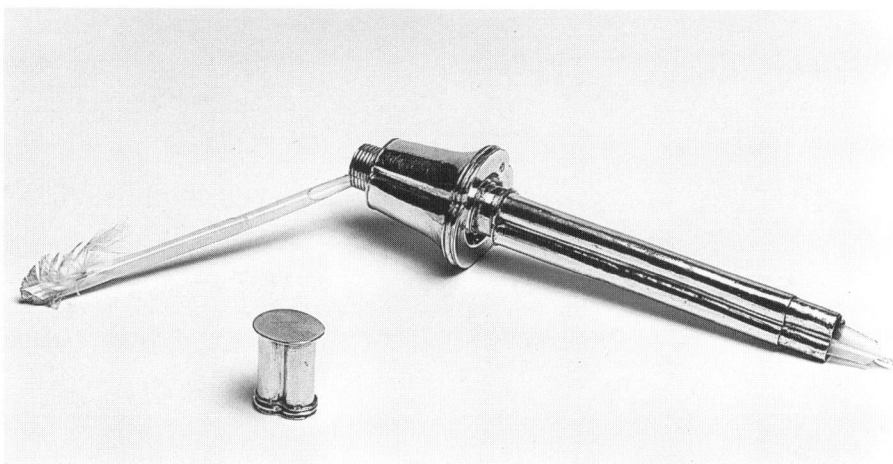

188
Similar silver penner. In this case the quill tubes can be screwed to the bottom of the inkwell to provide a handle. English, circa 1680, maker's mark only, IC in a heart. 160 mm long.
Courtesy Gerald Sattin, Esq

189
Eighteenth century horn penner. The pounce-pot has a simple nail-pierced iron plate typical of most penners made from horn, wood and other humble materials. 185 mm high.

Two horn penners, each having a screw-on **190** inkwell, pounce-pot and space for a quill pen, eighteenth century. This type of inkhorn, suspended from a coat button by a leather strap, would be used by the professional writer.
Courtesy of the Trustees of the Museum of Science and Industry, Birmingham, Charles Thomas Collection

191
Portable horn inkwell with screw-on cover, the neck of the finial showing considerable wear from a cord or strap, eighteenth century. 70 mm high.

192
Well-used home-made mahogany portable inkwell with glass bottle. The surface has been incised with the name or initials of successive owners 'Mr S. Atterby', 'H.G.' and 'P.M.P.'. Eighteenth century. 88 mm high.

193
Fine rootwood penner of unusually large size. The inkwell and pen case are horn-lined and the joints have horn ring mounts. Eighteenth century. 273 mm high.

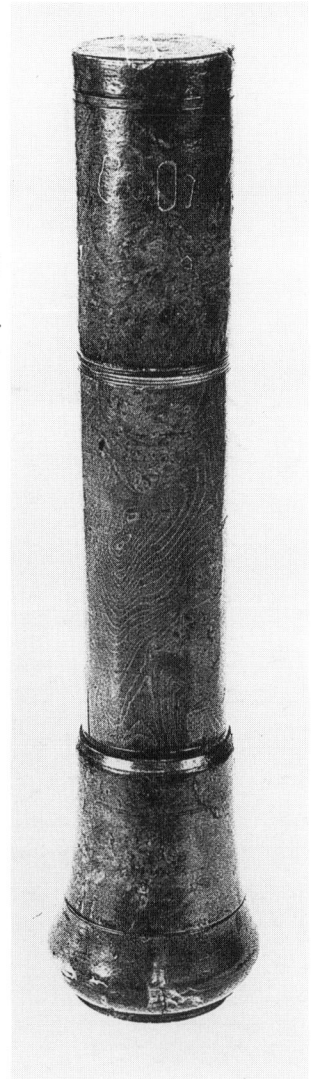

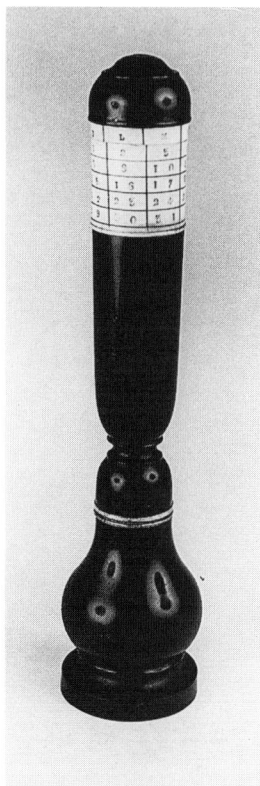

194
Ebony and ivory penner with gilt-metal mounts and a perpetual calendar, having a domed cover housing two interchangeable pen-knife blades which screw into the end, a gold-nibbed ivory pen and a chequered wafer seal. Below the pewter-lined inkwell, the foot is a wafer-box. French, late eighteenth century. 147 mm high.

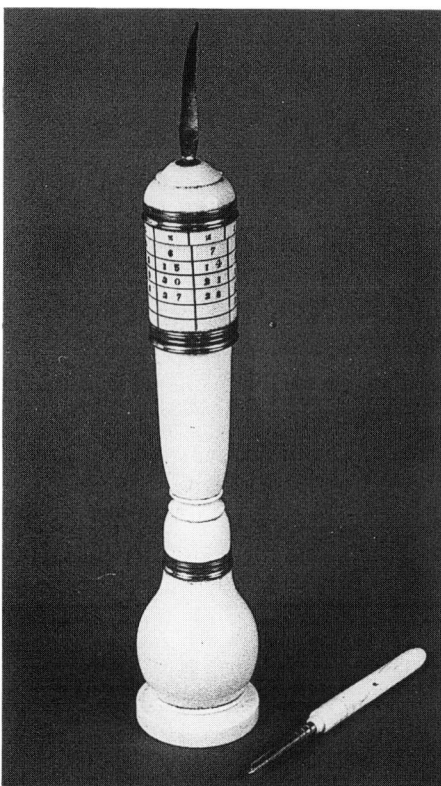

195
Similar ivory penner or inkhorn, French, late eighteenth century. 159 mm high.

196

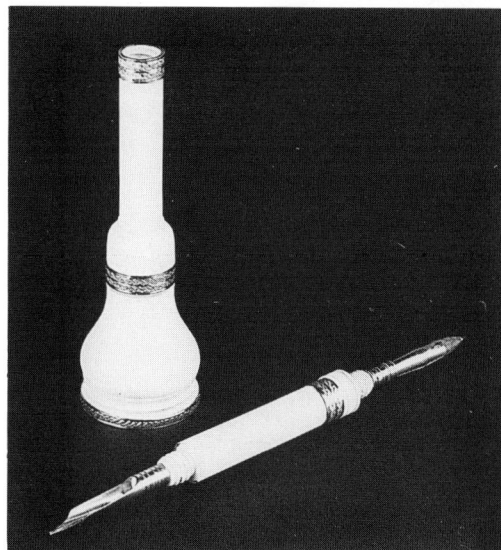

196a
High quality French gold-mounted ivory penner with inkwell and wafer-box, reversible gold pen and *porte-crayon*; there is no provision for a quill. Late eighteenth century. 133 mm high.

197
Simple inkhorn in turned bone with stoppered ink-bottle, the pen-case cover chequered as a wafer-seal, eighteenth century. 142 mm long.

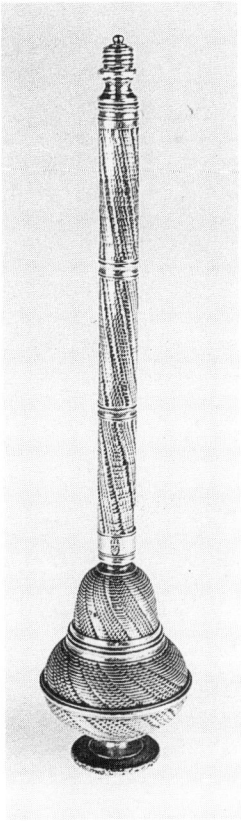

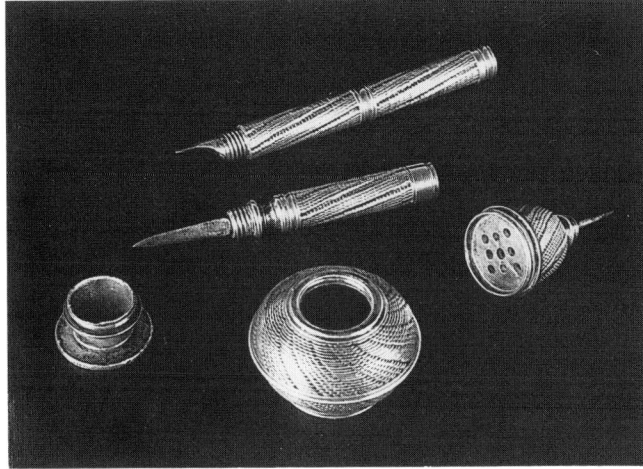

198
Fine German cast silver penner in
seven parts, the base a seal and
inkwell cover, the third section a
sander with pricker; the handle in
three sections, one with an
integral pen nib cut from the
solid and therefore lacking in
flexibility, the reversible finial
having a pen-knife blade.
Hallmarked Augsburg, 1739-41.
145 mm high.

199
Dutch or Flemish silver inkhorn
having a covered inkwell,
pounce-pot, pen-case and sealing-
wax box, each end engraved with
an armorial seal, mid-eighteenth
century. 108 mm long.

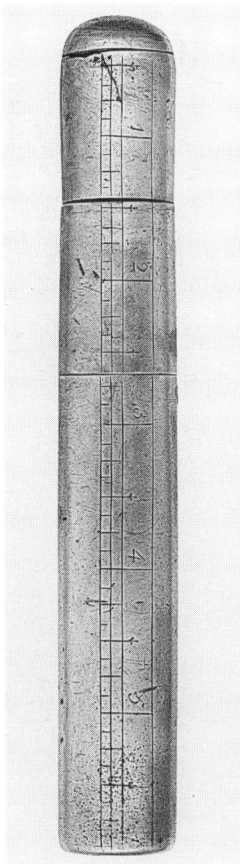

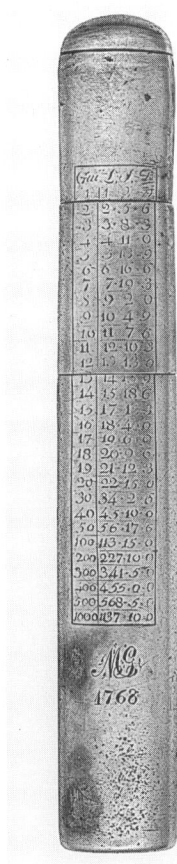

200
Silver writing compendium of
oval section, in three parts: cover,
pen-case and inkwell with
chained stopper. Engraved with
six inch ruler and currency
conversion table and dated 1768.
153 mm long.
Courtesy Sothebys

201
Leather inkhorn with glass bottle, the pen-case impressed 'GEORGE FISHER, MAKER', late eighteenth/early nineteenth century.
Courtesy of the Trustees of Northampton Museums and Art Gallery, Museum of Leatherwork

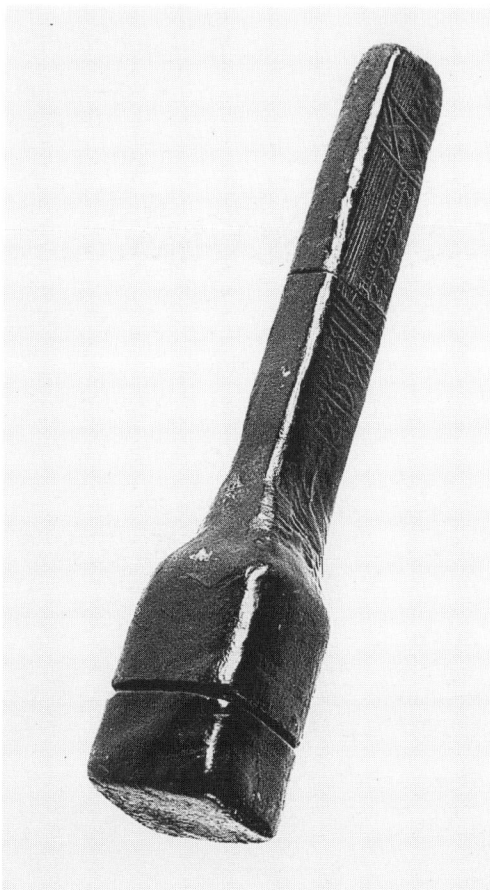

202
Leather inkhorn with black-glazed earthenware inkwell, pen-case and cover, eighteenth century. 168 mm long.

202a

146

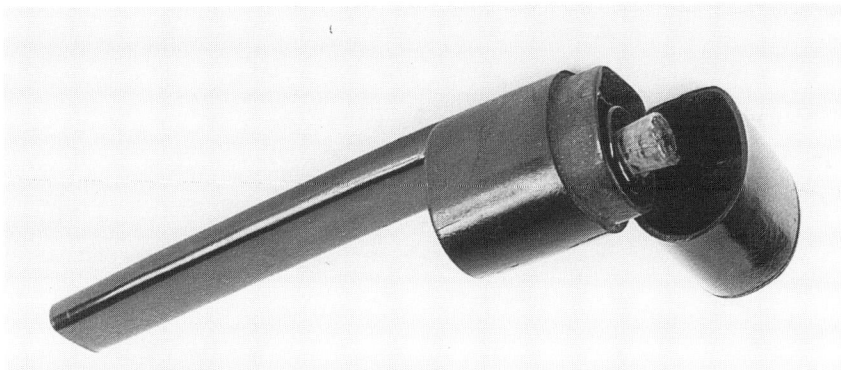

203
Leather penner with hinged cover
enclosing a pale green glass ink-
bottle and pen-case, late
eighteenth century. 175 mm long.

204
Pigskin penner with red
earthenware ink-bottle, (the neck
and shoulders black lead-glazed),
two quill holes and a cavity for a
folding pen-knife, circa 1800.
127 mm high.

205

205
Leather penner with glass bottle
and cork stopper, the hinged
cover of the pen-case impressed
T. CLARK, EDR. A Thomas Clark,
Paper Ruler and Law Bookseller
worked in Edinburgh from 1817
until at least 1831. A penner of
such simple and serviceable form,
the ideal working tool of a
scrivener or law writer, would no
doubt be part of the normal stock-
in-trade of a law stationer. Early
nineteenth century. 216 mm.

206
Paper penner with black-glazed
red earthenware ink-bottle
flanked by two quill
compartments; the bottle has
concave sides to accommodate the
quills. Late eighteenth century.
124 mm high.

206

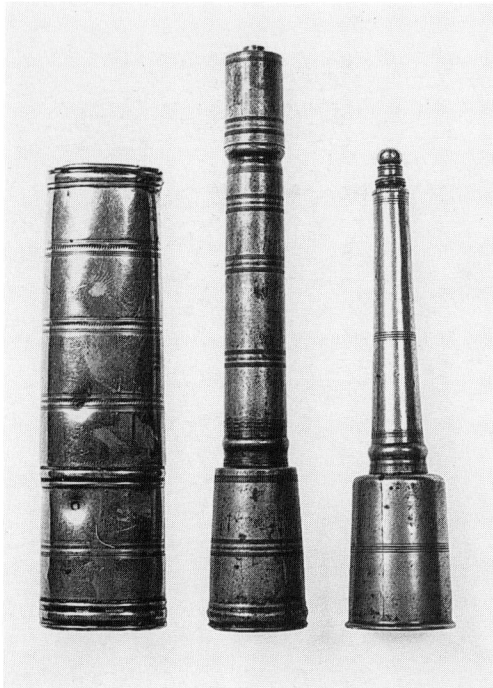

207

207
Three Sheffield-made penners:
a
Brass penner with black-glazed red earthenware ink-bottle flanked by two quill holes, the base impressed MYCOCK, late eighteenth century. 116 mm high. Note: Mycock, John and Joseph, of Burgess Street, are listed as makers of BRASS INKPOTS in Gale and Martin's *Directory of Sheffield*, 1787.
b and detail
Brass penner with lead-glazed pottery inkwell liner, the upper section containing a steel straight edge/sharpener, pen-blade which screws into the end, and a brass pen. Impressed under base with the mark of Mycock. Late eighteenth century. 147 mm high. Similar penners are found impressed JESSUP, who also appears in the 1787 Sheffield Directory.
c
Brass penner, with glass-lined inkwell, the finial reversible with pen-blade, the base impressed S. BARKER, late eighteenth century. 123 mm high.

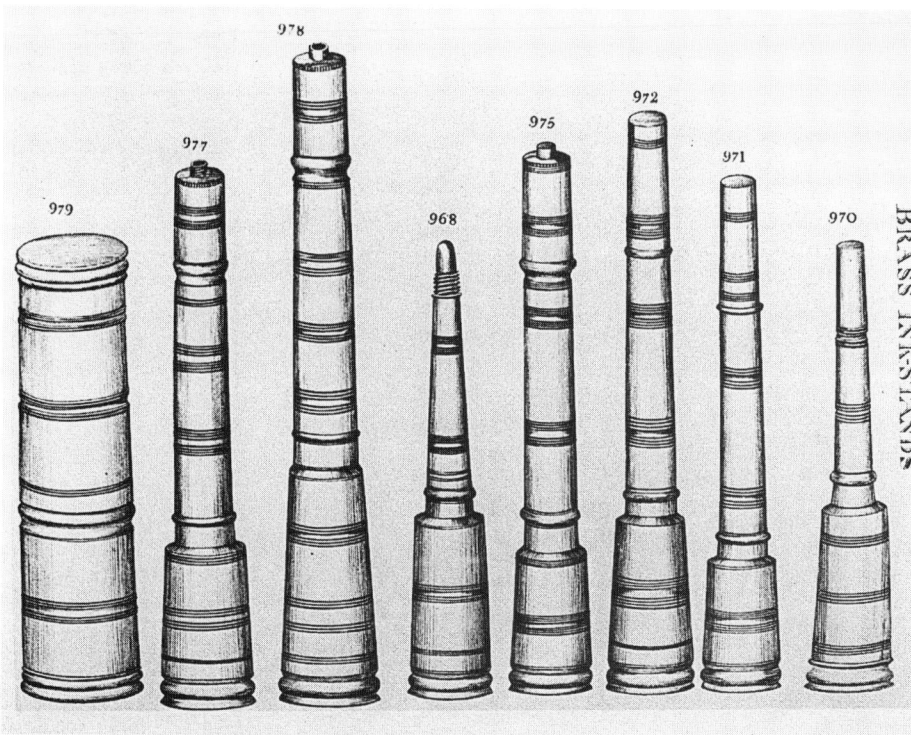

208
Group of penners, then known as BRASS INKSTANDS, an engraving from Joseph Smith's *Explanation or Key to the Various Manufactures of Sheffield*, 1816.
Courtesy of Sheffield City Libraries

209
Bilston enamel penner with fluted inkwell, painted with figures in landscapes in gilt bordered cartouches on a *bianco sopra bianco* ground and having gilt-metal mounts, circa 1770. 136 mm long.
Courtesy Christies

148

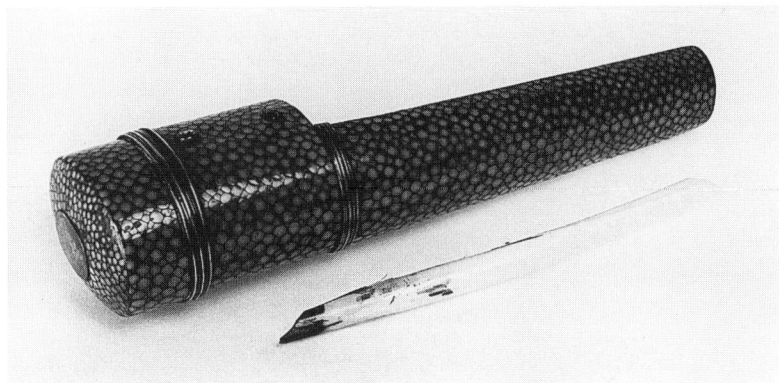

210
Green shagreen penner with silver mounts, the hinged cover enclosing a glass inkwell and D-section pen compartment, late eighteenth century. 162 mm long.

211
Gold-mounted travelling writing compendium in green shagreen, the square cut-glass inkwell and sander having spirally-fluted covers, with three interchangeable gold nibs, fluted holder with pencil, pen-blade and hardstone seal, English, circa 1770. 70 mm long.

211

212a

212
Three views of a silver-mounted green shagreen travelling writing case with cut-glass inkwell and sander, four pen nibs and holder with pencil and rock-crystal seal. English, circa 1775. 71 mm long.

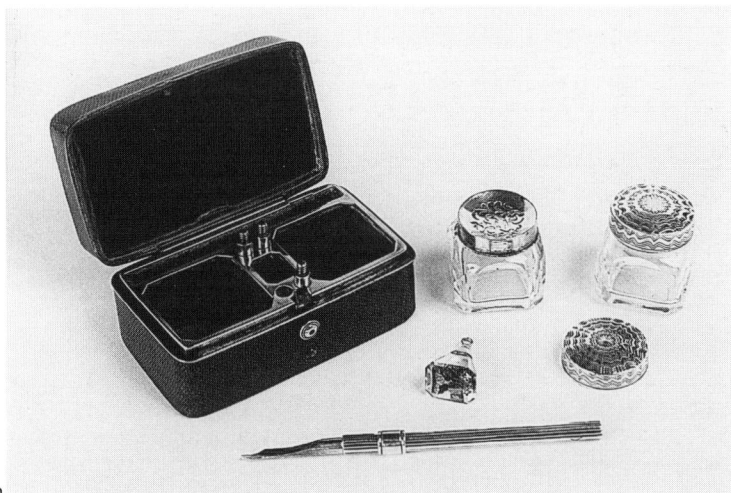

212b

149

214
Silver-gilt writing compendium with inscription dated 1814, the case calibrated as a six-inch rule. (The large knife blade in silver is for fruit, the smaller a steel pen-blade). Early nineteenth century. 152 mm long.

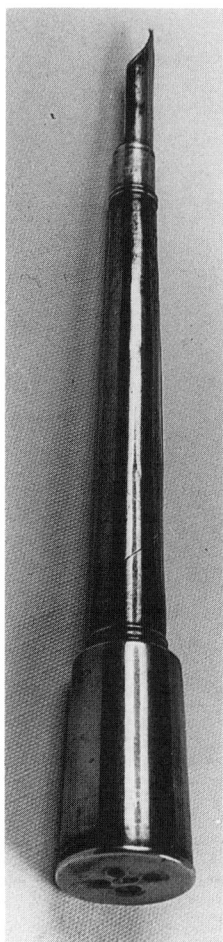

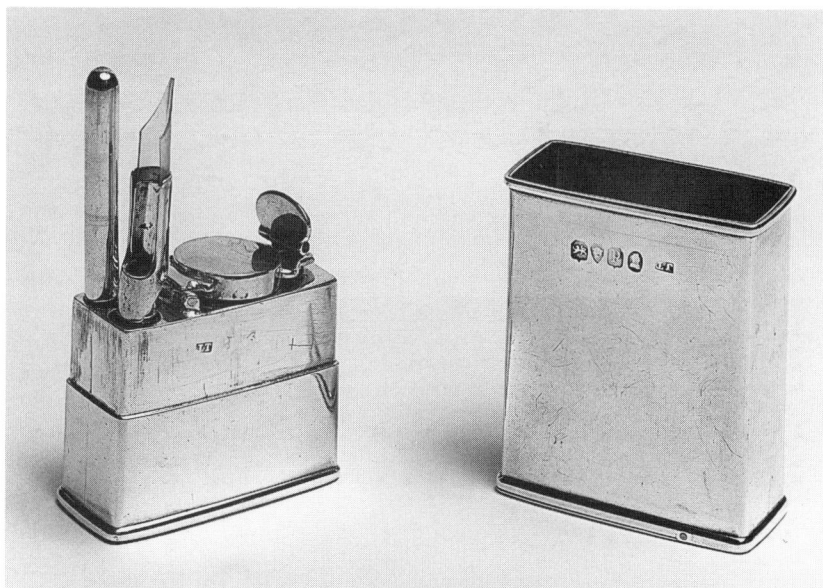

213
Silver penner with screw-on ink-bottle and reversible pen nib, hallmarked Birmingham, 1791, maker Samuel Pemberton. 111 mm long.

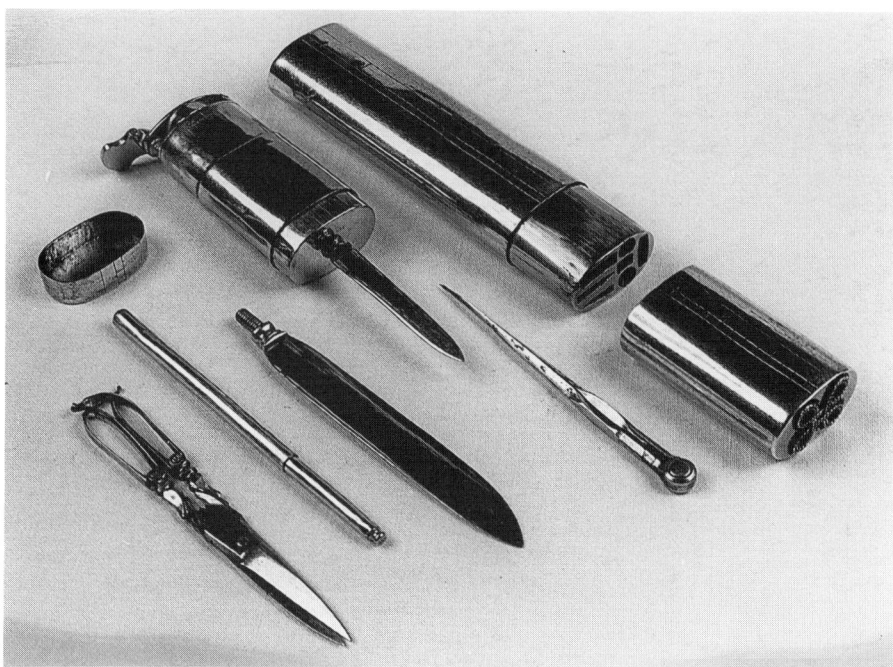

215
Portable silver inkwell hallmarked London, 1830, maker John Teare, with collapsible pen, the holder of the type patented by Joseph Bramah in 1809. 65 mm high.
Courtesy Gerald Sattin, Esq

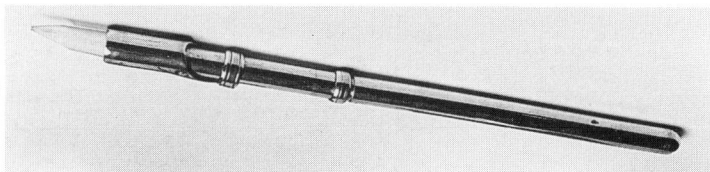

216
Glass excise ink-bottles, so-called because of their use by excise duty collectors, have funnelled necks to prevent spillage and could be worn either in a buttonhole or on a suspension cord. Nineteenth century. 59-70 mm high.

218
Fragments of two Admiralty pattern square glass inkwells with screw-on pewter covers. One lid has been cleaned, the other, showing its Admiralty broad arrow, still has its barnacles as it was salvaged from the wreck of the *Stirling Castle*, sunk in 1693.
Courtesy W. H. Lapthorne, Esq, Naval Historian

219
Portable inkwells:
Screw-topped glass desk inkwell with brass cover, mid-nineteenth century. 40 mm square.
Silver-covered cut-glass inkwell from a gentleman's travelling case, hallmarked London, 1841, maker GR. 36 mm square.
Similar brass-lidded glass inkwell from a travelling case or lap-desk, first half nineteenth century. 40 mm square.

Manufacturing and Export Stationers. **41**

GLASS INKSTANDS.

ROUND CONE INKS, STAR BOTTOM.

PLAIN.						s.	d.	
1½-inch	...	...	...	...	...	0	10	each
2 ,,	...	...	...	...	...	1	0	,,
2½ ,,	...	...	...	...	...	1	3	,,
3 ,,	...	...	...	...	...	1	6	,,

CUT.								
2 inch	...	...	...	...	...	2	0	,,
2½ ,,	...	...	...	...	...	2	6	,,
3 ,,	...	...	...	...	...	3	0	,,

SQUARE DESK INKS, REVOLVING TOPS.

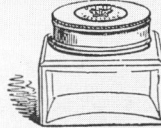

	s.	d.
Cut, 1½, 1⅝, 1¾, 1⅞, 2-inch, Bronzed Top ...	1	6
Cut, ,, ,, ,, ,, ,, Plated ,, ...	2	3
Cut, ,, ,, ,, ,, ,, Gilt ,, ...	3	6

This is the most secure Ink made.

SOLID, WITH BRONZED HINGED TOPS.

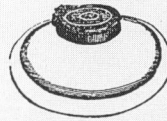

					s.	d.
3-inch	...	...	...	...	1	0
3½ ,,	...	...	...	...	1	3
4 ,,	...	...	...	...	1	9
4½ ,,	...	...	...	...	2	0
5 ,,	...	...	...	...	2	3

SOLID ROUND INKS.

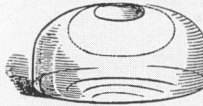

				s.	d.
2½-inch	...	...	...	1	3
3 ,,	...	...	...	1	6
3½ ,,	...	...	...	2	0
4 ,,	...	...	...	2	9
5 ,,	...	...	...	3	9

EXCISE INKS.

PLAIN.						s.	d.	
Small	...	...	...	...	...	2	6	per dozen.
Large	...	...	...	...	...	3	0	,,

CUT.								
Small	...	...	...	...	...	3	0	,,
Large	...	...	...	...	...	3	6	,,

59, Pall Mall, London.

217
Page from a wholesale stationer's catalogue, of Harrison & Sons of London, circa 1860-80, showing Excise Inks and Desk Inks.

220
Portrait of a Merchant, by Jan Gossaert
(called Mabuse),
*Courtesy National Gallery of Art,
Washington, Ailsa Mellon Bruce Fund; [circa
1530, wood, 636 x 475 mm, 25 x 18.75 in]*

222
Paduan bronze inkstand and oil lamp
from the workshop of Andrea Riccio, in
the form of Atlas supporting a globe of the
Universe which serves as a lamp, the
inkwell formed as a shell at the corner of
the base, second half sixteenth century.
254 mm high.
Courtesy Sothebys

221
Thought to be the earliest English silver
standish extant, this example has a
detachable inkwell and pounce-pot, with
two tubes and two covered boxes.
Hallmarked London, 1630-31, maker W. R.
132 mm high.
*Theodore Wilbour Fund in Memory of
Charlotte Beebe Wilbour, Courtesy of the
Museum of Fine Arts, Boston, 54,87*

223
Paduan bronze inkstand and candelabrum after
Severo da Ravenna, in the form of a kneeling satyr,
the shell inkwell on a triangular base, early
sixteenth century (the base perhaps later). 245 mm
high. *Courtesy Sothebys*

224
Venetian bronze inkwell from the workshop of
Roccatagliata, the cover formed as a young triton
astride a dolphin, the well supported by three
sphinxes, early seventeenth century. 202 mm high.
Courtesy Sothebys

226
Italian bronze circular inkwell
having a frieze of repeated panels
of cherubs in foliage, on three feet
in the form of recumbent lions,
circa 1600. 65 mm high.

227
Urbino maiolica inkwell from the
Fontana workshop, decorated
with polychrome arabesques,
grotesque human and animal
figures and classical cameos, circa
1650. 260 mm across.
Courtesy Sothebys

225
Venetian bronze inkwell, the lid a
seated putto holding behind him
a cornucopia as a quill-holder, the
well on three heavy paw feet
between satyr masks, early
seventeenth century. 131 mm
high.

228
Charles II silver inkstand of
casket form, engraved with
chinoiseries, hallmarked London,
1682. 273 mm long.
Courtesy Christies

229
George I plain oblong silver
inkstand with pounce-pot,
covered inkwell and quill-holder,
engraved with the Royal Arms
and those of Rushout; hallmarked
London, 1716, maker Philip
Rollos. 324 mm long.
Courtesy Christies

230
George I oblong silver inkstand
with pounce-pot, bell and covered
inkwell; hallmarked London,
1720, maker Augustine Courtauld.
320 mm long.
Courtesy Christies

231
George II oval silver-gilt inkstand with fluted booge and shell-and-scroll border, having an inkwell, covered seal-box with taperstick and pounce-pot. London, 1741, maker Eliza Godfrey. 343 mm long.
Courtesy Christies

232
George II shaped oblong silver inkstand with rococo style gadrooned shell-and-scroll border, with inkwell, taperstick, pounce-pot and pen depressions. London, 1744, maker Paul de Lamerie. 370 mm long.
Courtesy Christies

233
George II silver inkstand in the high rococo style, cast and chased with dolphins and winged cartouches, with baluster inkwells and a central pen-vase. London, 1744, maker John Edwards. 420 mm long.
Courtesy Christies

234
Fine and large George III inkstand
in the neo-classical style, having
two cut-glass inkwells flanking a
matching sander, hallmarked
London, 1784, maker Burrage
Davenport, 73 ozs troy.
Courtesy Asprey

235
Chamberlain Worcester porcelain
inkstand with *rocaille* decoration
of applied shells on a gilt ground
of formalised seaweed design;
script mark in red. 320 mm.
Courtesy Phillips

236
Minton porcelain inkstand of
serpentine oval shape with two
covered wells flanking a pen-vase,
decorated with panels of exotic
birds in landscapes on a gilt-
enriched mid-blue ground.
315 mm.
Courtesy Phillips

237

237
Carved fruitwood inkstand of box form, with glass
wells, the lid having a silver escutcheon engraved
Edward Mattison, 1663.
Courtesy of the Trustees of the Museum of London

237a

157

238
Tôle peinte inkbox with gilt chinoiserie decoration on a black ground; it is complete with its square inkwell, pounce-pot and wafer-box with hinged lid in the same material, and belonged to Rebecca Eves (1784-1874). Circa 1800. 155 mm long.

239
Tôle peinte inkstand of 'Treasury' form, the lid painted with an amusing scene of a bespectacled gentleman trimming his outsize quill pen after completing a prodigious amount of correspondence; complete with two removable toleware glass-lined inkwells. Circa 1830. 205 mm long.

240
Pewter double-lidded 'Treasury' inkstand; the second lid covers a cavity for pens, etc. Eighteenth century. 163 mm long. (Inkstands of this form were made from the seventeenth century virtually unchanged until the early twentieth. They were still being advertised in 1911 in Sir Joseph Causton's Stationery Catalogue, at prices from 8s 6d to 12s each.

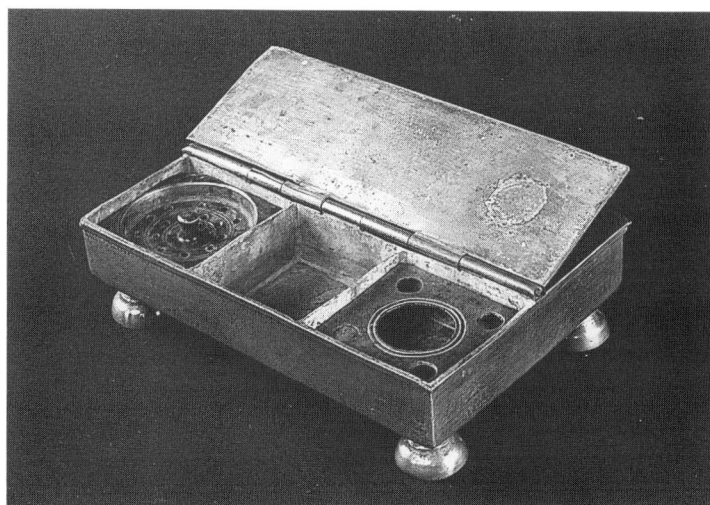

158

242
George III silver cube inkstand; although relatively common in pewter, such inkstands are rare in silver. London, 1787, makers Phipps and Robinson.
Courtesy Phillips

241
Pewter cube inkstand of Irish type with covered inkwell and drawers for wafers and pounce, eighteenth century. 88 mm high.

243
Swiss pewter inkstand with detachable inkwell and pounce-pot and tubes for two quills, eighteenth century. 124 mm long.

244
Perhaps the commonest of all pewter inkwells, the capstan or loggerhead type, also found on a broad flat circular base. This lidded example has a pot liner and holes for six quills; the Royal Cypher of George IV indicates its use in government service. Circa 1825. 86 mm diameter

245
Simple unlidded pewter capstan inkwell with pot liner and five quill holes, circa 1800. 103 mm diameter.

246
Documentary Bow porcelain blue
and white inkwell, inscribed
'MADE AT NEW CANTON' and
dated 1750. 90 mm diameter.
Courtesy Christies

247
Worcester porcelain inkwell of
capstan form painted in
polychrome enamels with
chinoiserie figures, circa 1760.
70 mm diameter.
*Courtesy of the Trustees of the
Victoria and Albert Museum,
C324a-1931*

248
French blue and white faience inkstand of
trefoil form, the three quill holes
integrated into the flowerhead decoration,
mid-eighteenth century. 120 mm across.
(The inkwell liner lacking).

249
Cream stoneware oval inkwell with central
well and two quill holes all with dark
blue enamelled edges, the sides moulded
with a neo-classical frieze between pale
blue moulded leaf borders. Staffordshire,
circa 1830. 93 mm long.

160

250
English earthenware inkwell of melon-fluted form enamelled with alternate stripes of crimson and bottle green, with three quill holes. Yorkshire or N. E. Coast, circa 1830. 70 mm diameter.

251
Treen inkwell of loggerhead type with glass liner and four quill holes, circa 1800. 81 mm diameter.

252
Unusual variation on a common type. The upper stage, with glass inkwell, unscrews to reveal a cavity for wafers or perhaps pounce, with four quill holes. Circa 1800. 70 mm diameter.

253
Treen inkstand, the square base with four quill holes. The glass liner is no longer present. Circa 1800. 97 mm square.

161

254
Exceptional George IV silver inkstand with
pneumatic action. Ink is pumped into the conical
well by rotating the crown finial, which operates a
piston. London, 1825, maker Archibald Douglas.
125 mm high.
Courtesy Sothebys

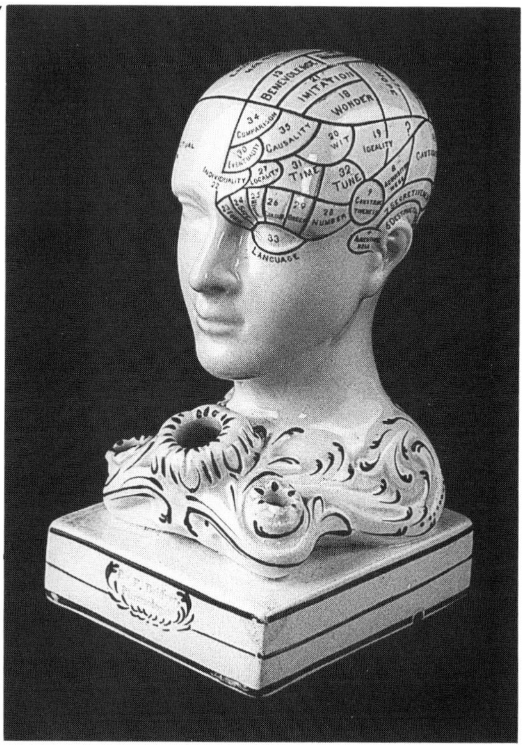

255
Patent inkwells, of which there were many in the
Victorian period:
Perry's Double-Patent Filter Inkstand, its china cistern
having polychrome floral sprays in gilt-bordered
cartouches reserved on a dark blue ground. The ink
was filtered as it was pumped from the cistern into the
covered conical well. Circa 1840. 98 mm high.
Perry's Patent Pneumatic Inkstand, its demi-china
cistern decorated in underglaze blue and iron-red with
Japanese style flowers, the gilt-brass mount stamped
with the Royal Arms. Operation of the plunger pumps
ink from the cistern into the conical well. Circa 1839.
90 mm high.

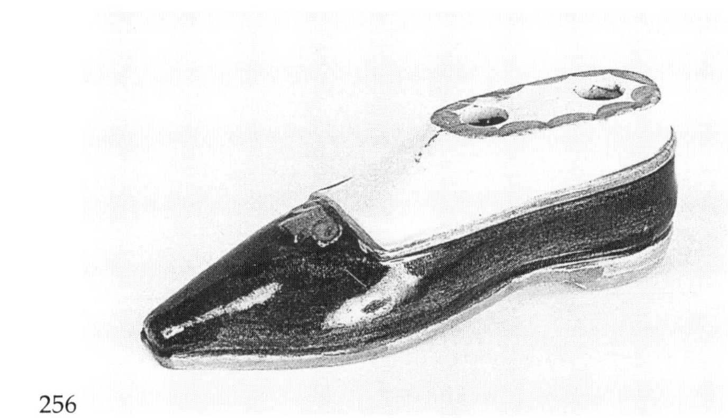

256
Prattware inkwell in the form of a contemporary shoe,
with brown and ochre decoration, late eighteenth
century. 110 mm long.

257
Demi-china inkwell in the form of a phrenological
head with central inkwell and two quill holes, the
plinth impressed 'BY F. BRIDGES, PHRENOLOGIST',
mid-nineteenth century. 150 mm high. (Similar inkwells
are found without the square base).

255

256

257

162

258
Trade card of Alexander Burges, a general merchant selling all manner of useful household objects, amongst which are 'Fountain-Pens'. From the style of the woodcut it can be dated to the late seventeenth or early eighteenth century, by which time the term was patently in common use.
Courtesy of the Trustees of the British Museum, Heal 52.24

ALEXANDER BURGES,
At the Red-Bull *and* Cafe *of Knives, the Corner of* Leadenhall-ftreet, *next to* Cornhill, LONDON.

SELLS all Sorts of Knives, Sciffors, Razors, Hones, Razor-Strops, Fleams; Tobacco-Boxes, Snuff-Boxes; Horn, Leather and Bath-Metal Buttons, and all forts of Buttons for Liveries; the beft Whitechapel Glovers and Packers Needles of all Sorts; Needle-Books, Needle Boxes and Cafes; Men and Women's Thimbles; Taylors and Glovers Shears, Paring-Knives for Glovers; Awl-Blades, and all forts of Shoemakers Tackle; Steel and Bath-Metal Shoe-buckles and Shoe-clafps; fine Stone and Bath-Metal Sleeve-Buttons, Spurs; Compaffes, Carpenters Rules and Penfils,Chalk-Lines and Line-Rowls, Whipcord; Combs, Comb-Cafes and Brufhes, Tooth-Brufhes, Stocking-Brufhes and Cloth-Brufhes, Toothpick-Cafes, and Squirril-Chains; Jews-Harps, Cork-Screws, Curtain-Rings, Hog and Pig-Rings; Knitting-Needles, Hooks and Eyes, Nutcrackers, Nutmeg-Graters; Horn Books and Primmers, Steel and Whalebone Busks; Tobacco-Tongs, Fire-Steels; Brafs, Glafs and Leather Ink-Pots, Ink-Horns, Powder-Horns, Hunting-Horns, Drinking-Horns, and Powder-Flasks, Shot-Pouches and Gun-Flints; Dog-Collars, Fountain-Pens, Pen-Cafes, Powder-Boxes and Puffs, Nacklaces and Pendants; Effence-Bottles, Dram-Bottles; Spectacles and Cafes, Profpective-Glaffes, Slate-Books, Vellum-Books; Clock-Lines, Brafs Jaggers, Hawk-Bells, Chamber-Bells, Ring and Poft Dials; Coopers Nippers, Spunges, with Variety of Bath Metal Toys; and all forts of *London Sheffield* and *Birmingham* Cutlers Wares, fold Wholefale or Retail, at Reafonable Rates.

N.B. Likewife all forts of *Tunbridge* Wares.

259
Engraving of a fountain-pen described by M. Bion, instrument maker to the French court, who died in 1715. This engraving which appeared in a translation of his work on scientific and mathematical instruments in 1723 was still being used in an edition of 1764.

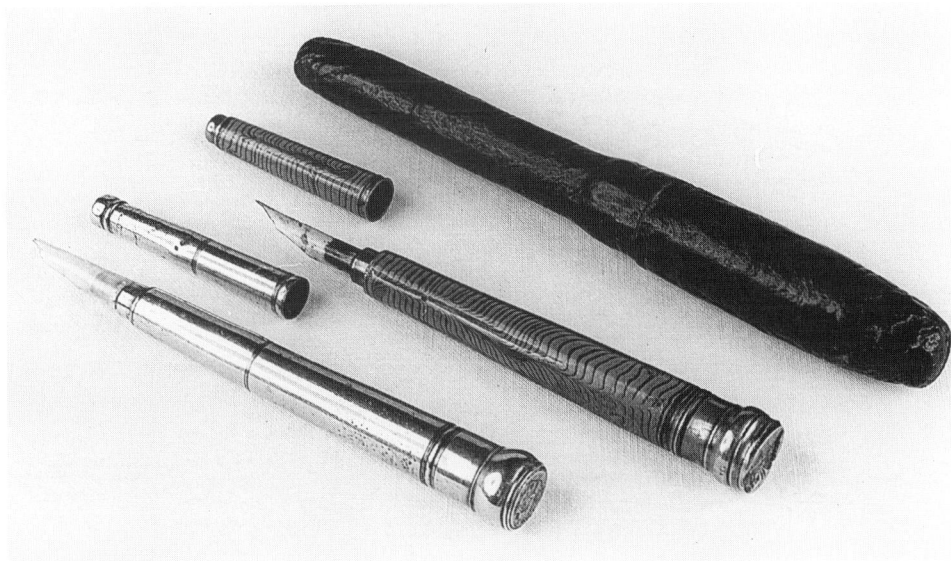

Fig. 2. FOUNTAIN-PEN.

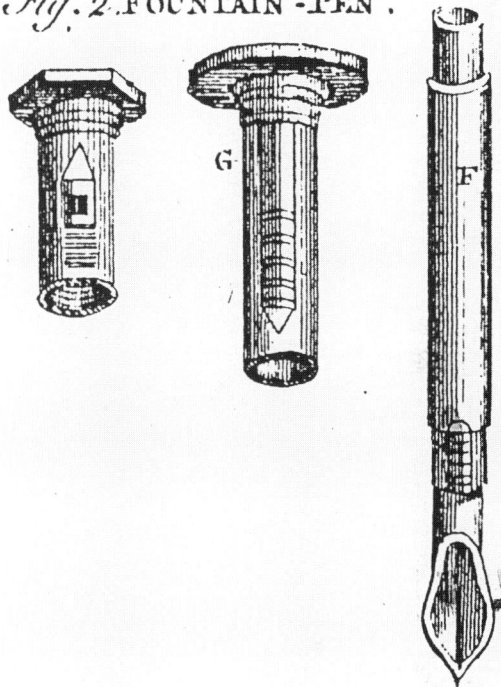

260
Two early brass fountain-pens on the Bion principle, each having a seal terminal, one with red and black hard wax decoration retaining its *cuir bouilli* case. Mid-eighteenth century. 122 and 129 mm.

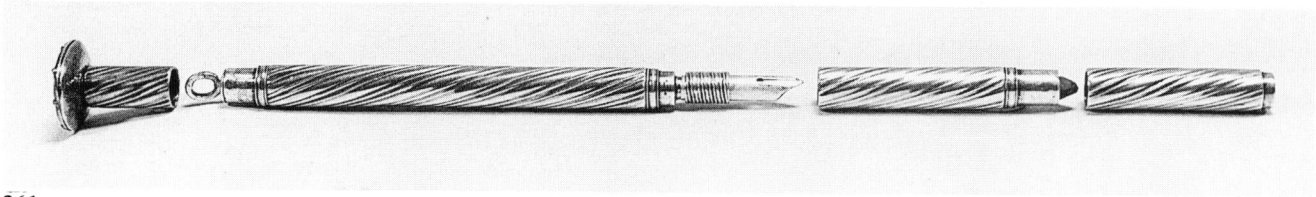

261
Silver fountain-pen with bloodstone seal
terminal and *porte-crayon*. Dating from the
mid-eighteenth century, it still uses Bion's
principle. Unmarked. 155 mm long.
*Courtesy Roger Bishop, Esq, William Bishop
Collection*

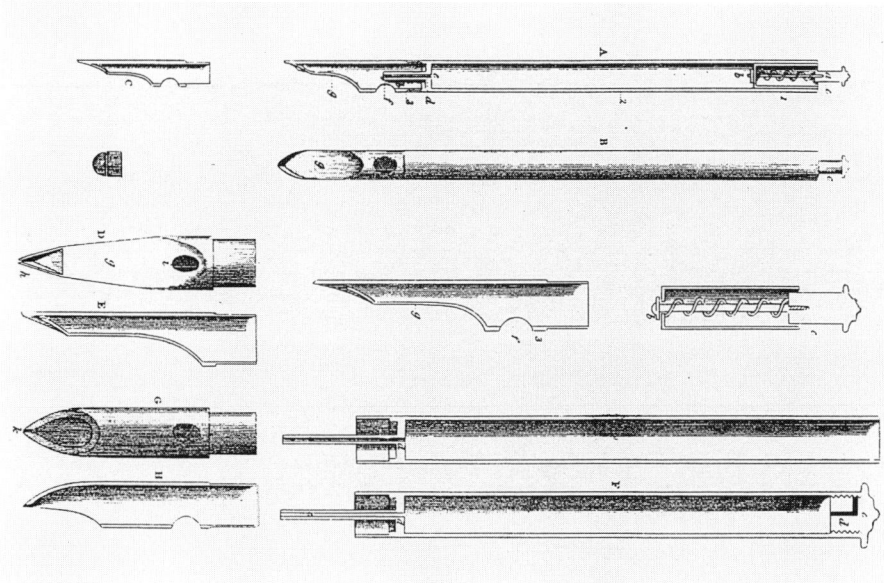

262
Engraving of Fölsch's patent
fountain-pen of 1809. Several
innovations helped to control the
flow of ink. From *The Repertory of
Arts, Manufactures and Agriculture*,
No XCII, January, 1810.
Courtesy Philip Poole, Esq

263
Scheffer's Patent Penographic or
Writing Instrument, which
controlled the ink-flow by means
of pressure on an internal
reservoir, and a lever-operated
feed cock. British Patent No 4389
of 1819.

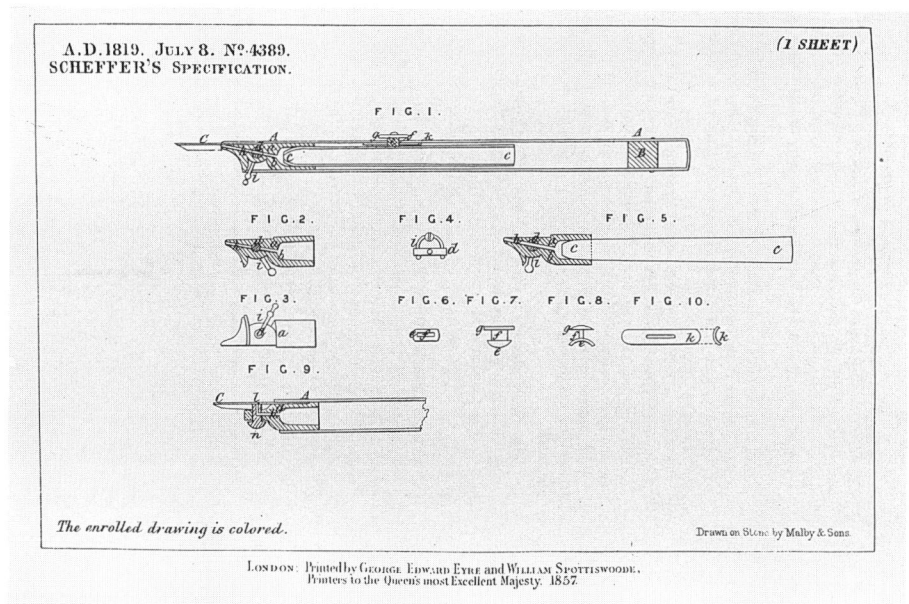

264
Advertisement for Scheffer's Patent Penograph, made by W. Robson, circa 1823.

SCHEFFER'S PATENT
Penographic or Writing Instrument,
PATRONISED BY
His Majesty George the Fourth.

MANUFACTURED BY
W. ROBSON & Co. Patentees, St. Dunstan's Hill, London.

The merit of this Instrument is, that it contains Ink and supplies itself as required, by which means the writer is enabled to use it for 10 or 12 hours with the same ease as with a pencil, without the aid of an Inkstand; and is manufactured in Gold or Silver in the usual size of a pencil case, and is so constructed that either a Metallic or Quill Nib may be applied.

DIRECTIONS FOR USING SCHEFFER'S PATENT PENOGRAPHIC.

When its use is required, take off the cover E, and to prevent its being mislaid place it on the top C, then propel the lever A, and press the projection B, which will cause the Ink to flow into the Pen D. It may be well to wipe the Nib when done with.

To replenish the Penographic with Ink, take off the top C, and draw the Stopple; then with some clear Ink fill it nearly to the brim, in order to exclude the air, which will necessarily occasion a small portion of the Ink to rise; this being removed, put on the top, and the Instrument will be found to contain Ink enough for 10 or 12 hours constant writing.

The Nib may be drawn out and renewed at pleasure.

Should the projection or the lever become stiff, immerse the Instrument in hot water a few minutes; afterwards allow the least drop of sweet Oil to enter the inner part of the lever by means of a feather. If the channel, through which the Ink flows, be stopped, apply a fine Needle, which will remove any difficulty that can possibly arise in the use of the Penographic, though it is presumed merely wiping it when done with will be sufficient.

N.B. Metallic Nibs and Boxes of Quill Nibs may be had of the Patentees.

265
Two rare silver fountain-pens:
a
Silver pen conforming to Scheffer's Penographic patent, hallmarked London, 1823 and made by W. Robson, who must have acquired the patent rights between 1819 and this time. It is impressed 'W. ROBSON & CO, PATENTEES, LONDON, 2945'. 123 mm long.
b
The first self-filling pen, patented by John Jacob Parker in 1832. (British Patent No 6288). Impressed 'PARKER'S PATENT, LONDON. No 6047' and hallmarked London, 1833, maker M.J.. 116 mm.

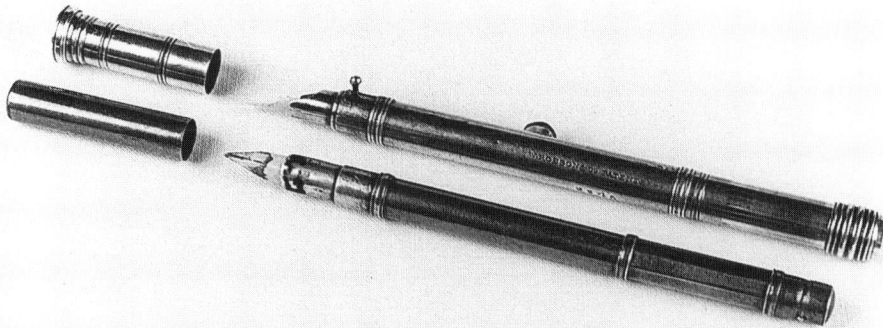

266
Parker's Patent self-filling pen, 1832. Illustration from the report of James P Maginnis's Lecture III, on fountain-pens in the *Journal of the Royal Society of Arts*, No 2763, 3rd November, 1905.
Courtesy Philip Poole, Esq

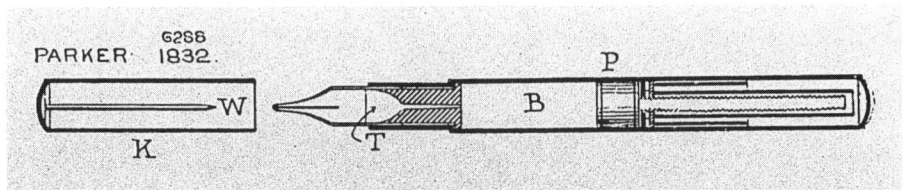

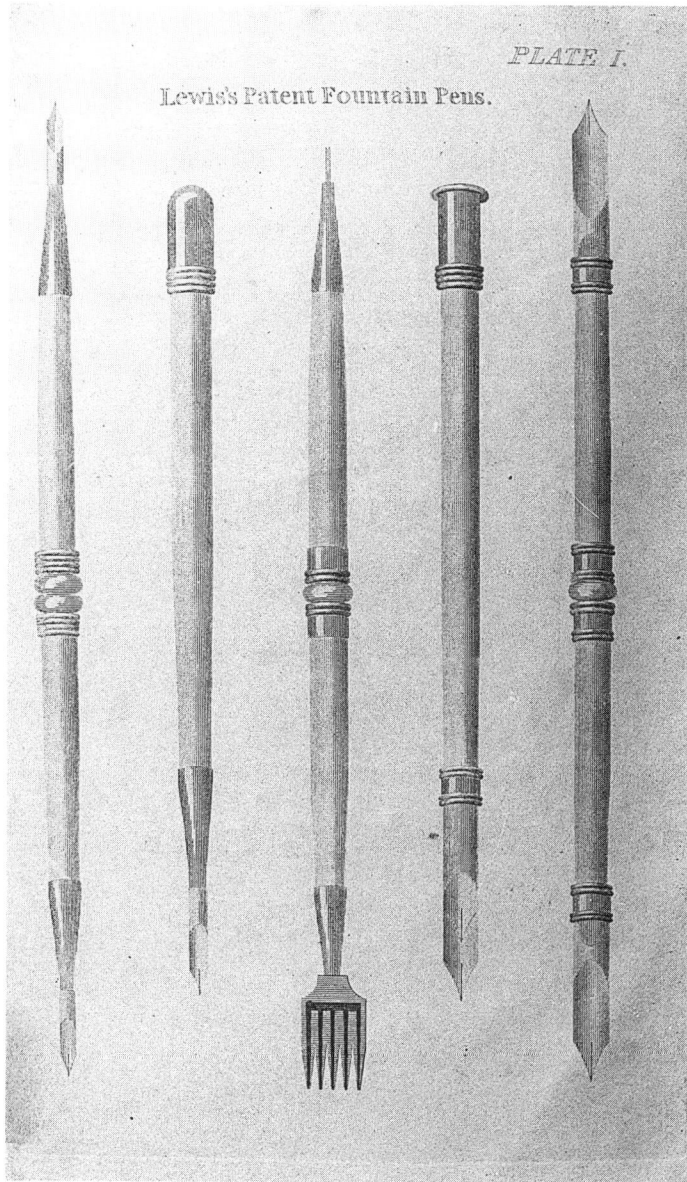

267
James Henry Lewis's Patent Fountain-Pens, from his *The Best Method of Pen-making . . .*, published circa 1826. (The five-pointed pen is a rastrum for ruling musical staves).

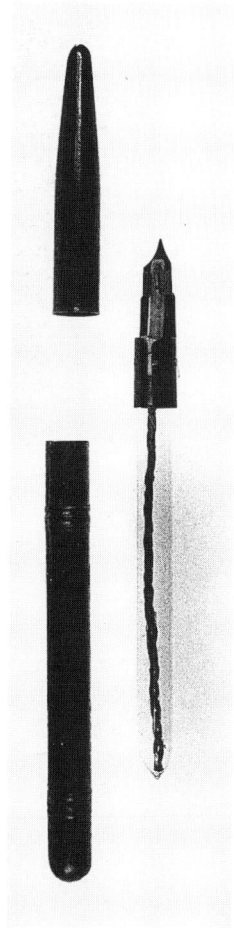

268
'The Little Imp Fountain-Pen', a late nineteenth century sheet-iron pen with glass liner and 'wick', on the Lewis principle.

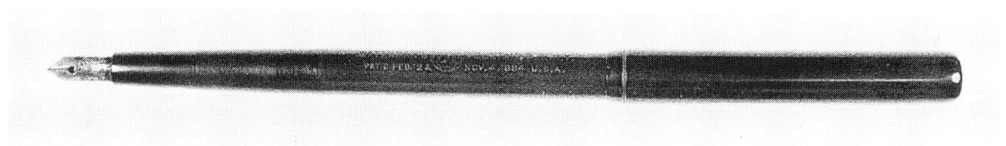

269
Early Waterman's 'Ideal' Fountain-Pen, model no 13, in black vulcanised rubber, filled by dropper. The barrel is impressed 'Pat'd Feb 12 & Nov 4, 1884, USA'. Circa 1898. 165 mm.

166

270
Two bronze pens of quill form, with split nibs, of a
type ascribed since the mid-nineteenth century to the
Roman period, but now thought to be probably
fourteenth or fifteenth century. The upper example was
found in the bed of the Walbrook, a stream which once
ran beside London Wall. Similar pens have been
excavated at both Finsbury Circus and Austin Friars.
The lower example 118 mm.
Courtesy of the Trustees of the Museum of London

271
Late medieval bronze pens with four-finned points, a
method of controlling ink flow revived in the
nineteenth century. Excavated at Wapping. 115 mm.
Courtesy of the Trustees of the Museum of London

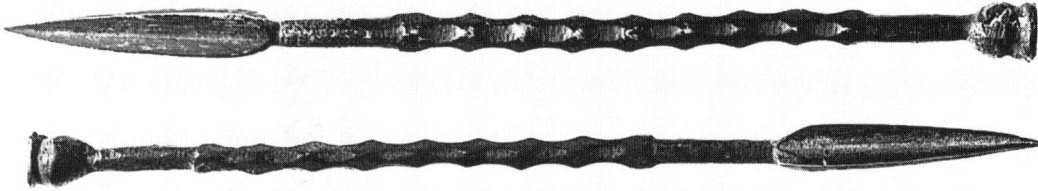

272
'Scofield's Original Crystal
Marking Pen', circa 1880. 110 mm.
Similar glass pens, which use the
principle of the medieval pens
above, were still marketed in the
1940s.

273
Steel barrel pen, the shoulders
split for flexibility, in turned bone
holder with screw-on cover,
stamped J. WISE. Jacob Wise was
making such pens by 1803.
102 mm.

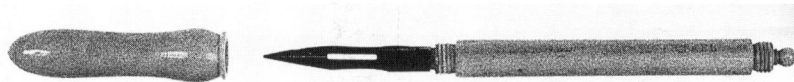

274
Steel barrel pen in turned bone
case, impressed IMPROVED
ELASTIC PEN, a term used by
Wise and other makers, early
nineteenth century. 107 mm.

167

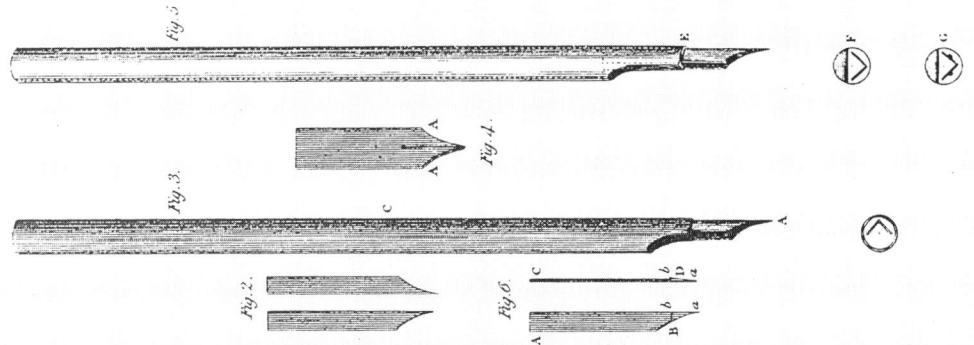

275
Advertising broadsheet of Daniel Fellow of
Sedgley dated in a contemporary hand, 28th June,
1805. At the time of its printing Fellow claims to
have been making steel pens for more than fifteen
years, making him certainly one of the earliest
English makers. 157 mm wide.

276
Bryan Donkin's Patent for a metal pen, British
Patent No 3118 of 14th March, 1808. These pens
could be made in 'Steel, brass, silver, gold or
platina'.

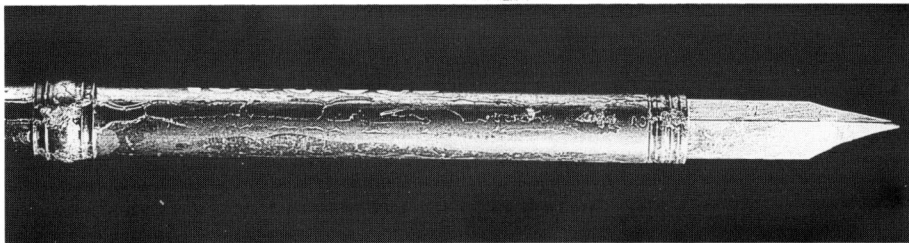

277
Two views of Donkin's patent
steel pen. The nib can be partially
retracted to vary the degree of
flexibility; the other end houses a
porte-crayon.
*Courtesy of the Trustees of the
Science Museum, London, Neg nos
639/86/20 & 21*

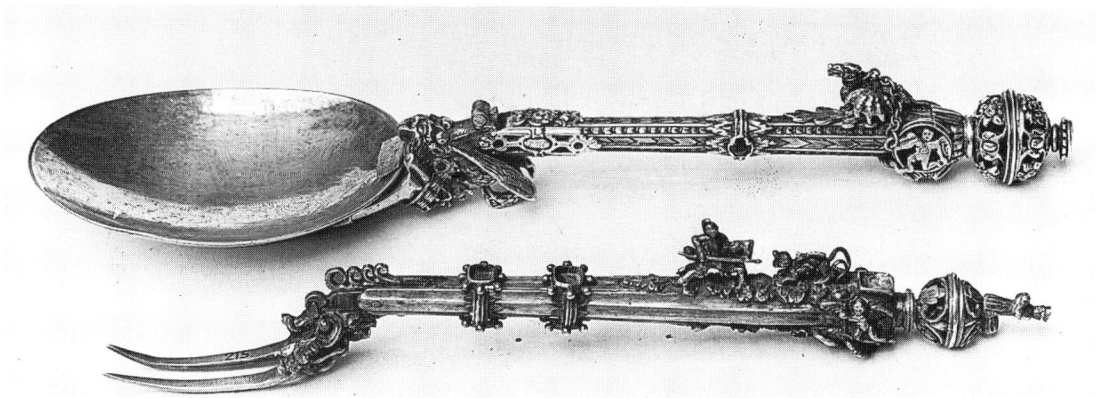

278

278a

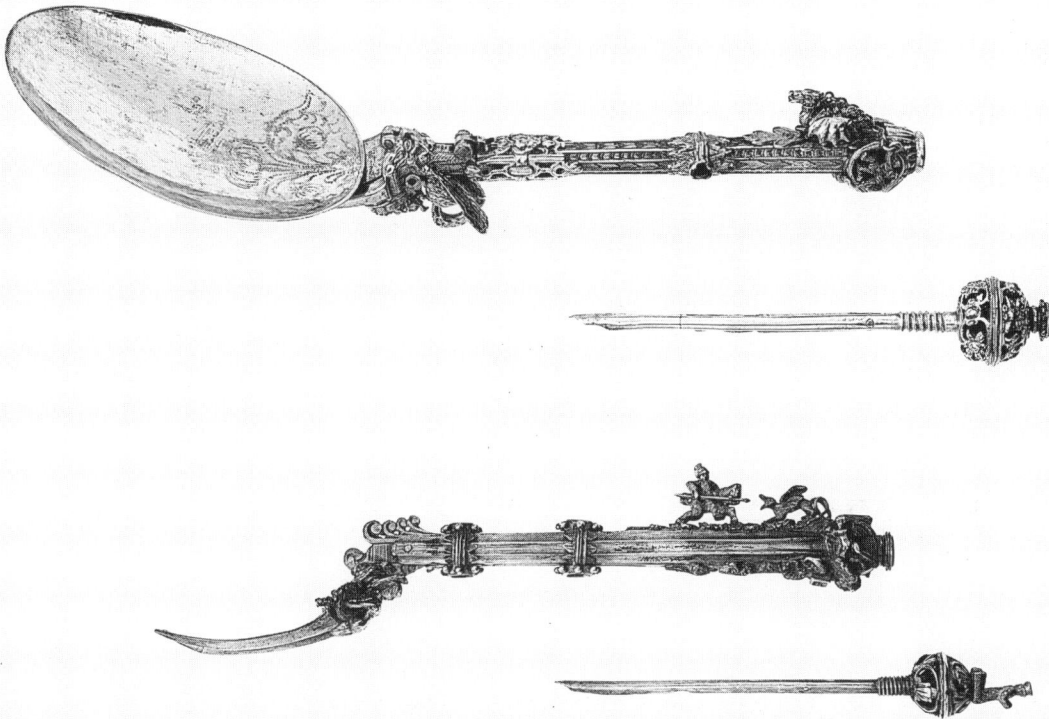

278
Exceptional silver-gilt fork and spoon. The finials unscrew to reveal silver pens; these in turn house folding tooth- and ear-picks. South German, late sixteenth century.
Courtesy of the Trustees of the British Museum, Waddesdon Bequest, 214 and 215

169

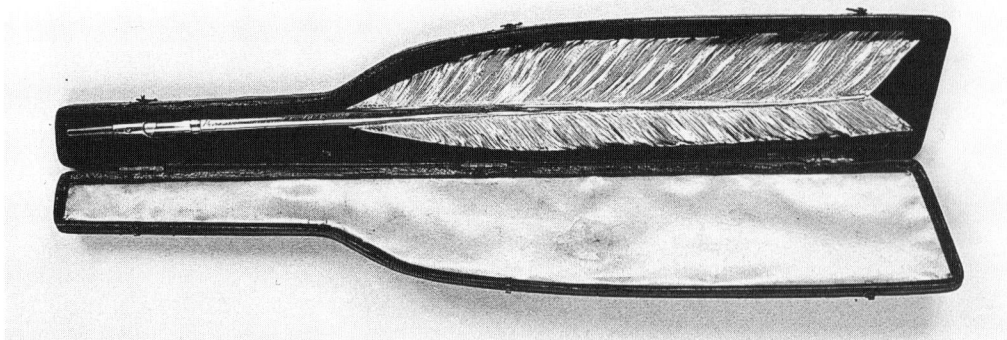

279
Parcel-gilt second-prize silver pen with holder of
the Bramah type for a quill nib, the barrel
engraved *'Prize at Tonbridge School, July 1838'*,
hallmarked London, 1838, makers Charles Reilly
and George Storey. In red morocco case. 310 mm
overall. (Whole-gilt and plain silver pens were
awarded as first and third prizes respectively.)

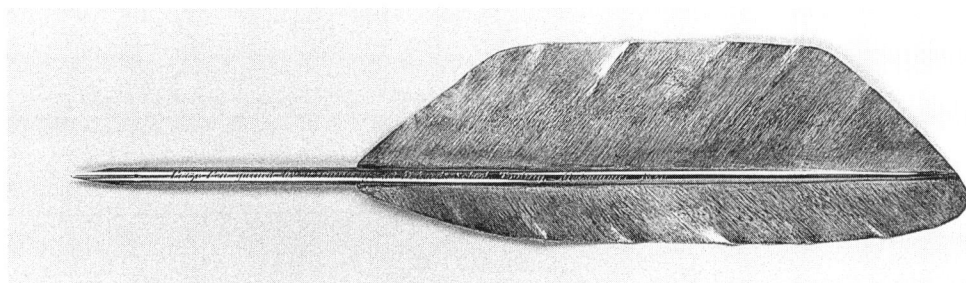

280
Plain silver quill pen with integral nib, engraved
*'Prize Pen gained by W. Banting at Dr. Lord's School,
Tooting, Midsummer, 1840'*, hallmarked London,
1839, maker's mark obscured. 281 mm. (Dr Samuel
Curlewis Lord, DD, a graduate of Wadham
College, Oxford, was curate at Tooting until 1833
when he resigned, and Churchwarden there 1839-
41. He was later Rector of Farmborough, near Bath,
from 1853 until his death in 1867. *Ex Inf:* Miss M.E.
Grimshaw, MA.)

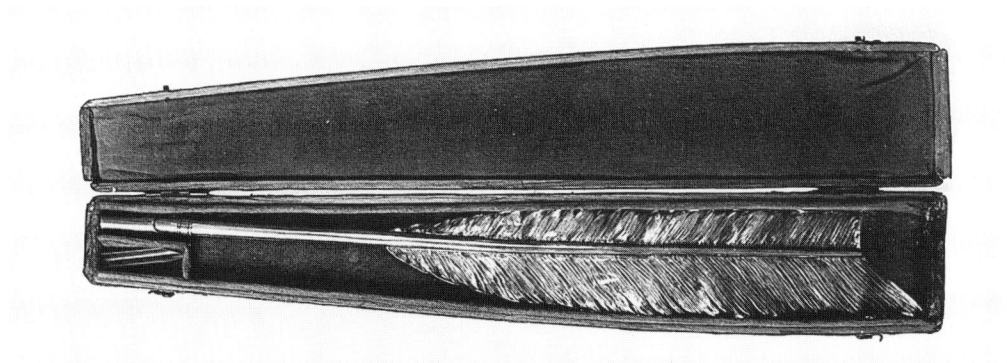

281
Plain silver quill pen with Bramah type holder,
hallmarked London, 1827, makers Mary Ann and
Charles Reilly, its red morocco case with
compartment for a quill nib. 272 mm long.

170

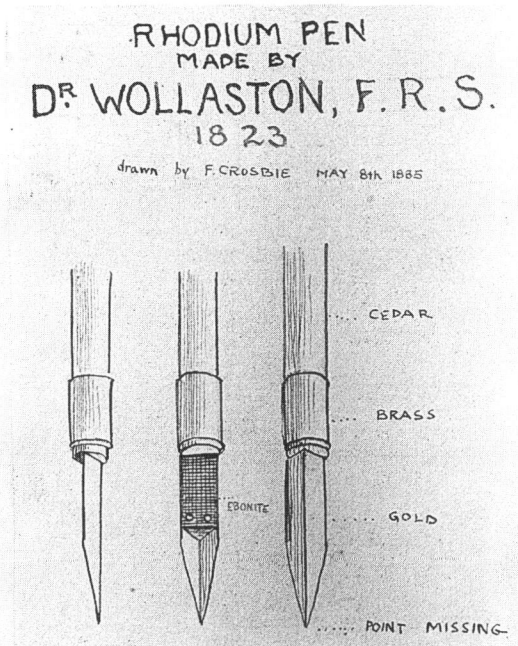

282
Illustration by Frank Crosbie, successor to
Francis Mordan & Company, of Dr
Wollaston's rhodium-pointed gold pen.

283
Advertisement for Doughty's ruby- and rhodium-
pointed pens, from *Robson's Directory*, 1830.

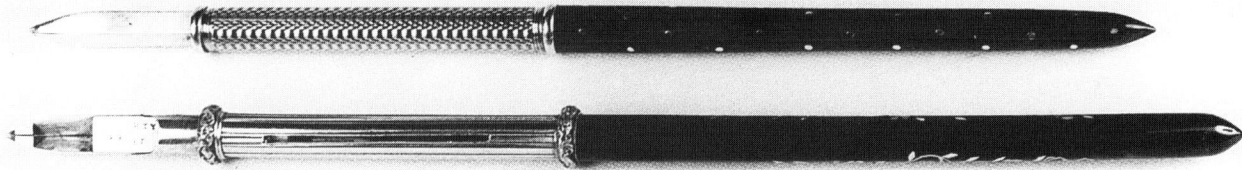

284
Two fine examples of Doughty's ruby-pointed gold
pens, the nibs retracting into engine-turned gold
barrels with tortoiseshell and piqué handles.

a
Detail showing Doughty's usual stamped signature.

b
Documentary example which identifies Doughty's
lapidary, Rose; a John Rose, Jeweller, worked at 427
Strand, a few steps from Doughty's later premises at
431 Strand.

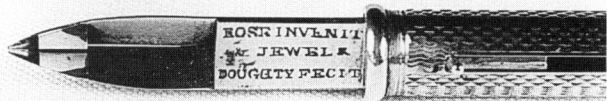

171

JOHN I. HAWKINS
INVENTED THE IRIDIUM
POINTED GOLD PEN IN 1834.

285
Silhouette portrait of John Isaac Hawkins,
inventor of the iridium-pointed pen; this
was no doubt executed using his
'Physiognotrace', a machine for taking
likenesses in profile.

opposite page –

287
Medieval bone parchment-prickers, used
for marking out skins prior to ruling up
writing lines. Centre example 91 mm long.
*Courtesy of the Trustees of the Museum of
London*

288
Scrivener's parchment-runner with brass
wheel, steel points and boxwood handle,
for marking out the writing lines at
intervals varying according to the number
of points, from five to fourteen. Early
nineteenth century. 117 mm (See plate
344).

TRADE MARK
F. MORDAN
LONDON

F. MORDAN'S
GUINEA
GOLD PEN.

In velvet-lined morocco case.

PRICE 21/- EACH.

This Pen is made with a *fine, medium,* and *broad* point.

Special Pens made for PHONOGRAPHERS.

Mr. T. A. REED in Pitman's *Shorthand Magazine*: "REPORTING
PEN.—I know of none better than MORDAN'S 21s. Pen."
Mr. HENRY PITMAN, the brother of the Inventor of Phonography,
had a Gold Pen in use for forty years.
"It cost me a guinea," he writes; "twice the nibs became bent by
accident, but I got them into writing condition again. From long wear
the inside of the holder containing the pen became loose and must have
dropped out. I was sorry to miss it."

286
Advertising page from a booklet entitled
The Everlasting Pen and How it is Made,
published by Francis Mordan & Co in
1892.

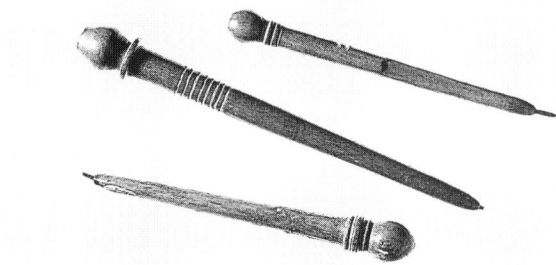

287

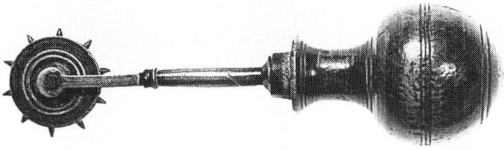

288

289

Two 'patent metallic books' bound in red morocco; the use of the special metallic pencil provided produced an indelible mark on the coated paper.

Harwood's Improved Patent Memorandum Book with Metallic Pencil, 'used in all the Government Offices', made by Alexander Cowan & Sons, 50 Cannon Street, London, complete with rosewood-handled metallic pencil. 176 mm long. Harwood advertised these books in *Pigot's London Directory* in 1832.

Henry Penny's Patent Improved Metallic Book, with bone-handled Metallic Pencil. 189 mm long.

290

Medieval ivory tablet. Coated with wax, it would be used with a stylus such as this pointed bone to jot down notes. 74 mm long.
Courtesy of the Trustees of the Museum of London

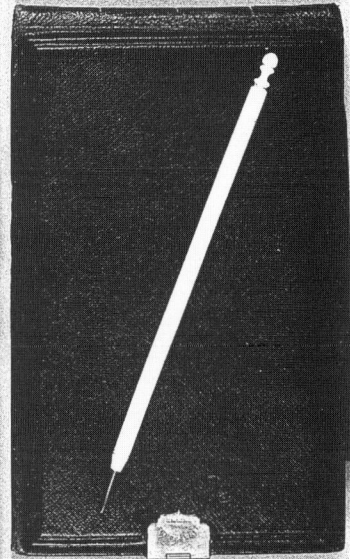

289

290

291
Large piece of pure plumbago
from the Borrowdale mine.
178 mm long.
*Courtesy of the Trustees of the Fitz
Park Museum, Keswick*

292
Two steel *porte-crayons* with
sliding cedar pencil or plumbago
holders; each has a seal terminal
with an engraved crest. The
shorter example is calibrated with
a four-inch rule. Circa 1770. 126
and 102 mm long.

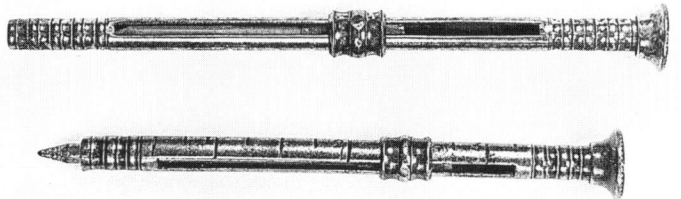

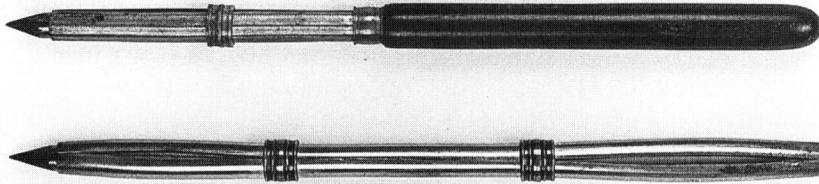

293
Porte-crayons:
 a
Unusual ebony-handled brass example,
early nineteenth century. 150 mm.
 b
Double-ended brass type, eighteenth
century. 149 mm.

294
The Young Artist, oils on canvas, by
Nicolas-Bernard Lepicie, (1735-1784),
showing the use of a brass *porte-crayon*
with both black and white crayons. 61 x 48
cm.
Courtesy Roy Miles Fine Paintings

295
Twentieth-century engraved billhead of
Banks and Co, Keswick, showing the
pencil mill established by Joseph Banks
on the River Greta in 1832.
*Courtesy Billinge Deposit, Cumbria Record
Office, Carlisle, DB/1/23*

296
Ann Banks's advertisement in *Slater's
Directory of Cumberland*, 1869.
*Photo: the author, courtesy Cumbria Record
Office, Carlisle*

297
Gold-tooled green morocco slip-case of
eight square-leaded pencils by Ann Banks,
Keswick, made for Alice Evans, on
September 12th, 1870. Both the pencils and
their case are of very high quality.

298

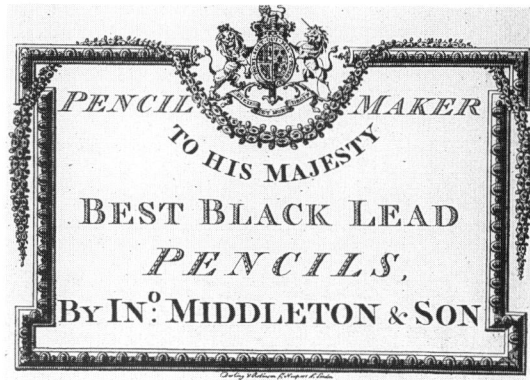

298a

298b

298c

298
Trade cards or labels of John Middleton,
late eighteenth/early nineteenth century.
*Courtesy of the Trustees of the British
Museum, Heal Collection, 92/19-22*

299
Brookman and Langdon trade card, early
nineteenth century.
*Courtesy of the Trustees of the British
Museum, Banks Collection, 92-2*

300
A rare survival – a block of compressed powdered graphite made by the Brockendon patent process and impressed with his mark, circa 1843. 57 mm.
Courtesy of the Trustees of the Fitz Park Museum, Keswick

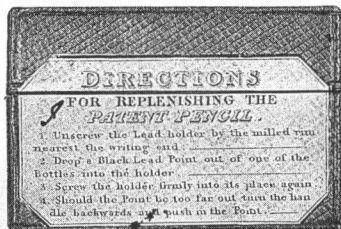

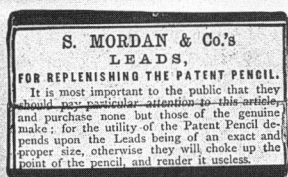

301
Sampson Mordan's Patent Leads: Red morocco slip-case of twelve pencil leads, circa 1832. 62 mm. Paper case of twelve leads, mid-nineteenth century. 50 mm.
In both cases the leads are individually housed in tiny glass tubes.
(a) Reverse view of same.

301

301a

302
Early silver propelling pencils: The 'Ever-Pointed Pencil' by Sampson Mordan and Gabriel Riddle, hallmarked London, 1829. The seal terminal, inset with an amethyst matrix finely engraved with a ducal crest, encloses a reserve of spare leads. 96 mm.
High quality pencil by Gabriel Riddle dating from the late 1830s. 92 mm.

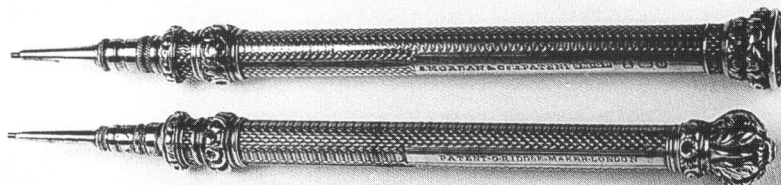

303
Lund's propelling pencils: Ivory propelling pencils impressed 'LUND PATENTEE LONDON', one having nickel mounts. 102 mm.
Cedar and ivory propelling pencil invented and patented by William Riddle in 1848. British Patent No 12383. The collar, moving along a helical groove, propels a series of leads. Made by William Lund, who subsequently acquired Riddle's patent rights. 170 mm.
Cardboard case containing thirteen inches of prepared leads for William Lund's 'Everpointed Pencil', priced at one shilling (5p). The leads are enclosed in fine brass tubes.

177

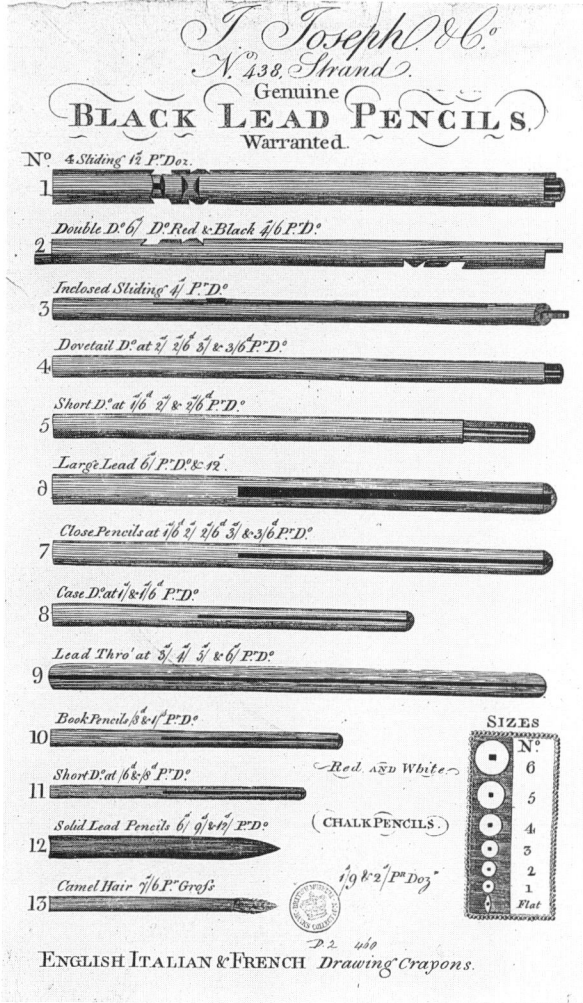

304

305

306

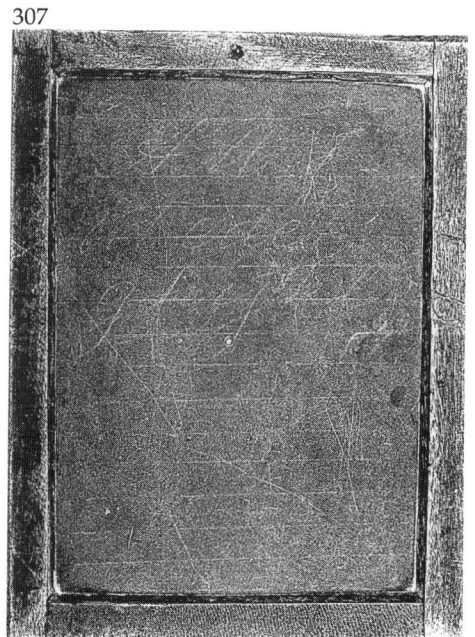

307

306
J. G. Dodd's Patent 'Everedy' sliding pencil, made by the American Pencil Company, New York, twentieth century. 175 mm.

307
Child's school slate in rudely-made fruitwood frame inscribed in ink with the owner's name John Dixon 1869 and carved with his initials. 160 mm wide.

304
Advertisement, circa 1800, for a variety of black-lead pencils including stop-sliding pencils.
Courtesy of the Trustees of the British Museum, Banks Collection, 92-5

305
Trade card of Jones, for stop-sliding pencils, late eighteenth century. A Jonas Jonas (probably a misprint for Jones) patented such pencils in 1783. British Patent No 1409.
Courtesy of the Trustees of the British Museum, Heal Collection, 92-17

308
'Liverpool Pocket Book' in green morocco,
gold-stamped with the name of its original
owner, Robert Greenhalch, Horrige and
dated 1777. It has the printed maker's
label of *'Joseph Rives, at the Black Cap in
Fenchurch Street, Liverpool'*. Such pocket
books were sold with and without slate
books; this example retains its slate pencil
in an iron holder. 199 mm long.

309
Green-stained vellum-bound pocket book
and almanac for 1700, with engraved silver
clasp. 167 mm long.

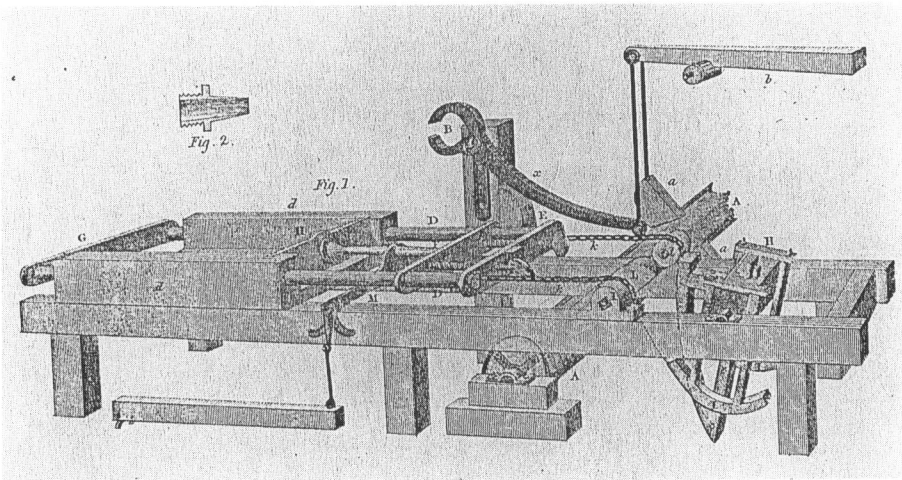

310
Engraving of a machine for
making slate pencils, invented by
J. Brockbank at Whirlpipin in
Cumberland. From the
*Transactions of the Society for the
Encouragement of the Arts,
Manufactures and Commerce*, 1811.
Courtesy Philip Poole, Esq

179

311

316

316a

311
Lead *bulla* sealing a papal bull of Calixtus III to the Bishop of Carlisle empowering him to determine a dispute between Christopher Morasby and the Rector of Kirkland concerning the latter's neglect of duty towards the Chapel of All Saints, Culgaith, dated 5th May, 1456.
Courtesy of the Cumbria Record Office, Ref: DRC 2/212, by permission of the Bishop of Carlisle

313
Great Seal of Queen Elizabeth I with Royal portrait, in ochre coloured wax.
Courtesy of Cumbria Record Office, Ref: D/ Lons/L Deed Box, by permission of the Lonsdale Estate Trust in whom copyright resides

314
Knight's seal of John de Warenne, obverse and reverse, from Exchequer, Treasury of Receipt, Barons' Letter, 29 Edward I.
Crown copyright photograph supplied by the Public Record Office, Ref: E26/Seal 57; reproduced with the permission of the Controller of Her Majesty's Stationery Office

314

315
Typically vesica-shaped seal of Robert Burnel, Bishop of Bath and Wells, (1275-1293).
Crown copyright photograph, supplied by the Public Record Office, Ref: E42/296; reproduced with the permission of the Controller of Her Majesty's Stationery Office

316
Medieval latten seal with pierced wedge for suspension; the inscription reads + S'(IGILLUM): D'(E) TORRVS : DE : RIRESCET. The crossed hammers may be tools of the original owner's trade. Fifteenth century. 29 mm diameter.

315

313

317
Gerbrand van den Eeeckhout, (1621-1674), *Four Officers of the Amsterdam Coopers' and Winerackers' Guild* and detail showing their seal and its impression, in a skippet.
Reproduced by Courtesy of the Trustees of the National Gallery, London, No 1459

312
Early Victorian envelope with embossed floral 'seal', 121 mm long.

318
Tinned-iron skippet containing the red wax seal of the Wernerian Natural History Society of Edinburgh, founded in 1808. Early nineteenth century. 77 mm long.

319
Group of fine Elizabethan seals of the Smith family of Saffron Walden, Essex. The gold signet ring has a crystal matrix engraved with an armorial, with painted and foiled backing. The larger silver-mounted desk seal is also engraved with an armorial, the smaller with a salamander and motto. Late sixteenth century. The desk seals 90 mm high.
Courtesy Christies

320
Silver seal, the handle a container for sealing-wax, engraved with a floral bowen knot between the initials K. M., maker's mark only T.W., late sixteenth century. 65 mm.
(For similar motifs on rings, see Taylor, Gerald and Scarisbrick, Diana, *Finger Rings*, Lund Humphries, London, 1978, plates 601, 603.)

320a

321

322

321
Ivory-handled desk seal with steel mount, the matrix engraved with an armorial, circa 1610. 100 mm.

322
Silver-mounted ivory-handled desk seal engraved with a cypher of the letters L, W and M under a coronet, seventeenth century. 105 mm high.

321a

322a

323

324

323
Steel desk seal engraved with an armorial of two luces, supported by Mercury beside a baroque style urn, seventeenth century. 55 mm high.

324
Steel desk seal engraved with a rococo style shield and monogram, under a coronet, mid-eighteenth century. 67 mm high.

323 a

324 a

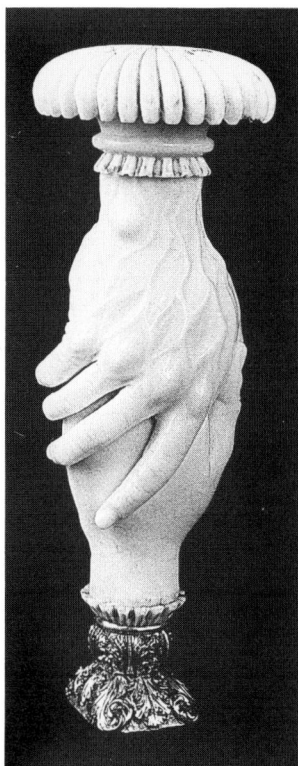

325
Silver-mounted *lignum vitae* desk seal with engraved armorial, hallmarked circa 1800, maker S.B. 98 mm high.

326
Dutch desk seal in spotted rootwood, the silver matrix engraved with an armorial, circa 1740. 65 mm high.

327
Fine gold-mounted ivory-handled desk seal carved with hands representing 'Age and Youth', the jasper matrix engraved with an armorial, circa 1840. 112 mm high. (See also Colour plate VII(i)).

325

326

327

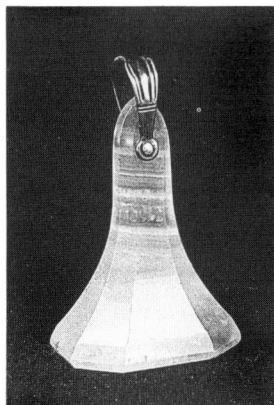

329
Chelsea porcelain fob seal of the Red Anchor period with copper-gilt mounts, in the form of a seated sportsman with fowling piece and dog, the base painted with the motto *'FIDELLE EN AMITIE'*, the carnelian matrix engraved with lovebirds in a tree and the motto *'FIDELLE'*, circa 1755. 38 mm high.

330
Agate fob seal of faceted bell form with gold suspender, the matrix engraved with a crest (a quill pen), the motto 'TRUTH' and ownership cypher G. S., circa 1790. 42 mm high.

331
Boxwood fob seal with brass matrix engraved with an armorial, eighteenth century. 44 mm high.

329

330

331

328
Fob seals of the eighteenth and
nineteenth centuries:
a. Silver fob seal of squared
baluster form, engraved with a
portrait of Queen Anne, circa
1710. 26 mm high.
b. Dark red stoneware fob seal
impressed with the name of the
maker, VOYEZ, an *immigré* French
potter who worked for Wedgwood
and Ralph Wood before setting
up on his own; engraved with
cypher G. M. Circa 1770. 22 mm
high.
c. Cut-steel fob seal engraved
with a rococo style armorial, circa
1755. 28 mm high.
d. Cut-steel fob seal of
exceptional quality, finely pierced
in the rococo style, the matrix
engraved with an armorial in a
neo-classical shield, circa 1770.
31 mm high.
e. Cut-steel fob seal engraved
with ownership cypher D. B., late
eighteenth century. 28 mm high.
f. Silver-mounted fob seal of neo-
classical scroll design, the black
basalt matrix engraved with an
intaglio head. Impressed
Wedgwood & Bentley No 73. (The
Wedgwood and Bentley Catalogue
of 1779 lists No 73 as
Demosthenes). Circa 1780. 31 mm
high.
g. Base-metal fob seal of neo-
classical scroll design, the
carnelian matrix engraved with
the cypher T. T. L., circa 1780.
26 mm high.
h. Gold fob seal of neo-classical
scroll design, the carnelian matrix
engraved with an intaglio head of
Neptune, circa 1780. 24 mm high.
i. Gold fob seal of neo-classical
bell-form strapwork, the carnelian
matrix engraved with an armorial,
late eighteenth century. 43 mm
high.
j. Fine quality gold fob seal of
fluted design, the bloodstone
matrix engraved with an armorial
and two crests, circa 1825. 32 mm
high.
k. Gold fob seal of C-scroll form,
the base fluted, the carnelian
matrix engraved with an armorial,
circa 1820. 27 mm high.
l. Gold fob seal of entwined
serpents design, the bloodstone
matrix engraved with a bird
escaping fron a cage, within the
motto *'QUI ME NEGLIGÉ ME
PERD'*, circa 1825. 18 mm high.

a   b   c   d

e   f   g   h

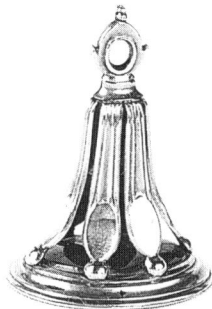

i   j   k   l

The Town in general will ftudy every poffible Accomoda-
tion for the Eafe and Satisfaction of all.

N. B. Where Sheep are not wanted to be taken away at
the Time, the Seller obliges himfelf to deliver them, at fuch
Place and Time as Parties may then agree. (c)

SEALS for SALE.

THE fo much Efteemed BLACK BASSALTES
SEALS, after the moft exquifite Works of Antiquity,
neatly Set in Roman Setting, at 3s. and 3s. 6d. each,
the Engravings of which, are equal to the fineft Engravings of
the Antients that have coft from Ten to Fifty Guineas each;
thefe Seals are not fubject to Ruft or Soil the fineft Linen,
they are fo hard as to cut Glafs, and no File can touch them;
making the Stone Red Hot in the Fire has no Effect on it.
Impreffions of Heads, Figures, Groups of Figures. Hiftori-
cal Subjects from different Gems of the Cabinets of the Cu-
rious of this and Foreign Kingdoms.

Any Perfon's Name in a Cypher, either for Watch or
Counting-Houfe Seals at 2s. each, Elegantly Engraved, in
the *Etrufean Black Bafaltes Stone*, and ready to be delivered
out in Five Minutes time by WILLIAM PENNY, *Brazier*
and *Tinman*, in the *Market-place*, *Whitehaven*, Agent to SA-
MUEL GREENWOOD, at *Burflem*.

The Ingenious are Requefted to come and View the Elaborate Works of the Antients, where Inimitable Engravings
are to be had in Everlafting Remembrance, and to be held in
the Higheft Efteem. (a)

Whitehaven, Auguft 10, 1778.

TO BE SOLD in public Sale, to the higheft
Bidder, at *Haile's Coffee-Room*, on *Wednefday* Even-
ing, the 26th of this Month;
The Good BRIGANTINE
HIBERNIA

332

333a

333

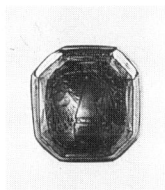

334

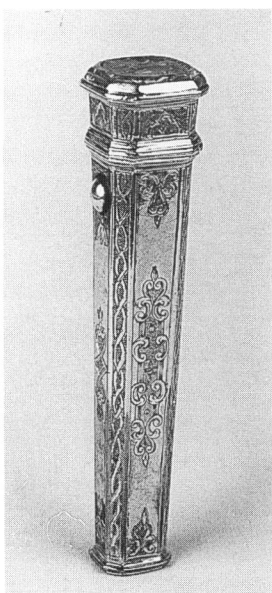

335

332
Advertisement of William Penny, from the *Cumberland Pacquet*, 11th August, 1778, for Samuel Greenwood's 'Black Bassaltes Seals' which were engraved 'in Five Minutes time'. ('Watch' seals are now usually referred to as fob seals and 'Counting House' seals as desk seals).
Courtesy of the Trustees of the Whitehaven Museum

333
Rare seal impression in gesso, which would have been given with the newly-engraved seal by the seal-engraver to his customer, circa 1785. 52 mm high.

334
Seal specimen impression in red shellac sealing-wax, in its turned *lignum vitae* box with the trade label of Butters, Seal Engraver, 8 Bridge Street, Edinburgh, the label itself engraved by John Robinson and dated 1820. 55 mm diameter. (Laurence Butters was working in Edinburgh from before 1809 until at least 1831.)

335
Fine quality silver-gilt sealing-wax box engraved with baroque style scrollwork and *guilloche* borders, the hinged lid inset with a pink-foiled crystal matrix engraved with an obelisk and the motto 'TOUJOURS AINSI', early eighteenth century. 85 mm long.

336

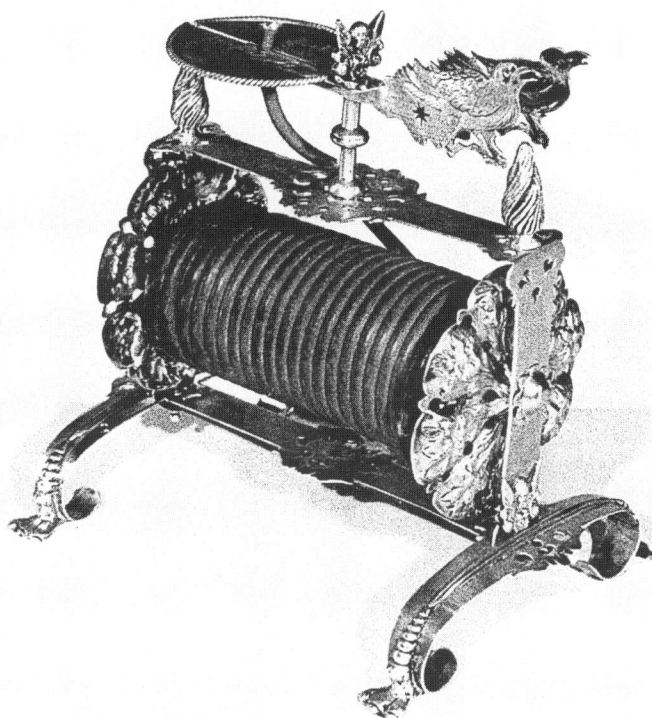

336
Silver bougie-box, maker's mark only
E.M., (possibly Edward Medlicott), circa
1730. 62 mm high.

337
Charles II silver taper-holder or 'wax-jack'.
London, circa 1680. 235 mm high. (Now in
the Museum of Fine Arts, Boston).
Courtesy Sothebys

337

338

339

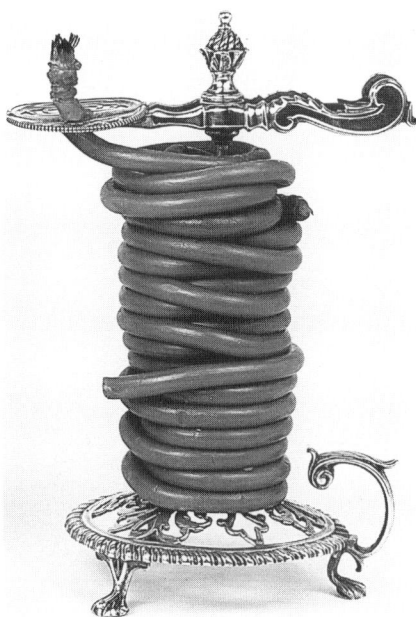

338
Silver 'wax-jack' on pierced
circular base with gadrooned
border and three claw feet, the
taper-holder spring-loaded,
hallmarked London, 1763,
possibly by S. Herbert & Co.
Courtesy Christies

339
Silver 'wax-jack' with open
wirework frame and conical
extinguisher, hallmarked
Newcastle-upon-Tyne, circa 1795,
makers Robertson and Darling.
Courtesy Christies

340

340
Lacquered brass spring-loaded taper-
holder manufactured by Thomas Wharton,
his design registered 28th August, 1846,
the base checkered as a wafer seal. 100 mm
high.

341
Victorian box of stick-on paper wafers
with the mottoes: 'Shall I expect', 'At Your
Service', 'Can I Prevail', 'Respect the
Truth', etc, 1840s.

341

342   343

344

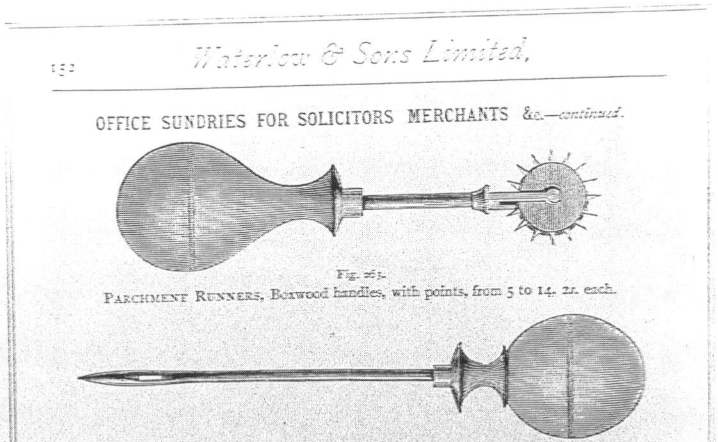

342
Ivory-handled steel seal-chisel, used to open letters sealed with wax, which retains its *cuir bouilli* and paper pocket case, eighteenth century. 90 mm long.

343
Silver-handled steel seal-chisel, the handle of navette section, hallmarked Sheffield, 1789, maker's mark indistinct. 109 mm long.

344
Page from Waterlow's wholesale stationery catalogue of 1882, offering seal-chisels at 1s 6d (7½p) each.

Waterlow & Sons Limited,

OFFICE SUNDRIES FOR SOLICITORS MERCHANTS &c.—*continued.*

Fig. 263.
PARCHMENT RUNNERS, Boxwood handles, with points, from 5 to 14. 2s. each.

Fig. 264.
BODKINS—Boxwood handles, with or without Eye, 9d. each.

Fig. 265.
PARCHMENT KNIVES, 6d. and 1s. each.

Fig. 266.
SEAL CHISELS, Boxwood handles, 1s. 6d. each.

Fig. 267.
EYELET PLIERS, per set of two, for punching hole and fastening Eyelet, with box of Eyelets, 6s.

95 & 96 London Wall; Finsbury Stationery Works, E.C.

Index

Page numbers in *italics* refer to illustrations

191

Finis